ADOLESCENT
SUICIDAL BEHAVIOR

ADOLESCENT SUICIDAL BEHAVIOR

David K. Curran

Public schools, Shrewsbury; Anna Maria College,
Paxton; University of Massachusetts Medical School, Worcester;
Private practice, Worcester; Massachusetts

● HEMISPHERE PUBLISHING CORPORATION

New York   Washington   Philadelphia   London

Dedicated to C.B., B.C., L.C., S.C., C.F., K.K., and D.W.
who have taught me much of what I know about adolescents
and are, among others, the inspiration for this book

ADOLESCENT SUICIDAL BEHAVIOR

2 3 4 5 6 7 8 9 0   E B E B   8 9 8

This book was set in Press Roman by Hemisphere Publishing Corporation. The editors
were Christine Flint Lowry and Eleana Cornejo-de-Villanueva; the production supervisor
was Miriam Gonzalez; and the typesetter was Rita Shapiro.
Edwards Brothers, Inc. was printer and binder.

Library of Congress Cataloging-in-Publication Data

Curran, David K., date.
    Adolescent suicidal behavior.

    (Series in death education, aging, and health care)
    Bibliography: p.
    Includes index.
    1. Youth—United States—Suicidal behavior.
I. Title. II. Series. [DNLM: 1. Suicide—in
adolescence. HV 6546 C976a]
HV6546.C87 1987   362.2   87-8650
ISBN 0-89116-618-1 (cloth)
ISBN 0-89116-781-1 (paper)
ISSN 0275-3510

A Short Life

She starts as a small seed,
embedded in rich, nurturing soil.
Slowly, she struggles to reach the sunlight and warmth of the
unknown world.
She pushes and nudges the loose dirt and pebbles aside.
She is exhausted but her aggressive perseverence pays off.
She thrusts an infinitesimal, dainty, limp sprout into the air she so
desperately wanted.
She extends her flourishing body into the vast unknown.
She is nurtured by the tender, loving hands of Mother Nature.

Days, weeks, pass.
She develops into a delicate, graceful, harmonious flower.
Her elegant petals shine in the sunlight with radiance.
Her tender leaves fluttered in the playful wind.
Mother Nature's adornment was immaculate!

As months pass things begin to change.
The warming sun no longer sent rays of sunshine to the flower.
The rain stopped offering his tasty drops.
The flower grew frail and unquenched.
Her long, sturdy stem began to languish.
Her dazzling petals grew arid and abandoned their home one by one.
The flower implored Mother Nature for succor.

Yet, there was no reply.
Still, the sublime leaves became juiceless.
Her roots desperately strived for the smallest amount of moisture.
All her efforts were in vain.
Now, she remains still.
Her body frazzled and lifeless.
So much toil and labor for such a brief life.

by Amy
age 16

Contents

Preface

This comprehensive book addresses the problem of adolescent suicidal behavior in America today. It devotes a great deal of attention to sublethal acts or suicide attempts, rather than committed suicides, for several reasons: Suicide attempts are far more common than committed suicides among adolescents; there is better research available on suicide attempters than committers; attempters are available to participate in research; adolescent attempted suicide differs—even more than committed suicide—in its dynamics, meaning, and intent from adult suicidal behavior, and is, therefore, less well understood by adults; most books in the field focus, as does the media, on committed suicide; and finally, the adolescent suicide committer is in most ways similar to the adolescent attempter. Many eventual committers have been attempters; some attempters will become victims of suicide. While differences between the two do exist (in sex for instance), the two groups are not mutually exclusive and there are far more similarities than differences. I believe a focus on suicide attempters will allow for a complete study of the nature of suicidal behavior among adolescents.

The book establishes a progression that discusses the scope and magnitude of the problem and an exploration of the meaning and reasons for adolescent suicide in the individual case. The opening chapter is a commentary on our society's injurious impact upon adolescents and adolescence. Chapter 4 develops a historical perspective in the study of the suicidal adolescent. Research that provides a validated picture of the troubled past of the adolescent who becomes suicidal is reviewed.

A distinctive feature of this work is the inclusion of an intensive study of the postattempt experience. The response by the human environment to the teenage suicide attempter and the reaction of the teenager to that response are evaluated and discussed. The plight of the chronic attempter is considered in light of the observation that for some disturbed adolescents, attempted suicide is a habitual form of acting out behavior, problem solving, coping, and communicating. Problems in the delivery of mental health services to the suicidal adolescent are reviewed and critiqued.

Chapter 7 discusses the controversial question of imitative suicides and addresses the frightening phenomenon of so-called "cluster" suicides among adolescents. New research on the degree of familiarity that adolescents have with suicidal behavior will be presented in demonstrating that suicide, like drugs and sex, has become a part of the experience of adolescents in the United States.

Recommendations and a review of strategies for assessment, referral, and treatment of the suicidal adolescent are presented, along with a call for suicide education and prevention programs in schools and hospitals, for adolescents, parents, and school and medical personnel.

A theme central to this book is the belief, supported by extensive research, that suicidal adolescents are significantly disturbed and historically troubled individuals. Adolescents' suicidal acts, no matter how seemingly impulsive or benign, constitute an acute psychological emergency and reflect considerable and probably long-standing emotional disturbance, exacerbated by adolescence and its vicissitudes. Normal, happy, well-functioning adolescents do not attempt or commit suicide, even though many cases are believed and appear to be so. Suicide attempters are often, paradoxically, attempting to solve a problem of living rather than hasten their death, to ameliorate rather than end their lives. Often, theirs is an attempt to communicate tremendous needs within an interpersonal context by means of actions rather than words. Farberow and Shneidman (1961) called this the "cry for help," a cry for caring and support from the human environment. All too often, however, their desperate acts are perceived by misunderstanding adults and peers as purposeful acts of simple coercion and manipulation, prompting responses of neglect and hostility. Ironically, it seems that adolescents are never more poorly understood than when they become suicidal—when they need understanding the most.

The positions established in this book are supported by review and evaluation of the research in the field; however, extensive use is made of the author's own clinical experience. Case material is used to give life to the material as well as to support the image of adolescent suicidal behavior offered here and supported by empirical research.

This book hopes to avert the danger of adolescents turning in increasing numbers toward quicker, more unequivocal, and less healthy means of coping, as adolescence becomes more difficult within the context of a more complex, fast moving society, increasingly lacking in familial and institutional supports. Suicidal behavior may join drug and alcohol abuse as a common means of escaping confusion and stress, eschewing mastery and growth in favor of nothingness. Its prevalence may signal viability to an ever increasing number of teenagers within an environment unprepared to respond in a helpful manner to the behavior.

I wish to extend special thanks to my wife, Patricia O'Keefe Curran, as the primary source of support, advice, constructive criticism, pre-editorial consultation, and typing. In short, she insisted I write the book. Dr. Hannelore Wass kindly offered much appreciated advice and encouragement. Mr. John Hodgen's skillfull and thorough proofreading proved invaluable and is much appreciated. John is an excellent proofreader for the same reasons he is a hopelessly fanatic Red Sox fan. He has great patience and is keenly aware but forgiving of errors. Finally, I must thank a very special group of friends who deserve acknowledgment as the inspiration for this book. They are a group of teenagers who have made my clinical work both challenging and joyful and the writing of this book a gratifying duty. They have taught me a great deal and it is to them that this book is dedicated. Also, thank you very much, Amy, for sharing with me your poem, *A Short Life,* and for granting me permission to use it here.

David K. Curran

Perspectives

HISTORICAL

Our Western culture, developed from Judeo-Christian and Greco-Roman values and traditions, has always harbored a deeply ambivalent attitude toward suicide and attempted suicide. Changing times and changing philosophical and religious fashions, however, have created alterations in the balance between sharply differing feelings about the question of suicide.

Suicide has apparently existed for as long as have people. Early societies sometimes forced certain members into committing suicide for ritual purposes. Suicide was used within the context of a magical belief in the workings of the universe, in order to control the fate of living beings (revenge), and of course, to control the fate of the suicide victim in the afterlife. Suicide was sometimes expected of the wives and slaves of husbands or masters who had died, as an expression of fidelity and duty. This phenomenon has existed in many societies, most notably and recently, India and Japan.

Modern Judaism, while officially regarding suicide as a sin, rests upon a long tradition of honoring "heroic" suicides. In spite of prohibitions, including the denial of full burial rites, Jews have recognized and revered suicides committed to avoid slavery, rape, or being forced into idol worship. The mass suicides of the Hebrew defenders of Masada in A.D. 73 in defiance of Rome and as an alternative to lifelong slavery, has been glorified by Jews and non-Jews alike as a triumph of courage and the will to freedom. The Old Testament makes mention of only four individual suicides; those committed by Samson, Saul, Abimilech, and Achitophel. In no case are their acts condemned in the scriptures (Alvarez, 1971). The suicide of Judas Iscariot, the only suicide recorded in the New Testament, also draws no negative comment in the gospel texts.

Attitudes toward suicide changed radically after the establishment of the Catholic Church and the leadership of St. Augustine in the fourth century. Prior to that time, however, Christian martyrdom was a common and accepted form of political protest and spiritual salvation. Many early saints achieved recognition primarily through suicidal self-sacrifice, some believing they were modeling their deaths after Christ's, who willingly accepted his crucifixion. St. Augustine, however, laid down rules against suicide that became the basis for Christian doctrine throughout the succeeding centuries. Augustine, drawing heavily from the philosophy of Plato and Aristotle, argued against suicide since it violated the sixth commandment "thou shalt not kill," and allowed no opportunity for repentence (Alvarez, 1971). At the council of Arles, in 452, suicide was censured as a homicide of an innocent person (Silviny, 1957). The Council at Braga, in 563, called for the denial of funeral rites of the Eucharist and the singing of psalms to any suicide. In 673, the Council of Hereford advocated the withholding of burial rites (Grullman, 1971). The teachings of Augustine and other early church leaders led to an institutional condemnation of suicide and attempted suicides within the society of the Roman Catholic Church and later the Anglican Church (Alvarez, 1971). Suicide was considered to be an act of the devil and a mortal sin. Though many of these laws remain in effect in Catholic and many Protestant Churches to this day, many priests and ministers find ways to modify them when circumstances appear to call for it.

The Christian churches found precedent for their thinking in this matter within the ancient writings of Greek and Roman philosophers, primarily Plato and Aristotle, though neither Roman nor Greek law considered suicide to be a crime, in most instances (Dublin & Bunzel, 1933). In fact, Athenian magistrates were empowered to provide hemlock to those who had obtained permission from the Senate to commit suicide, indicating quite clearly that the state condoned suicide in certain cases. For Aristotle, however, suicide appeared socially irresponsible in that it deprived the state of a potentially useful individual and was, therefore, tantamount to an offense against the state. Plato likened it to a soldier deserting his post, a disgraceful and cowardly act. From this we see the seeds of our own American mentality of toughing out one's problems despite their hardships.

Many other classical intellects felt very differently about suicide, among them, Seneca, Plutarch, the two Pliny's, Musonious, Marcus Aurelius, and Diogenes. Some of antiquity's greatest personages died of their own hand, including Cleopatra, Lucretius, Lucan, Brutus, Cassius, Atticus, Hannibal, Nero, Cato, Seneca, Zeno, and Socrates (albeit under duress), to name a few.

Nevertheless, societal opposition and defamation of suicide in Christian communities continued and gathered strength throughout the Middle Ages, until the Renaissance and especially the Age of Enlightenment broadened thinking on the subject. Always, however, public and private opinion remained far from unanimous. Along with a growing romanticization of suicide in the writing of Dryden, Hume, Donne, Goethe, Montesquieu, Montaigne, and Rousseau, continued violent opposition to the act. A rather gruesome incident in 1860 England, reported by a Russian traveling abroad, in a letter home, will help to establish the dichotomy. Apparently, a man was to be hanged for the crime of having attempted suicide, by cutting his own throat. Though the court was warned by its physician that hanging would prove fruitless since the man's mended throat would tear open from the hanging, allowing him to breath through the aperture and survive, he was, nonetheless, hanged anyway. He survived. Amidst much consternation and dismay, the officials deliberated upon what to do next. Ultimately, the man's neck was bound up below the wound and held tight until he died, executed for suicide. The Russian observer comments in his letter, "Oh my Mary, what a crazy society and what a stupid civilization" (Alvarez, 1971, p. 41). This was occurring at the same time that Nietzsche and Schopenhauer wrote in support of a person's moral right to commit suicide.

American law, based on English law, has always been more liberal in regard to suicide, though attempted suicide is considered a felony in nine states: Alabama, Kentucky, New Jersey, North and South Carolina, North and South Dakota, Oklahoma, and Washington.

Though devoid of the power of legal censure in all but very rare cases, attitudes against suicidal behavior remain strongly negative in the United States. The stigma, originating in early times, remains. It is a stigma, however, which is not now and has never been, absolute or well defined. There has always been, existing alongside even the most prolife attitudes, a glorification and romanticization of suicidal behavior which adolescents, past and present, have responded to rather than created. Men and women who have behaved suicidally and committed suicide may find themselves enshrined forever in our folklore as courageous, heroic figures. Our military history is replete with incidents, from the awarding of congressional medals of honor to soldiers who throw themselves onto grenades, to those who make suicidal and hopeless charges, to the captains who are expected to go down with their ships. Honor and freedom are considered worthy causes. Patrick Henry's "give me liberty or give me death" and the New Hampshire state motto of "live free or die" which is emblazoned on every New Hampshire state license plate are considered laudable sentiments. Confederate Civil War general

Richard Garnett, accused of cowardice by Stonewall Jackson a year earlier, helped lead Pickett's famous charge (more of a walk, actually) at the battle of Gettysburg, on horseback, fully exposed to the enemy and against direct orders from Lee, thus gaining the death he desired and the restoration of his previously tarnished honor. Garnett, like many others, was "allowed" his suicide when the quality of his life became intolerable.

Suicidal behavior can be the most American or un-American of behaviors, depending on the circumstances, but the circumstances have never been specifically delineated. American males, especially, must endure an ethic which allows for suicides of "honor," along with contiguous demands for quiet steadfastness and perseverance in the face of any adversity: "Death before dishonor," side by side with "never say die."

Adolescents grow up in the absence of any firm adult concensus on the issue of suicidal behavior. As with so many other issues of life and death they have been left to develop their own. Alarmingly, they appear more attracted to it as a viable mode of problem solving than their peers of preceeding years. Adolescents are increasingly choosing suicidal alternatives to an intolerable quality of life. This is a baffling and intensely upsetting realization to adults whose feelings about adolescent suicide stem in large part from their attitudes, beliefs, and prejudices about adolescents, in general. Adult attitudes toward adolescents feature a combination of admiration, resentment, and annoyance, which somehow congeal into the adult promulgated notion that the adolescent years are "the best years of their lives."

ADULT

While adults have historically struggled with the issues of suicidal behavior among their peers, they appear quite solid in their opposition to suicidal behavior among their young. There are a variety of complex reasons for this. Adult attitudes toward adolescent suicidal behavior and their subsequent response to and management of it cannot be fully understood without some understanding of their attitudes toward adolescence and adolescents. Haim (1974) discusses the dynamics of adult attitudes toward youth and the young at length in his book, *Adolescent Suicide:*

> *The attitude of the adult to the adolescent is never a neutral one: the adolescent arouses in the adult contradictory feelings, conflicts of a more or less violent and anxiety inducing kind. He tries to avoid anxiety in stereotyped reactions, which not only force the adolescent to play contradictory roles, but also impose stereotyped attitudes on the adult himself. This conflict makes him incapable of understanding the adolescent's experience. (p. 120)*

Lack of understanding can breed alienation, prejudice, and fear. Irrational and erroneous beliefs may be created and maintained which obscure accurate assessment of adolescent behavior. Adult misperceptions and subsequent mishandling of adolescent suicidal behavior have been documented at length in this book. For many adults, their inaccessibility to an understanding of adolescence derives from anxiety associated with their own adolescent experience. Anna Freud (1958) and Lampl de Groot (1960) have described the particular difficulties attendant upon having patients in analysis relive their adolescent experience. Adults often appear to energetically avoid reflection on their own adolescence, and in so doing, support their ignorance of adolescents presently in their midst.

Adolescents, by their mere existence and by the process of their normal development, can create a threat to the adult psyche. Teenagers, by virtue of their youth and vitality tend to confront adults with the fact of their own aging process and ultimate mortality. Adults come to realize that they are not young enough to be love object for the adolescent or strong enough to hold them. Adolescents often provoke feelings of unattractiveness, unloveability, and impotence in the adult. Frustration and, finally, anger often ensue.

Adolescents, as growing, individuating entities are in a position to stand in critical contrast to the sense of identity and purpose established by adults for themselves. They cause adults to question the meaning and quality of their lives, and to face the inevitability of their death. These are unpleasant thoughts, indeed, and are often neutralized in the adult by overinvestment and identification with the potentialities of the adolescent. The adolescent becomes, at times, the bearer of the adult's ego ideal. Adults project upon the adolescent much of their own unfullfilled wishes and aspirations, just as they may project their sexual and aggressive fantasies onto the burgeoning sexuality and power of the growing adolescent. The parent's or adult's hope of seeing their unsatisfied desires fulfilled is intensified. There is a great temptation to manipulate the adolescent in a manner that will apparently fulfill all the possibilities that adults feel are in them, to make them all that one would have liked to have been oneself. However, adolescents will not play and in their demand for autonomy, deliver a hurtful blow to the now confused and angered adult.

The separation of the child from the adult in adolescence often prompts mourning both for the loss of the child and the loss of childhood potentialities and hopes in the adult. Adolescent separation may be viewed as a rejection of the individual adult, his culture, his life and all that it stands for. It is a separation which often is not without acrimony, fear, and resentment.

While there is much in adolescents that repels adults, there is also much that attracts them. Remembrance of youth, though anxiety provoking in analysis, may be glowing in revised form. Many of us recall adolescence in a

manner which is idealized and legendary. As a time of excitement, ex-
hilaration and hope where fun was easy to come by. Much of what is
new and daring in our language, music, and apparel comes from the young.
Their manifest gaiety, effervescence, and activity call forth images of
unbounded joy and a life without worries. Adults give lip service to an
acknowledgement of the troubles kids have today, while secretly blaming
them entirely for their drug, alcohol, suicide, and sex problems. Adults
resent the notion that the teenager's life is in any way more difficult than
their own. To be responsible for a teenager would seem in and of itself
a greater task than being a teenager. Recently, I attended a high school
awards ceremony in which the keynote speaker, addressing a predominantly adult audience, spoke on the difficulties of parenting teenagers
today, saying that if there is anything harder than being a teenager in the
1980s it was being a parent of a teenager. The thunderous applause he
received as he finished seemed to say, "Yes, it's about time *our* plight was
acknowledged."

Many adults appear to resent the problems of adolescents and the
attention devoted to them. Not only are they held responsible for the
problems of youth, but in the process, their own adult problems tend to
become ignored. For many reasons, then, adults have difficulty seeing
adolescents and adolescence clearly. Adolescents can provoke fear, anger, and
uncertainty in adults which may cause them to retreat from a realistic
appraisal of adolescents and their relationship with them

> *Adolescence is certainly the awkward age but it is so above all for
> the adult, since it disturbs his tranquility and reassuring organiza-
> tion. Not knowing the adolescent, not understanding his experience,
> replacing the reality of his experience by a stereotype, is certainly a
> way of avoiding anxiety. (Haim, 1974, p. 124)*

Stereotypic thinking allows the adult to trivialize and simplify the problems
of adolescents. It allows them to suppose that adolescents are just naturally
"crazy" anyway and in so doing obscures their capacity to see the truly
troubled among them. It allows them to simply not take adolescents and their
behaviors very seriously, believing in the shallowness and transience of their
various upsets. The suicidal behavior of adolescents is, therefore, more easily
impugned, ignored, and misunderstood. If adolescence, by its very existence
is able to shake and destablize the adult, how much more so does adolescent
suicide? It appears to the adult to be a profound error, a monstrous coupling
of two incompatible facts, youth and death. It throws our sense of meaning
and order into chaos

It is hardly surprising that the voluntary death of an adolescent arouses the maximum reaction of flight in the adult. Adolescent suicide has the sad privilege of arousing the most extreme intolerance. It would seem that no subject arouses more defenses. (Haim, 1974, p. 140)

Suicide is a very powerful manifestation of rejecting behavior. Adolescent suicide, occurring as it does within the context of separation and individuation from parental figures (itself a rejection), may be felt as a particularly emphatic rejection. Durkhiem (1897) has suggested that an increase in the suicide rate is a sign that the group is in trouble. Increasing rates of adolescent suicidal behavior implies that something is wrong with the environment established and maintained by adults. Adults, therefore, are apt to feel responsible.

Finally, as adolescence confronts adults with the fact of their own mortality, adolescent suicide virtually screams it at them. Understandably, the adult's feelings of failure, rejection, responsibility, and fear, will be defended against as they threaten to become intolerable. As adults protect themselves, so too do they promote their own ignorance of the meaning of the adolescent's suicidality. As a result, they are often left with little to respond with but denial and anger. Both serve to maintain or increase the distance and alienation that the teenager had probably hoped to ameliorate with his self-destructive behavior.

SOCIOCULTURAL CONTEXT

Adolescents today live at a time in which adolescence as a stage in development and a way of being is glorified by preadolescents and postadolescents alike. There exists in our society a push exerted upon the very young to emulate teenagers and pull upon the older to be as youthful as possible. In some ways it would seem that everyone wants to be a teenager except the teenagers themselves. At the same time, adolescence is becoming more prolonged, more complex, and more difficult. It is, of course, an essential task of adolescence for the adolescent to separate and establish for himself a new and genuine identity. However, identity is, as are all things, relative and must exist in relation to or in juxtaposition with something else, some other clearly defined identity. This task is made more and more difficult as roles and values in our society become less well defined. Teenagers often experience themselves as an entity within a darkened room attempting to discern boundaries and dimensions, confused and rather frightened by the lack of solidity, predictability, and clarity in their environment. Necessarily then, for adolescents who experience their world in this manner it is harder to find roles and values to gravitate toward or against. Adolescents, therefore, have found it necessary to range further and further afield in service of their natural rebelliousness, until they are finally able to divine the countours of their world and are opposed by firm societal boundaries. The boundaries of approved social functioning are often defined and developed by our institutions: courts, representative government, the military, church, police, and leaders of all types. All of our institutions, however, have been seriously tarnished and have lost a good deal of credibility and respect over the past two generations. The adolescents of today are to a considerable extent, the offspring of that generation which first witnessed the fall into relative disrepute of all our cherished societal icons, the dismantling of many of our revered role models. Cynicism and a lack of faith and trust in the virtue, equity, and workability of our society and its values is for the first time shared by parent and adolescent alike. The effect that this has on the adolescent must be significant.

As heroes have ceased to exist, the antihero has sprung forth and blossomed. Joe Namath was referred to as an antihero in the late 1960s for his irreverent attitude toward accepted norms of humility, respect for elders, and conservative conformity in the world of sports. Antiheros are those who thumb their nose at conventional society. They appear to be saying that society does not work. It is these individuals who we, along with our teenagers, find ourselves drawn to, with whom we identify. "Dirty Harry" is applauded for taking the law into his own hands and delivering justice unto the "lawless" ones against whom the courts, the law, and "legal" police procedure have proved impotent. Rock stars are the most popular and numerous antiheroes for today's youth and constitute the only heroes of any type generally accepted by adolescents. Movies such as "Taxi Driver" (1976) with Robert DeNiro as the alienated and frustrated taxi driver symbolize the desperation shared by so many adults and adolescents in our society. Compare "Taxi Driver" with the 1946 Frank Capra film classic, "It's a Wonderful Life" starring Jimmy Stewart. Both films depict the workings and workability of American society. Both films feature a lead character, disgruntled, disillusioned, and discouraged by his life and his immediate environment. Jimmy Stewart is saved from suicide by a society which is shown ultimately to work with fairness, justice, and love. Robert DeNiro, on the other hand, demonstrates that society cannot save itself or the individual and that only extraordinary measures can hope to gain some sense of satisfaction for the hero and resolution to his problem. Society will not help. DeNiro embarks as a one man demolition team to murder the pimps, addicts, and pushers who inhabit his environment, symbolize its rot, and appear to have the upper hand. His solution is both violent and suicidal as are those increasingly chosen by our more disturbed teenagers who experience a similar sense of anomie, frustration, isolation, and anger.

Not all cultures' and societies' adolescents have such a difficult time of it. Primitive cultures, closed societies, societies in which choices are much more limited than ours, of course, tolerate little, if any adolescence at all. Adolescence, as a stage in development is a relatively recent phenomenon and a luxury of affluent, predominantly democratic societies. Only recently, with expanding professionalism and greater demand for educated skilled labor, have childhood and adolescence emerged as full-blown life stages characterized by a prolonged preparation for adulthood (Robertson, 1980). Teenagers today are both blessed and cursed with an almost infinite variety of choices as to who, how, and what to be and do. They do not have to go off to work at an early age or fit into predetermined roles. They are free to find their own niche based on the actualization of their own unique abilities and potential. They are also free to become hopelessly confused, overwhelmed. They are free to fail. When choices become unlimited, choice is very hard. Many flounder, or avoid the issue altogether by means of readily available drugs or alcohol. Those who are the focus of this book may become suicidal as well, as they attempt to live their problematic lives within the context of modern America.

Adolescents today experience, more than their predecessors, a heightened sense of marginality and confusion. Paul Goodman (1960), a generation ago, wrote that a major problem of adolescence in an industrial society is that they are freed from the responsibilities and rights of adults. Consequently, the teenagers' greatest problem is their "uselessness" as they wait to enter adult life. As society has become more complex and the need grows upon the individual for increasing amounts of education in order to function effectively, adolescence will be prolonged. It is difficult for many adolescents to tolerate the seemingly endless period of waiting in a society they feel offers no guarantees and perhaps little support. Teenagers today seem less idealistic and more cynical. Their vision of the future clouded, in part, by the threat of nuclear war, can be a demoralizing one. Feeling unable to influence society it is not surprising that many adolescents appear to have grown more alienated from society. Alienation has been implicated by Wenz (1979) as an important factor in the individual adolescent suicide attempt as well as the increase in its incidence across the country. He states that "adolescent attempted suicidal acts are part of an active response to a situation of alientation" (p. 28).

Active responses to psychological conditions such as alienation and depression are, of course, endemic to adolescence. These active responses, however, often do not include healthy, effective coping, or problem solving strategies. Instead, the response may tend toward acting out behaviors or other forms of avoidance. White (1974) speaks of "a greater tendency for public acting out in the face of frustration" (p. 33) among adults as well as adolescents. Television and other media forms, present adolescents with countless examples of unhealthy responses to stress.

The number of teenagers who use alcohol and other drugs is on the rise. The Metropolitan Life Insurance Co. reported in 1984 that 93 percent of high school seniors had tried alcohol and 59 percent had tried marijuana. Though the percentage of seniors smoking pot on a daily basis has apparently declined from a peak in 1978, the percentage of seniors using marijuana and alcohol may have reached an all-time high. Indications are that experimentation is beginning at an increasingly young age.

Alcohol and drug abuse has long been associated with suicidal behavior. Peck and Litman (1973) ranked drug and alcohol abuse as the number one cause of increasing adolescent suicide rates, followed by "alienation" and "increased stress." Greuling and DeBlassie (1980) report that at least 50 percent of teenagers who commit suicide were involved in moderate to heavy drinking and abusive use of dangerous drugs prior to their death. Drugs and alcohol are also, of course, commonly utilized in the actual suicide attempt itself as well as playing a role in the decision to attempt suicide (Robbins & Alessi, 1985).

An even greater danger, however, is the general proliferation of the means and acceptability of avoidance methods of coping. These include drug and alcohol abuse as well as sexual acting out, running away, and even attempted suicide. As adolescents turn toward nonmastery behaviors, they cripple their capacity to cope effectively with stress. They cease to grow and mature in a manner which will provide them with the means to successfully struggle within an increasingly stressful and unsupportive environment. Instead, increasing numbers may be literally medicating themselves against these pressures and demands, thus weakening their ability to deal with them. Jacobs (1971) and Novick (1984) have demonstrated that the progression toward suicidality often features a progression of ineffectual problem solving strategies, including withdrawal, running away and, finally, suicidal behavior.

The erosion of the stability of the nuclear family is, perhaps, the most critical factor involved in adolescent suicidal behavior. More and more families are overstressed in our society as are individuals and increasing numbers of families cannot cope with it. As such, they are less able to support and care for those who are dependent on it. Divorce, separation, the two working-parent family, increased mobility, lack of extended family ties, and the diminished sense of community present in many localities, all contribute to the reality of families less able to provide the support and communication needed by its young in a society such as ours. The rapid tempo of change, combined with feelings of insecurity and instability within the family exposes many of our young to a continuing state of anxious overarousal. The simplest and most effective solution may, at times, appear to be drugs and/or suicide. The very young teenager is at very great risk, since they are exposed at ever younger ages to the means of escape, before they have an opportunity to master age appropriate tasks of development in personality strengthening ways.

Regardless of societal stresses, suicidal behavior in our culture, in past years, has generally been regarded as unacceptable, immoral, even illegal behavior. Peer pressure and general societal sanctions against it have always been strong. This attitude may be weakening, at least among the young, who appear more accepting of suicide than their parents' generation. Curran (1984), has reported that, while adolescents do not hold positive attitudes toward peer suicide attempters, their feelings may be less negative than adults or even college age individuals. In short, while adolescents may not actually approve of suicidal behavior, they may not be as frightened of it or as unsympathetic to it, as their parents.

Adolescents are very familiar with suicidal behavior. Most have been exposed to it. Many know a friend who has tried it (Curran, 1984; McIntosh, Hubbard, & Santos, 1985). The behavior has, therefore, been modeled for them. Modeling has been reported to be a factor in the development of suicidal alternatives in disturbed individuals (Ashton & Donnan, 1981; Barraclough, Shepherd, & Jennings, 1977; Bollen & Phillips, 1982; Hewitt & Milner, 1974; Niemi, 1975; Phillips, 1974, 1979; Surtee, Taylor, & Cooper, 1976) and in disturbed adolescents (Corder, Shorr, & Corder, 1974; Jacobs, 1971; Kerfoot, 1979; Paulson & Stone, 1974; Shafii, Carrigan, Whittinghill, & Derrick, 1985; Teicher, 1973). As the incidence of adolescent suicidal behavior grows, so too will modeling and familiarity. This may contribute to an increase in suicidality within a subgroup of adolescents bearing a high level of readiness for such an act.

In conclusion then, we have before us an impressively dangerous formula for self-destruction among our young. There exists in combination, a highly stressful, fast-paced society, which our more troubled young feel both compelled to enter and at times hopelessly alienated from, an increasingly prolonged (beginning earlier and ending later) and complex adolescence, a proliferation of the means and acceptability of nonmastery, avoidant and self-destructive methods of coping with challenge and stress (i.e., drugs, alcohol, and other forms of acting out behaviors), the diminished ability of the nuclear family to bear up under the strain and provide necessary support to their young, reduced fear of suicide among the young, increasing modeling of suicidal behavior and subsequent familiarity with it. These factors may act together in creating fertile ground for the growth and spread of suicide as a response to problems in living.

Still, it is only the seriously troubled adolescent who, having exhausted a number of other strategies is apt to attempt suicide. Most adolescents will survive their attempt. Committed suicide in this age group, while becoming more frequent is still quite rare. Survivors, however, are greeted, postattempt, with a number of problems as they face a human environment often ill disposed toward responding to the young attempter in the manner that he or she may have wished. As a communicative gesture designed to elicit caring within an interpersonal context, attempted suicide, especially when perpetrated by the young, seems an exceedingly ineffective, even counterproductive way of getting one's needs met. Unfortunately, the attempter has no way of knowing this ahead of time. The adolescent suicide attempter frequently places himself in a position in which he is apt to be more misunderstood, more alone, and feel more rejected after his attempt than before it. The challenge, therefore, to the mental health profession, educators, health care personnel, and family members is enormous and likely to grow as suicidal behavior among adolescents remains on the increase. Obviously empathy and concern need to be at a high level within those in a position to respond to the suicidal adolescent. Empathy and concern, however, will be impossible to muster unless responders understand the behavior. Too often, adolescent suicidal behavior is denigrated, trivialized, ignored, denied, or rejected due to attitudes and beliefs that promote prejudicial and stereotypic notions of adolescents and their behavior.

In the immediate future, adolescents are likely to become more, rather than less, suicidal. We must be prepared to educate ourselves and others as to the meaning of the phenomenon in the individual case as well as the issue at large. A conciousness raising concerning the problem is under way, with a veritable explosion of research being devoted to an area referred to in 1973 as the "deserted field" (Brown, 1973).

2

Scope of the Problem
in the United States

RISE IN RATES

Adolescent suicide has leapt into the consciousness of the American lay and professional public in dramatic fashion in recent years. The spectacular prominence of suicidal adolescents in our midst would have been difficult to ignore. Its darkening shadow has spread too far. Prior to 1960 there was little to be found in the scientific literature pertaining to adolescent suicide. The steady rise in reported committed and attempted suicide among adolescents combined with intensive media attention to epidemics of suicide "clusters" or groups of deaths in single localities has yielded a national response. Research has greatly expanded in recent years. Governmental intervention has created the National Committee on Youth Suicide with representatives from every state to act as a clearinghouse for information on programs which are effective, focus public attention on the issue, and push for federal legislation to fund research, compile accurate, up-to-date national statistics on youth suicide, and provide information on existing suicide prevention programs. Research projects on adolescent suicide are receiving priority attention from the National Institute of Mental Health. The National Center for Disease Control in Atlanta has launched a major research effort into adolescent suicide. The Senate Subcommittee on Juvenile Justice called a congressional hearing in September 1984 to determine what action the federal government should take to stop the rapid rise in adolescent suicide.

Several states, most notably California and Florida are implementing or considering plans for school-based suicide education and prevention programs. Many town and county school systems have already begun to do this on their own. Television movies and talk shows have begun dealing with the subject in a serious and meaningful way. Professionals who work with adolescents applaud these efforts but ruefully note their slowness in coming. National attention, it would seem, has been dragged kicking and screaming toward a confrontation with this most unpleasant condition. As Haim (1974) and others have rightly pointed out, adults harbor an almost pathological aversion toward recognizing that young people intentionally end their lives or attempt to do so at an alarming and increasing rate.

Suicide now ranks as the second leading cause of death among persons aged 15-19 and the leading cause of nonaccidental death. Teenagers have not only become more suicidal, they have become apparently more reckless and self-destructive in general. As the suicide rate has risen steadily over the past 20 or so years, so too has the rate for motor vehicle accidents (the leading cause of death), accidents of other forms, and homicides (U.S. Vital Statistics 1981).

While suicide rates for teenagers have risen 72 percent since 1968, most other age groups have experienced a reduction in rate. It would be safe to say that while America as a whole has become slightly less suicidal over the past five years, teenagers and young people in general (30 and under) have become dramatically more suicidal. For teenagers the increase has risen most steadily and most consistently.

Still, death by suicide remains a relatively rare event among teenagers. The latest government figures show a rate of 8.7 per 100,000 which is only half that of 20-25 year olds and far less than any other measurable age group except 10-14 year olds (.8 per 100,000). Adolescents are, however, distinguished by their rate of increase relative to the other age groups and by one other resounding distinction: their rate of attempted suicide.

PREPONDERANCE OF ATTEMPTED
VS. COMMITTED SUICIDE

While committed suicide among adolescents increases at a disturbing rate, attempted suicide has become a phenomenon of truly epidemic proportions. Data on attempted suicide is particularly elusive and difficult to quantify with certainty. However, it is clear that teenagers in particular, and young persons in general, are greatly overrepresented in national and worldwide figures on rates for attempted suicide. Weisman (1974) attributes 50 percent of all attempted suicides to those under the age of 30 and points out that the modal age is dropping. Birtchnell and Alarcon (1971), in a study of emergency room admissions in Aberdeen Scotland reported 25 percent of the suicide attempters to be under 20 years old.

Attempted suicide is far and away the most common and characteristic form of suicidal behavior among teengagers and to a lesser degree, for persons in their 20s, while attempted suicide among the middle aged and elderly is relatively rare. In other words, the ratio of attempted to committed suicide reverses itself with increasing age.

Over the past 20 years the incidence of attempted suicide among adolescents has been seen to increase. This would reflect both the actual increase in the behaviors and greater accuracy and completeness in compiling data. An early ratio of 8:1 (Farberow, & Shneidman, 1961) for attempted to committed suicides was long cited by writers on adolescent suicide as an estimate of the ratio for that age group. However, this ratio was intended to reflect the rates for the general population and not a specific age group and therefore is largely meaningless since it grossly underestimates the rate of attempted suicide among adolescents while overestimating the rate for the older age groups. Over the years the ratio has crept toward a more realistic version, from 50:1 (Jacobziner, 1960; Schrut, 1964) to 220:1 (McIntire, Angle, & Schlicht, 1980). McIntire et al.'s ratio is especially helpful since, unlike many others, it is based exclusively on data on adolescents under 19 years of age. Angle, O'Brien and McIntire (1983) cite a ratio of 200:1 for persons aged 15-24. Curran (1984) reported a ratio of 312:1 based on data gathered from 15- to 18-year-olds. Clearly then, coupled with the rise in the rate of deaths by suicide is a corresponding rise in both the relative and absolute number of attempted suicides. The phenomenon of attempted suicide requires more attention. The meaning of the overrepresentation of adolescents among the nation's suicide attempters and the reasons why only a small percentage of teenagers who make what are called suicide attempts actually die, need to be explored. These two issues, among many others, point to the very different and special quality of adolescent suicidal behavior which set it apart from that of older age groups.

NATIONAL STATISTICS AND GENERAL POPULATION STUDIES: ARE THEY ACCURATE?

The figures for adolescent suicide and attempted suicide are impressive and rising. However, the bad news is that they are unanimously judged to be grossly underestimated. The actual rates of committed and attempted suicide are unknown and in the case of young persons, especially difficult to ascertain. Schrut (1964) estimated that the actual rate of adolescent suicide was 50 percent greater than the official figure. This seems to be a figure generally accepted as reasonable (Frederick, 1971; Mishara, 1982; Weiner, 1970).

Widespread acknowledgement of official underestimates of suicide rates, both in the U.S. and abroad, have spawned some interesting research. Burvill, McCall, Stenhouse, and Woodings (1982), in Australia, studied reports of deaths classified as undetermined or accidental. It was estimated that Australian suicide rates were possibly underestimated by 5-10 percent for males and 10-20 percent for females by categorizing some deaths from poisoning (drug overdoses) as being undetermined or accidental, rather than as suicide. Malla and Hoenig (1983) searched the Registrar of Births and Deaths in Newfoundland, Canada for death certificates in which no cause of death was recorded. Further investigation by a forensic pathologist revealed that 13 percent of these deaths were unequivocal suicides but had not been recorded as such.

Underreporting is an accepted fact. It occurs in a multitude of ways, from a variety of motives. Physicians, coroners, pathologists, family members, and the surviving perpetrators of suicide attempts all have compelling reasons to obscure or deny the fact of suicidal behavior. Committted suicide is still a crime in some states. The Roman Catholic Church has only recently begun to permit Last Rites for the nonpsychotic suicide victim. Suicide has long been considered a mortal sin. Insurance companies may retain discriminatory clauses in their policies, including lengthy waiting periods of one to two years, after the beginning date before the actual amount of the policy will be paid for a suicidal death, if at all. Less formally, the stigma associated with suicidal behavior, for the family and/or the surviving suicide attempter is very strong and decidedly negative. Shame and guilt are attendant upon the surviving familial or collegial associates of the suicide victim. For the survivor, research has proved nearly unanimous in discovering that people of widely differing ages, occupations, education, and socioeconomic levels and sex are predominantly negative in their attitudes toward persons who survive suicide attempts. (Ansel & McGee, 1971; Barber, Hodgkin, Patel, & Wilson, 1975; Bell, 1978; Boldt, 1982; Curran, 1984; Frederick, 1971; Ghodse, 1978; Ginsburg, 1971; Gordon, 1979; Haim, 1974; Hawton, Bancroft, & Simkin, 1978; Hawton, Marsack, & Fagg, 1981; Kalish, Reynolds, & Farberow, 1974; Limbacher & Domino, 1986; Linehan, 1971; Nicol, 1973; Patel, 1975; Sale, Williams, & Clark, 1975; Stillion, McDowell, & Shamblin, 1984; Stillion, McDowell, & May, 1984.)

This is especially true when one deals with adolescent suicide. Adults are responsible for identifying and recording causes of death. It is clear that ascribing suicide as a cause of death or a reason for injury in the young demands that the adult confront a painful realization. Haim (1974) states that suicide and attempted suicide are most often concealed in adolescent cases and offers three reasons as to the cause.

First, the family, especially the parents, have stronger motives for concealing the suicidal behavior of an adolescent than have the family or neighbors of an adult. Second, and related to the first, in the case of young people under age 21, there is the fear on the part of those responsible for the young person that they may be held responsible to some degree for the suicidal behavior of that person. The significant adults must feel not only concerned and fear being held morally responsible but there may also be a question of legal responsibility. This pertains not just to the parents but to adult supervisors if the teenager is in an educational or other specialized institution. Third, adolescent suicide, unlike suicidal acts of other age groups, offers the adult greater latitude for interpretation and more opportunity for ascribing accidental or nonsuicidal reasons for the act. The suicide of the adolescent is typically of a quality which often gives the appearance of accidental death (e.g., motor vehicle accidents and drug overdoses). Emergency room personnel and physicians often dismiss, due to ignorance as much as to attitudes, the adolescent suicide attempt of relatively low lethality and ambivalent intent as a "gesture" rather than dignifying it with the label of attempted suicide.

It is quite easy for the well-meaning individual to purposely assign accidental rather than suicidal reasons for a young person's injury or death, feeling for the sake of the victim, the family, and perhaps acting in the service of his own needs for denial. Burvill et al.'s (1982) study citing a higher level of underreporting for women pertains to the young as well since the young and the female favor a method of suicide (self-poisoning) which can more easily be taken as accidental especially when alcohol is used as well.

But considered more broadly, as Haim (1974) has elaborated at some length, adults struggle with conflicting emotions and beliefs concerning adolescence and adolescents in a manner that makes clear thinking concerning adolescent suicide a most difficult proposition. Adults often view the teenage years through lenses of wistful romance. These years are called by adults "the best years of your life," to which an unhappy teen might well respond "you mean it gets worse?!" To the adult who feels his or her youth is going, gone, or even worse, misspent or squandered, the teenage years stand as a time of unlimited potential, hope, and vigor. To then confront the teenager who would, with seeming indifference throw it all away or attempt to, is to the adult incongruous and maddening. It strikes to the heart of his world view. Making matters worse, the teenager's suicidal behavior is often precipitated by events which may seem trivial in comparison to the woes through which the adult must continually slog. It is not surprising then that adult physicians, parents, and others in a position to recognize and identify adolescent suicidal behavior, regularly fail to do so.

Circumstantial evidence for the presence of a vast number of undetected or disguised suicides and suicide attempts among teens has long existed and is being increasingly documented. Holinger (1979) called attention to the uniform fluctuation of death rates by suicide, homicide, and motor vehicle accidents among the young. The death rates for all three causes of death tend to rise and fall together. Lately they have been on the rise. Bollen and Phillips (1982) and Phillips (1979) have confirmed the association in great detail. In their research on the effects of modeling and suggestion on suicidal behavior in the general population, they have made an extensive study of the incidence of imitative suicides following publicized suicides (see chap. 7). Auto accidents and suicides are linked in a variety of ways. After highly publicized suicides, the suicide rate in the area of publication increases significantly. Single vehicle auto accidents increase but not multiple vehicle accidents, and in the area of publication only. The percentage of fatal, single vehicle accidents increases. The age of those involved in the accidents correspond closely with the age of the person whose suicide was published. The persons involved in the fatal crashes died more quickly than usual. Police often found no skid marks suggesting that the victim's foot was on the accelerator and not the brake, thus allowing for a more traumatic collision. There seems to be no question that auto accidents harbor a significant number of suicides both among the general population and the young. Given that persons aged 15–24 have by far the highest rate of death by means of motor vehicle accident (U.S. Vital Statistics, 1981) this association is especially relevant to the young. If it were possible to know precisely how many adolescent deaths officially registered as due to auto accidents or other forms of accidental or undetermined causes were actually suicides, suicide would certainly creep closer to accidental death as the leading cause of mortality among teenagers and the young.

Accurate data on adolescent attempted suicide is more difficult to ascertain and compile than committed suicide. There exists no national system for gathering and organizing statistics in this area. We are left largely to theoretic guess work, clinical experience, and a small number of studies based primarily on emergency room admissions to formulate an impression of the rates of attempted suicide in the young. As data-finding methods have improved, the reported rate has increased. However, all methods currently in use for gathering data have their limitations.

Attempt rates based solely on emergency room admissions must fail to yield a complete picture of the extent of attempted suicide. Medical staff often misdiagnose self-destructive behavior in the young as accidental or nonsuicidal. Moreover, suicide attempts, especially among teenagers often go unrecognized and untreated. Attempts of low lethality may be undetected by adults and no medical intervention will be involved. Hudgens (1975) found that 31 percent of the hospitalized adolescents who attempted suicide prior to admission had made an attempt without having any psychiatric or medical care associated with their action and without telling any adult about it until much later. Smith and Crawford (1986) reported that 90 percent of the 351 teenage suicide attempters studied had received no medical attention. This finding is consistent with the author's clinical experience in which it is fairly common to hear of suicide attempts by teenagers which are of a sufficiently minimal health risk so as to make possible their being hidden from parents, or if known to parents, it would be unnecessary to seek hospital care. These teenagers either treat themselves or obtain first aid assistance if necessary from friends or parents who are so often conveniently and not coincidentally nearby.

Lisa, at the time of her attempt, was a 15 year-old girl who attempted suicide by swallowing approximately 16 capsules of her allergy medicine at 9:00 pm at home with her parents present in the house. After taking the medication she lay down initally hoping for a more permanent peace. However, as time passed, her resolve to die dissipated and by 10:00 she was up and about the house interacting with her parents and appearing as though nothing was wrong except for what her parents described later as a heightened activity level. By 11:00, frightened of the effects of the medication and afraid to go to sleep lest she perhaps not awake, Lisa called a friend and spoke with her for another hour, never mentioning her suicidal behavior or thoughts. The effects of the medication were fairly powerful, but in the opposite direction from what she had anticipated. Rather than put her to sleep, it was keeping her awake. She roamed restlessly through the house. Her mother kept her company and tried to relax her, thinking that Lisa was agitated over some private circumstance as she often was. Early in the morning, still sleepless, she vomited a couple of times but maintained silence as to what was bothering her. Still, she insisted upon going to school the next morning which is where she first reported her suicidal behavior to me at 8:00 that morning. At that time she also gave me the suicide note she had written much earlier the night before.

Lisa's behavior is typical of the kind of suicidal behavior that never reaches public attention. She received no medical attention. Though in close proximity to her parents at all times that evening, she told them nothing. It was I who, 12 hours after the fact, informed them of what had happened. Even her best friend with whom she had spoken the night before was kept in the dark.

Hudgens' use of a self-report format for obtaining information about prior suicidal behavior in the histories of psychiatric patients has been used by others with interesting results. Mishara (1975) elicited data relevant to past suicide attempts from a population of 20-year-old college students. He found that 15 percent reported having made, at some point in their lives, a suicide attempt, in most cases, during their high school years. A later study by Mishara (1982) yielded a 13.6 percent rate of undergraduate respondents who had attempted suicide. Other studies using a similar self-report format for undergraduates report lower but still noteworthy rates of past suicide attempts (Limbacher & Domino, 1986; McIntosh, Hubbard, & Santos, 1985). All of these rates are considerably higher than those found in most studies of the general population for attempted suicide (McIntosh, Hubbard, & Santos, 1985). While some college populations have typically been found to have a higher incidence of suicidal behavior than noncollege populations (Ishii, 1985; Seiden, 1969), the findings are nonetheless striking. Curran (1984) questioned high school students, grades 10–12, and reported 12.5 percent admitting to having made suicide attempts. Smith and Crawford (1986) reported a rate of 10.5 percent. However, the question can be fairly asked, "Do these kids know what a suicide attempt is?" It is important at this point to define "suicide attempt" since the term clearly has different meanings to different persons. The definition in this book follows Stengel's (1964) as "any act of self-damage inflicted with self-destructive intent however vague and ambiguous." This definition includes any act, irrespective of the extent of physical injury but excludes gestures or self-mutilation where death is clearly and purposefully not intended. Examples of non-suicidal self-harm would include acts such as self-mutilation to relieve stress, overdosing to become "high" or intoxicated, or purely feigned self-injury for the purpose of dramatization. The critical element which distinguishes the "suicidal" act from the harmful nonsuicidal one is psychological rather than physical. The person must have in mind, subjectively, the attitude that death is to some extent anticipated and welcomed.

However, there is apparent in teenage suicidal behavior a broad continuum of degrees with reference to the commitment to death. Teenagers are usually highly ambivalent about the intended lethality of their attempts. Some merely gamble with death not really caring if death or life ensues from the act. But death is always an element in the motivation for the act, be it a 1 percent or 100 percent commitment. If the teenagers being questioned believe that they have made a suicidal attempt, then in the author's view they probably have. Certainly methods of data gathering involving objective adult evaluators in emergency rooms are imperfect as well and likely to represent only a portion of adolescent suicide attempters and can never represent them all. More extensive and refined use of self-reporting is recommended to help explore the nature and extent of suicide attempts among teenagers and to render more accurate the statistics on attempt rates. These studies need to include noncollege populations of post–high school age young persons as well as more study of high school age students. Studies of undergraduates, while logistically more appealing, will always be of limited value. Underreporting exists not merely as a testament to the complexities and problems involved in the gathering of accurate health statistics but, in the case of adolescent suicidal behavior, it attests to psychological and attitudinal complexities as well. Underreporting is not only harmful in that it prevents a full appreciation for the magnitude of the problem but speaks as well of a profound reticence in our culture toward acknowledging the conditions and reality of the need on the part of some to act upon themselves in such a dramatic way. This aversion is particularly strong for adolescent suicide.

EPIDEMIOLOGY

Race, Class, and Community

Suicidal behavior among adolescents remains, as it has consistently for decades, a behavior in which whites (Vital Statistics of U.S., 1986) and the middle and upper middle classes (Peck, 1986; Wiessman, 1974; White, 1974) have long been overrepresented. Among the 15-19-year-old age group for whom complete national figures are available up to the year 1981, white teenagers as a whole were reported as having a suicide rate of 9.1 (per 100,000) as compared to a rate for blacks of 4.5. However, suicide among blacks would appear to be on the increase.

Several theories have been offered as to the reason for black/white disparity in suicide rate. It has been suggested that black adolescents may have available more family support. Blacks, given the context of disadvantaged peers within which they often reside, may feel less out of phase from others in their community and have less of a problem with relative status. They may derive a hidden benefit from a "we're all in this boat together" kind of attitude. A "vicissitudes of aggression" theory has been promoted to account for black/white differences. Groups which externalize their anger are expected to have high homicide rates and lower suicide rates while those who internalize their anger should show the reverse pattern (Henry, & Short, 1954). Recent reviews of this theory has been somewhat critical (Sudak, Ford, & Rushforth, 1984), but it remains true that blacks maintain a much lower suicide rate than whites.

Geography may help to explain the difference. Suicide is more prevalent in rural areas than urban communities. This trend has progressed steadily since the early part of the twentieth century when the reverse was true (Stack, 1982). There are two major reasons offered for this difference. One possibility is that population movement into more rural areas affects the suicide rate by overwhelming and thereby limiting the effectiveness and supportiveness of community organization. Another possibility is that the reversal of the direction of migration toward rural rather than urban regions causes "structural disturbances" in formerly stable communities (Wilkinson

& Isreal, 1984). A more simple common denominator might be that people are being pulled away from one another.

For the more rural or suburban adolescent, what this means is greater social isolation and loneliness (Berman & Carroll, 1984). Depressed adolescents are intensely intolerant of loneliness, isolation, and anomie. Adolescents typically seek active, social avenues as a means of distracting themselves from their periodic depressions. Seriously depressed adolescents crave such diversion and can become seriously at risk without it.

Plano, Texas, the home of the Southfork Ranch of T.V.'s "Dallas" is a fast-track, white-collar Dallas suburb whose population has jumped at a rate of 10,000 annually. Plano experienced 8 teenage suicides in 15 months from February 1983 to May 1984. While Plano is unusual both in its rate of growth and its recent rate of adolescent suicide, it represents what occurs all across America on a small scale, all the time. The results for teenagers are often unhealthy doses of competition, uncertainty and instability in peer relations, insufficient support from over taxed communities, and alienation both from family and peers.

Educational Status

Suicide in adolescence has been associated with above average intelligence (Schaffer, 1974), and college students (Ishii, 1985; Fox, 1971; Lester & Lester, 1971; Pinkerton, 1969; Ross, 1969; and Seiden, 1969). However, others have presented findings rebutting the general statement that college populations are at significantly greater risk and have offered important qualifiers (Peck & Schrut, 1971; Senseman, 1969).

Most teenage suicidals are attending school though a disproportionate amount of them have found the complex and tremendous demands of high school to be too much. Rohn, Sarles, Denney, Reynolds and Heald (1977) and Teicher (1973) have reported 35 percent and 36 percent, respectively, of school age adolescent suicidals to have been school dropouts. McIntire et al. (1980) however, found only 5 percent dropouts in her teenage population. Those still attending school were found to be experiencing significant and debilitating problems with attendance, peer relationships, or grades, either singly or, more typically, in combination. An interesting and consistently reported finding relative to associations between class, education, intelligence, and suicide is the observation that suicide rates correlate positively with the exclusivity of the university that one attends. Higher suicide rates at "name" universities have been reported in Japan (Ishii, 1985), England (Lyman, 1961), and the United States (Black, 1971). In a report by Sorrel (1972) the suicide rate among Ivy League students was calculated to be twice the rate of the remaining college students in America and twice again the rate of noncollege peers. These findings speak forcefully of the added pressures and heightened expectations that the more gifted must sometimes face.

The suicidal adolescent in the high school environment wears many faces and evades a stereotypic description. It can, however, be said of all that they struggle to cope with a prodigious burden because nowhere in their teenage lives is a greater or more persistent level of energy and concentration required than in the typical high school experience. High schools demand of their students a high level of self-organization, self-monitoring, independence, adaptability, efficiency, and self-control. It insists that thoughts and feelings be effectively compartmentalized. For example, thoughts and feelings related to home and family, self-image and peer and love relations must be kept separate from thoughts related to class and curriculum. Each class must be thought of separately and organized separately. Adult support, while usually available must be sought out. Depressed, perhaps suicidal adolescents attempt to cope with this complex, sometimes chaotic environment in a variety of ways.

Cara was a 17-year-old senior and the embodiment of the perfect high school student when things began to slip and I came to know her. She was ranked in the top five in her class, was a class officer, member of the student council, National Honor Society, debating club, was involved with theatre productions, the yearbook, Math team, and numerous other student organizations during her high school years. She was pretty, articulate, apparently self-confident, and popular. On paper she looked great, so it came as rather a shock when she burst out of class one day yelling that she had "had it" and "I'd just like to kill myself." The explosion was both startling and without a clear precipitant. In fact, Cara was quietly and secretly (for she had no close friends), dealing with enormous pressures. Her father was a selfish, childish, rejecting alcoholic whose inconstant behavior and employment yielded a family that was chronically anxious and insecure. Cara's heavy investment in the school and its activities provided her with structure and certain rewards. However, her reticent and superficial nature as regards relationships prevented her from forming close supportive attachments in place of the absent supports from home. In short, Cara, despite outward appearances and obvious strengths, was a lonely, unsupported, overextended individual who derived little pleasure from her activities and accomplishments. For her, it was all hard, joyless work, and it failed to fill up the void in her life as intended.

When Cara attempted suicide it came as an enormous shock to those very few adults and students who knew of it. Being familiar only with the outer contours of her life, they found it hard to understand. Given their partial knowlege of Cara it seemed incongruous, reminding one teacher of the poem about "Richard Corey," the man who had everything and who went home one night and put a bullet through his head.

Cassandra went through high school quite differently. While high school was for Cara a place to bury one's self and one's feelings and thoughts in work and more mainstream activity, for Cassandra it was a place to bury oneself in drugs and socializing. Needless to say, Cassandra was not a good student nor did she involve herself in any school sanctioned activities or clubs. Nonetheless, Cassandra was nearly always at school, if not in class, and was at least as well known there as Cara. Further, she had many more and closer friends. Cassandra was fun and had fun, something Cara could never do. Cassandra, however, was virtually incapable of work. In fact, she was nearly incapable of attending school or class at all without the calming and fortifying influence of marijuana. Cassandra was a daily user. Drugs were her priority. She once complained, in all seriousness, during a group session to incredulous peers that her only problem in school was the price of pot. Asked to elaborate, she explained that since the price in the area had gone up and her hours at work had been cut back she could no longer afford to get high both before school and during lunch: "So that's why I'm having trouble going to class. I can't concentrate without pot. I'm nervous. I can't think. I feel weird. I can always get high at lunch but the morning is shot. I don't even bother to come. That's the problem with school."

More accurately, Cassandra was and is a seriously depressed girl who abused pot, alcohol, and cocaine in an effort to medicate herself against her depression. She was intolerant of tension and avoided most challenges. She was obviously not insight-oriented and relied almost entirely on external sources of support. School was way too much for her and she left during her junior year. Her suicide attempts (there were two) came as a surprise to no one but herself, because Cassandra's problems and Cassandra herself were wide open and fairly easy to observe and understand, not hidden like Cara's.

Both girls, however, found the high school experience to be more than their limited abilities to cope could handle. Cassandra could handle the social aspects, but not the work. And in this sense I mean not just the assignments, but the arduous and constant tasks of self-organization, compartmentalized thinking, independent functioning toward goal achievement, the tasks of making yourself do what you do not want to do and doing it often and to someone else's schedule and taste. Cara could handle the work, usually, but could not fit in, could not open up and learn about people and let them learn about her, thereby gaining the support outside the home which she needed and sought. Both are tasks of adolescent development which are experienced in intense and concentrated fashion in the typical high school environment. Adolescents who are disturbed to the point of being suicidal are also likely to find some, if not many, aspects of high school demands and challenges to be too much for them.

Sex

Among the general population, males have for decades outnumbered females approximately 3:1 in suicides committed. Recent findings suggest that this disparity may actually be increasing (McIntosh, & Jewell, 1986). For adolescents in America, national figures for 15-19 year-olds (U.S. Vital Statistics, 1981) show a rate for males of 13.8 and for females of 3.0, a ratio of more than 4:1. The difference was even greater among white male and female teenagers (males 14.6, females 3.4). Attempt rates show major sex differences in the opposite direction. Attempted suicide among adolescents appears to be a largely female phenomenon. The literature, based on general population studies, consistently cites female:male ratios of at least 3:1. Ratios of 4:1 have been cited by Jacobziner (1965), Teicher (1973), and White (1974) in reference to purely adolescent populations. Much more disparate ratios for adolescents have been reported by Birtchnell (1971) 9.5:1, Curran (1984) 5:1, Hawton, Cole, O'Grady, and Osborne (1982 a) 9:1), McIntire et al. (1980) 9:1, and Toolan (1975) 10:1. The ratios that are consistently the highest in terms of female attempters over males have been studies based on self-poisoning or drug overdoses as this is the method preferred by females, while males have tended to favor the more violent means including firearms, hanging, and auto accidents. However, clinical observation suggests that women are adopting more violent and historically masculine means of attempting suicide.

The fact that males attempt suicide with less frequency, but commit with greater success than females in the teenage years has been taken as evidence that suicidal adolescent males constitute a significantly more disturbed population than suicidal adolescent females (Hawton, 1982; Otto, 1972; Sudak et al., 1984; Teicher, 1973). On the other hand, higher rates of male suicide may have more to do with choice of methods or their perception of receiving a more negative response to an unsuccessful attempt. There are several inferences which can be drawn from these figures and observable clinical phenomena in adolescence. Girls in our culture still are permitted fewer outlets for the release of aggression externally. For males a multitude of socially sanctioned activities and endeavors exist, such as sports and rough play. Behaviors which are deemed inappropriate for girls, such as fighting, obscene language and certain types of delinquent behavior are tolerated as a quasi-normal stage of development in boys. For many males, these behaviors are indeed seen as admirable traits so long as they do not do serious damage or persist too long into late adolescence. Thus, anger and aggression are encouraged toward external objects and provisions are made for their almost ritual release. For adolescent females the reverse is generally true. Girls are encouraged to control angry feelings and withold aggression. Far fewer outlets are provided for the sublimation and discharge of aggression through acceptable channels onto acceptable objects. Girls risk femininity and censure for creating their own means for externalizing their anger. At the same time they are permitted and encouraged to internalize their feelings, to turn their anger upon themselves. It would seem that our culture has deemed depression to be the psychological affliction or condition of its females while assigning to angry males the role of "disorderly persons."

Further, males are expected to respond differently from females to psychological and environmental stress. It is unseemly for males to manifest low self-esteem. It is often attractive for women to do so. Males are expected to not give in to or even acknowledge painful or disturbing feelings or anxiety. They are encouraged to use repression, denial, and displacement, leading often to somatization (heart disease, high blood pressure, ulcers). Females are allowed to cry, feel and manifest sadness, depression, grief. Our culture prepares men to respond to problems with vigor and forthrightness, or at least stoicism. To acknowledge or give in to problems connotes weakness and a lack of self-reliance. Males are expected to pull themselves up by their bootstraps. Females are encouraged to rely on others, to accept weakness and dependence on external sources of support, to *not* be strong internally.

In short, suicidal behavior is for girls more consistent with societal expectations than it is for males. For a teenage boy to attempt suicide he must step further outside cultural norms and expectations than a female does. They must go more against the cultural grain, so they make fewer attempts

> *It may be that females expect more sympathy and empathy than do males and, therefore, feel less restraint in attempting to end their lives. Males on the other hand, may expect less environmental support after an attempt, thereby increasing their determination to succeed if suicide is attempted. (Stillion, McDowell, & Shamblin, 1984, p. 75)*

Studies by Topol and Reznikoff (1984) and Walch (1977) confirm certain aspects of these sex based differences in adolescent suicidal behavior. Topol and Reznikoff found that teenage female suicide attempters tended to be more dependent on outer sources of support than did their male counterparts. They were seen as especially dependent on peers. Walch found that female suicide attempters manifested lower self-esteem than the suicidal teenage males in the study and cited data in agreement with Topol and Reznikoff's findings on greater female dependency on external sources of support.

Though our society is apparently changing and young girls are encouraged to take on more "masculine" roles, adolescent females remain distinctive in their suicidality. They tend to engage in more, and less lethal, suicidal behavior. They overwhelmingly prefer drug ingestion as the method of attempt. The suicidal act tends to occur as part of an interpersonal conflict or loss. Though less disturbed they are more depressed. It will be interesting to see how this changes with the next generation if women become more aggressive and, unfortunately, more violent.

Methods

It is a common and inevitable feature of suicidal behavior, be it adult or adolescent that committed suicides are associated with more active and lethal methods. However, there are important sex and age related differences. For males, adult or adolescent, use of firearms easily leads all other methods of comitted suicide, followed, according to most studies, by poisoning by means of alcohol and barbiturates and by hanging. Females however, favor more passive, less violent methods. Self-poisoning and the use of carbon monoxide gas are the leading methods, with firearms second, and hanging third. Adolescents as a group, however, favor less active, less violent methods than adults. They utilize firearms less frequently than adults (though it is still their leading method) while using hanging and self-poisoning through alcohol and drugs more than do adults (Peck, 1986).

Suicide attempts, on the other hand, typically involve self-poisoning, regardless of sex, though for females, especially adolescent females it is the overwhelming favorite among all other methods (McKenry, Tishler, & Kelley, 1983). Most frequently used are the analgesics (pain relievers), but nearly any household prescription or nonprescription drug will do. Adolescents are largely ignorant of their own physiology and the interactive effects of drugs. They have only the vaguest notions of what might constitute lethal dosages. The teenager who is made drowsy by two Tylenol is fully prepared to believe that 4 or 5 times that dosage may cause permanent sleep. Other methods less frequently used by adolescents in their suicide attempts include wrist slashing, strangulation, and a hidden method, automobile accidents. The means adolescents adopt in engaging in suicidal behavior reflect their ignorance of the effects of drugs and medications and their ambivalence concerning their own deaths. These are distinctive features of adolescent suicidal behavior, features that are often misunderstood but are often central to an appreciation of its meaning.

Psychiatric Status

Historically, adolescent suicidal behavior has been viewed as age-related behavior of an impulsive and rather frivolous nature, often indulged in by relatively normal teenagers for consciously manipulative purposes. More recently, adolescent suicide and suicide attempts have come to be better understood and, as a result, taken far more seriously. However, formal diagnostic labels often fail to capture the character of the disturbance that is present or to encapsulate teenage suicide into any homogenous diagnostic category. Lester (1972) reviewed earlier studies trying to establish personality correlates to suicidal behavior among adolescents and reported that no methodologically sound conclusions could be drawn. Hudgens (1974) stated, "considered by itself, the fact that a teenager has attempted suicide or made a serious suicidal communication tells little about him except that he probably has a psychiatric disorder" (p. 131). It is becoming increasingly clear, however, that despite the failure of current diagnostic nosology, teenage suicide attempters are significantly disturbed individuals who upon close inspection often have a history of family, school, social, and affective dysfunction that is impressive if not easily labelled.

Crumly (1982) states quite emphatically and accurately in speaking of suicidal adolescents that "adolescent symptoms in general are often unrecognized, minimized, and underdiagnosed" (p. 158). There remains a tendency on the part of many in the mental health profession who are inexperienced with adolescents to expect "craziness" from adolescents despite the work by Oldham (1978) and Offer (1979) who have shown clearly that most teenagers do not experience adolescence as particularly traumatic or tumultuous and do not present symptoms of any significance during this stage of development. Smith and Crawford (1986) found marked depression in only 1.7 percent of nonsuicidal adolescents as compared to 42.4 percent of adolescent suicide attempters. Oldham (1978) and Haim (1974) emphasize this point in asking that adolescent symptoms be taken seriously and that self-destructive or suicidal behavior of any kind regardless of the apparent lethality of intent is to be viewed with great concern. Normal, happy, well-functioning teenagers do not attempt or commit suicide. Finch and Poznanski (1971) in their review of the literature stressed that "the emotionally healthy adolescent does not either commit suicide nor attempt to do so" (p. 160). This much would seem obvious. However, the nature of their disturbance is sometimes elusive. McIntyre et al. (1980) reported that 31 percent of the over 1000 adolescents studied by her group were categorized as having "no significant problems." Porot, Covdert, and Collett (1968) found no "identifiable" psychiatric disorder in a group of 40 adolescent females who had taken overdoses. White (1974) states, however, that "formal psychiatric nosology is often inappropriate in considering the problems and needs of this group of patients" (p. 33).

While adolescent suicidals constitute a heterogenous group of significantly and historically troubled youngsters it is possible to assign to them certain general qualities. First, the feature most often seen and reported is depression (Crumley, 1982; Gould, 1965; Hodgman, 1985; Robbins, & Alessi, 1985; Smith, & Crawford, 1986; Tishler, & McKenry, 1983; Toolan, 1975; Triolo, McKenry, Tishler, & Blythe, 1984; White, 1974). Though its manifestation in adolescence can take many forms, Gould (1965) described depressed adolescents as experiencing "a felt loss of love," emanating from a specific relationship or relationships but sometimes generalized to the human environment as a whole. There is commonly a profound and progressive sense of abandonment, loneliness, and isolation, coupled with hopelessness, a loss of faith in the future, and a feeling of being trapped permanently in the present. Jacobs (1971) speaks of a progression of familial and social failures and dysfunction which culminate in social isolation, depression, and eventual suicidality. Depression, however, is often difficult to spot in the adolescent. It is often masked and acted out in ways that look like anything but depression. It is more difficult to assign diagnostic labels to these teenagers. Nonetheless, the disarray of their lives and the quality of their familial and interpersonal relationships will always reveal, if one has the opportunity to study them, significant and chronic disturbance. These relationships have not been able to gratify the needs of these adolescents. Further, it may be that the mental health status of the adolescent suicide attempter and committer is now more disturbed than in previous years. Schneer, Perlstein and Brozobsky (1975), in a comparative study of adolescents admitted to the same hospital thirteen years apart (1957 and 1969–1970), found that not only was there a doubling of the rate of admissions for adolescent suicidal behavior but that the typical attempter presented a more psychologically disordered and aggressive suicidal adolescent.

Despite the stated position of this work that suicidal adolescents are significantly disturbed and that certain generalizations can be made about them in terms of their affective, interpersonal, and family histories, they remain a group whose heterogeneity and varied symptomatology make them difficult to both diagnose or identify. Their behavior is especially difficult to accurately predict. Many teens who manifest many or all of the traits mentioned will not become suicidal. More research is needed in order to better identify those most likely to become seriously self-destructive in order to educate and protect this very much at-risk population.

Family

Considerable research has been devoted in recent years to the constitution, dynamics, and histories of the families of suicidal adolescents. Much of this research has been fruitful in distinguishing the characteristics which set the family of the suicidal apart from normal families and the families of disturbed but nonsuicidal teenagers. Briefly (Chapter 3 will address the issue in greater detail), any analysis of the antecedents of suicidal behavior in a child or adolescent must include an assessment of family history and family functioning. It has been shown that the families of suicidal adolescents experience significantly more dysfunction, disruption, mobility, and loss than the families of normal teens. Parental losses tend to occur at an earlier age for the suicidal teenager than in comparison groups of disturbed nonsuicidal adolescents. (Stanley & Barter, 1970). Higher incidences of abuse, neglect, and incest have been reported (Deykin, Alpert, & McNamara, 1985; Green, 1978). Serious impairment of communication and relationship between father and daughter is being noted and treated with increasing importance in the dynamics and etiology of female adolescent suicide. Jacobs (1971) stressed in writing of the progressive etiology of suicide in adolescents that they often feel like a "burden" to their families. They feel that the family would be better off without them. In many cases the perception was covertly or overtly reinforced by family members. Adolescent suicide attempts typically occur within an interpersonal context as a form of maladaptive communication. More specifically, the interpersonal context is often a familial one.

Peers

Good peer relationships are, of course, important to adolescents and it is a quality of teenage life that peer relationships become invested with greater meaning and urgency than at any other age. This is at a time when familial ties may be slackening and the teenager's search for identity, validation, and self-esteem are most effectively clarified and supported within their peer relationships. This may be especially true for the disturbed, suicidal adolescent for whom family life has often been inadequate. These teenagers characteristically turn with greater urgency to their peers in order to have enormous needs met. Their relationships become supercharged with a degree of desperation and need that is often not shared by their friends and lovers. They tend to have fewer close friends but much more intense couplings (Teicher, 1973). Ruptures in these rather top heavy relationships are both inevitable and devastating to the suicidal adolescent. They tend to feel that they have so little else in their world to support them and with the departed person goes their own sense of worth, self-esteem, and purpose. This can often be the precipitant to what to others might seem an unjustified suicide attempt. Observers view the broken relationship far less seriously than does the damaged victim, and therefore, have difficulty understanding the magnitude of the suicidal response. However, to the suicidal teenager, with a history of felt loss and rejection, this response to this latest blow is far from being the dubious, attention-seeking ploy, that adults and peers may deem it to be.

Research has shown that peers hold a place of very special importance in the emotional and object life of the suicidal adolescent (Topol and Reznikoff, 1984; Walch, 1977). It has been further demonstrated that peer problems are considered to be a critical factor in the development of adolescent suicidal behavior (Dashef, 1984; Jacobs, 1971; Rohn et al., 1977; Teicher, 1973; Tishler, McKenry, & Morgan, 1981; Walch, 1977; Wenz, 1979).

The story of the popular, competent, brilliant star of the school who inexplicably attempts or commits suicide is a myth. Such are merely outward appearances as in the case of Cara and certainly not the subjective experience of the suicidal person. Suicidal teenagers are failures to themselves, if not to others. Apparently popular ones may maintain only superficial, unsatisfying relationships. They feel alone even in a crowd. Their unhappiness seems all the more frightening and inexplicable given their popularity and apparent competence. They, like their suicidal peers are not engaged in relationships that effectively comfort them or fulfill their needs.

The Role of Drugs

Adolescents today are often described as being subject to greatly increasing amounts of stress. Certainly there are symptomatic adolescent behaviors which tend to confirm that belief. Suicide and substance abuse are two such behaviors. As the level of stress in the life of the adolescent has become more plentiful so too has become the availability and use of drugs and alcohol. The Metropolitan Life Insurance Company report of 1984 found that 93 percent of American high school seniors had used alcohol, with 70 percent reporting that they had used it during the previous month. The report stated that 59 percent of high school seniors had used marijuana with 29 percent having used it during the previous month. Further, one in sixteen seniors were reported to be daily pot smokers. While no significant differences were noted among whites and blacks in terms of drug use, blacks appeared to drink considerably less with 37 percent of black seniors being abstainers while only 20 percent of white seniors could claim that distinction. The sample group for this enormous study included 17,700 12th-graders from all regions of the country in 140 public and private high schools.

Clearly, adolescents are using drugs, including alcohol, at an alarming rate. A significant and increasingly younger minority is using them as a way to cope with the stress of adolescence and are becoming abusers of drugs in the process. The wider availability and abuse of psychotropic drugs and alcohol have long been associated with an increased incidence of suicide in adolescents (Greuling & DeBlassie, 1981; McIntire, Angle, & Schlicht, 1980; Weissman, 1974).

In fact drug abuse and suicidal behavior appear linked in a variety of ways. Overdosing is the prevalent mode of both completed and attempted suicide in the young. Both behaviors are usually responses to levels of depression with which the individual cannot effectively cope. Crumley (1981) has called drug and alcohol abuse the most common and characteristic symptom of the suicide attempter. Frequent use of drugs and alcohol was found in a large majority (70 percent) of a group of adolescent suicide attempters while found in only 29 percent of the adolescent comparison group of nonsuicide attempters (Shafii, Carrigan, Whittinghill, & Derrick, 1985). Research focusing on the family lives of teenage suicide victims have often noted a higher incidence of drug and alcohol abuse and addiction in their parents as compared to the parents of nonsuicidal teens (McKenry, Tishler, & Kelley, 1983). Adolescents will often use their parents' drugs in their suicide attempt (McKenry et al., 1983).

Substance abuse has been found to be not only significantly associated with adolescent suicide but a serious symptom contributing to increased suicidal risk and more medically serious attempts (Robbins, & Alessi, 1985). Adolescents who seek to cope in such a maladaptive way may be those with less access to healthier means such as family and social supports. Substance abuse itself with its own corrosive and isolating effects may produce not only poor adaptation to primary problems by adolescents, but may produce numerous secondary problems as well. As such, substance abuse appears to be both a concomitant and complication to what may be a primary affective disorder. It is often both a contributor to the suicidal process and the means for the suicidal act.

However, while substance abuse has been associated with adolescents at higher risk for suicide it is also cited as a substitute for suicide. Ironies, contradictions, and inconsistencies abound in the study of adolescent suicidal behavior. Stanton (1977) suggested that drugs are perhaps an alternative to or an equivalent of suicide. For many adolescents, substance abuse serves as their form of self-prescribed medication against depression or even decompensation to psychotic or near-psychotic states as with the borderline personality. In so treating their underlying disorders some adolescents ward off as well the threat of suicide, albeit in a dangerous and ultimately maladaptive way. These adolescents take their suicide instead in smaller, more temporary, and more frequent doses. Teenagers have been largely responsible for coining the majority of slang terms for intoxication and they are a disturbingly self-destructive array of derogations when taken literally. Some favorites include, "smashed," "wasted," "obliterated," "stoned," "wrecked," "shit-faced," "gonzo," and "totaled," to name a few. Of course, few teenagers take these terms seriously, but some undoubtedly do. For some, the goal *is* obliteration, to act upon oneself in such a way as to blot out one's conscious existence, at least temporarily to become insensate, unthinking, unfeeling.

I have known more than a couple of teenagers who, if suddenly deprived of their "medications," would instantly have been at very high risk for suicide, at least in my mind. While their manner of coping left a great deal to be desired, hindered the progress of therapy and produced other problems as well, it also bought time. For the teenager whose life-threatening stresses are largely phase specific regarding, for instance, family, school, and the intensity of adolescent social life, the time bought can make an important difference. Time bought in this manner, however, exacts a heavy price. Sometimes the damage can be repaired to a reasonable extent, often it cannot. Adolescents who avoid healthy mastery by coping with drugs may forfeit their maturation. They often remain at the level of maturation at which drug abuse began, and with abuse beginning at increasingly early ages, this is a frightening prospect. The average age of first use of alcohol, for example, is down to 12 to 13 years according to the National Institute on Alcohol Abuse and Alcoholism. Teenagers who turn from use to abuse may remain permanently crippled in their capacity to deal in a strong, healthy, and adaptive manner to the demands of growth, having failed to learn during adolescence, that is one of the things adolescence is meant for.

Suicide among American teenagers is increasing at an alarming though underestimated rate. Specific determinants of race, class, sex, intelligence, education, personality, family, and peer relationships have been briefly reviewed in order to describe the problem and to put a face on its victims. However, none of these characteristics of suicidal adolescents adequately explain the phenomenon or its increase. Seemingly, each is too circumscribed, and even together fail to address this rising tide in a way which can allow us to perceive its source or course. These include a greater tendency for public acting out in the face of frustration, lower frustration tolerance, and a demand for more immediate gratification on the part of the young, as well as the greater use and abuse of drugs and alcohol by increasingly younger segments of society. Many teenagers opt to avoid the challenges of growth in this manner, failing therefore to develop healthy and mature coping mechanisms and problem solving strategies. Maturation is in these cases arrested while stresses may continue to accrue. These ill-equipped teens become highly vulnerable to external and internal stresses with which they have not learned to deal. American families are failing at an expanding rate to provide stable, predictable, secure, and nurturing environments for the growth of healthy, confident children. Instead, they are becoming ever more fragmented, broken, mobile, disorganized and, as a result, less effectively loving and supportive.

Things change quickly in our time. Rapid and continuous adaptation is being demanded of our young at younger and younger ages. While our society and technology may indeed have advanced in impressive ways, it is not at all clear that the human organism has changed all that much in recent years, or that it is capable of standing up to these demands. It is not surprising that increasing numbers of teens may respond by hunkering down, turning to drugs or alcohol, and waiting for all this to pass, electing not to jump on the merry-go-round. Some who have ridden the dizzying ride to exhaustion may risk themselves by simply jumping off.

I have noticed in my clinical experience with teenagers that most of the ones I work with do not use drugs or alcohol primarily to experiment, have fun or get high. Rather, they use them for relief, tension or stress reduction, or escape. They appear to be attempting to medicate themselves against their noxious environments. The problem of the rise in suicide rates needs to be addressed not just by the essential study of the minutiae, but by a more global perspective as well. We must create an environment that is liveable before expecting our young to be able to live in it.

3

Meaning and Reasons:
The Balance of Life and Death

DEATH CONCEPTS AND ADOLESCENCE

Ascertaining the meaning, intent, and precipitants of adolescent suicidal behavior is a tricky business. However, before we can begin to explore the meaning of the adolescent's suicide attempt, we must evaluate his notion of the meaning of death itself. One's concept of death or of any complex idea develops over time, with the support of accumulated experience and the expansion of intellectual capacities. The child's, and eventually the adolescent's, understanding of the meaning and personal relevance of death proceeds in a systematic sequence. Piagetian developmental psychology applies to the development of the death concept as it does to most other areas of cognitive development. Take as an example the issue of irreversibility in death. Children at the preoperational level of intellectual development (approximately 2-7-years-old) have not completed an accurate understanding of the permanence of death. Rather, they appear to view death as a temporary, reversible event such as sleep (Stillion & Wass, 1979). Even children at the concrete level of mental operation (approximately 7-12-years-old) often struggle with the concept of the irrevocability of death (Wass, 1984).

By the time a person has completed adolescence they should not only have reached the stage of Piagetian formal operations and become capable of adult levels of abstract thought but should have acquired an adult understanding of death as well. If properly cognitively advanced the adolescent should understand that death is natural, universal, and irreversible, both as an abstract and personal reality. However, not all individuals progress at the same rate though they may proceed along the same track. As Wass (1984) points out,

> There is little variation in the sequence *provided the environment is constant but as with all growth, children vary in the* rate *of cognitive development; that is, children differ widely in chronological ages at which they reach higher cognitive levels of understanding, including the understanding of death. (p. 17)*

Variable environmental and emotional conditions, however, are a given in human life; so too is variability in the level of understanding of death among adolescents. Adolescents' potential for abstract, reality-based thinking is often compromised by conflicting needs which can cause him to essentially deny the limitations of reality and confabulate his thought. The issue of his own mortality is a prime example. Research has shown that comprehension of death can be interfered with by a high level of anxiety (Orbach & Glaubman, 1979; Orbach, Grass, Glaubman, & Berman, 1985; McIntire, Angle, & Struppler, 1972). Speaking in regard to the death concept of the adolescent, McIntire et al. (1980) write

> The adolescent has a sense of personal immortality no matter what his stated concepts are, because his own death is so remote in time; he enjoys the invincibility of youth. (p. 74).

Indeed denial of death or personal injury is a major dynamic in adolescent drug use and driving habits. This sense of invincibility and immortality, so strong and typical in the adolescent, is reinforced within our culture by the attitudes of aversion and denial. The subject of death is taboo. Euphemisms such as "put to sleep," "passed on," and "took a long trip" substitute for and stand in the way of an affirmation of the finality of death. Television and the movies regularly depict reversible, clean deaths as characters are killed in one show and reappear on another. A lifetime of exposure to death, Western style, can impede development of a "formal operations" level of death concept. It is little wonder that teenagers entertain such hopes that Jim Morrison of the "Doors" yet lives. For whatever reasons, many teenagers contemplating suicide may be doing so without a clear understanding of what it is they are getting into. This can make the behavior more possible and perhaps more dangerous.

Recently I had referred to my practice a 17-year-old whose father had become very concerned over what seemed to be numerous signs of suicidal intent. She had been depressed for several months and had not yet gotten over a broken relationship with a boyfriend which occurred a year ago. She had just quit school and her job. A friend of hers had hung himself a month before from his parents' front lawn tree in a much publicized incident. Her father had, on the morning he called me, found a butcher knife in her drawer; and it was Spring. If ever a teenager had seemed at risk, this one did. I was encouraged by her statement that she wanted someone to talk to and was very willing to make an appointment for the next morning. I met an attractive, articulate girl of well above average intelligence who confirmed during the session the impression of major depression which her father had reported but not of high suicide risk. The reason for this, aside from her honest and urgent desire for therapy and an ability to make good use of it, was her description of her feelings about her friend's suicide. "I'll admit I've thought about trying to kill myself, but I've always been too afraid. But after Tom did it and I went to his funeral, I know I won't. It's too final. I want a chance to see if things can get better later on."

It came as a shock to this intelligent girl that death was final, and so too would be hers. Stillion, McDowell, & May (1984) have written "It is reasonable to assume that adolescents with greater development of their formal operations in a Piagetian sense would better understand the finality of death and would be less likely to romanticize suicide (p. 90)." Adolescents, and particularly suicidal and therefore disturbed adolescents, do not function on a solely intellectual plane and though they may not always be subverted into romanticizing death, they are highly susceptible to faulty reasoning and perceptions about it.

LETHALITY OF INTENT

A cursory examination of the rates of adolescent committed and attempted suicide reveals a distinctive quality of adolescent suicidal behavior. Their self-destructive acts are typically nonfatal. The ratio of attempted to committed suicides favors attempts among teenagers to a far greater extent than for any other age group. Only a small percentage of teenagers who make what are called suicide attempts actually die. The relative infrequency of successful suicide attempts in teenagers raises a question as to the actual meaning and intent of their apparently self-destructive acts.

The literature is often highly contradictory in its assessment of the dynamics and motives involved. It matters greatly whether the assessor is an adult or a teenager, the attempter him or herself, or an objective evaluator. It matters whether the evaluator him/herself is a former suicide attempter or one who is not. Ascribed reasons will vary depending on whether the attempter is asked to cite a reason for the attempt or whether they are asked to choose from a list of most often given reasons for suicidal behavior. Research has been carried out utilizing all of these methods of inquiry. In reviewing and clarifying some of the conflicting data, two points become quite clear. First, there exists a significant and dangerous level of misunderstanding among adolescents and adults as the meaning and intent behind adolescent suicide and suicide attempts. Second, the lethality of suicidal acts exist along a life-death continuum, which is also inadequately understood. For many suicidal persons, especially the young, the commitment to death is less than 100 percent. Most teenagers who attempt suicide harbor along with their self-destructive urges, a wish to live of varying strength, or at least a wish not to die. Suicidal and depressed teenagers feel, at least for a time, that life is not worth living. They are tired of struggling. They want to quit. They do not want to keep living. However, they are often not fully committed to either life or death. Several whom I have known have expressed the feeling that if death somehow took them by chance they would be relieved. They are, however, very passive about it. These individuals do not wish to be the active agent in their demise.

Bob, a boy with whom I worked, lived in a mid-sized city through which ran a four lane elevated, windy, and dangerous highway which is fairly heavily traveled even late at night. Bob lived very close to this highway. When he felt especially depressed and hopeless about his life predicaments (and there was a good deal to be depressed about), he would get out of bed, leave his home, and walk once across the highway and once back again. He would not stop for traffic or even acknowledge it. He would simply step over the guard rail and walk at a steady pace, eyes forward heedless of any oncoming cars. If he made it (he always has), either by virtue of the fortuitous coincidence of no cars traveling at such a time and place as to intersect his path or by alert and avoidant drivers, then fine. He took it as a good sign that perhaps things for him might improve. On the other hand, if he were to be hit and die then so be it. He could not lose, not in the frame of mind which would bring him out to that road.

Charlene, a girl who I once knew well would subject herself to great danger after fights with her boyfriend, her only supportive attachment in an otherwise desolate life. On one occasion she purposely went out of her way to walk, late at night, through a very dangerous part of her city where a month earlier a teenage girl had been raped and murdered. One final example, and among the most common forms of self-destructive behavior, involves purposefully reckless driving; the cause of many unrecorded suicides.

Suzanne, a very disturbed, probably borderline, and probably alcoholic 18-year-old with a history involving, among other traumas, two earlier suicide attempts, had a special road in her town which she used for a special purpose. Alone at night, drunk to some degree, and in the possession of her one true friend, her car, she would sometimes feel drawn to her road as to death.

She generally had a particular speed in mind when she would begin her descent down this long winding and narrow road. Once the starting speed of 50 or 60 mph was decided upon she would not fall beneath it no matter what, as she flew like a bobsledder down her course. Like Bob and Charlene she took a very passive attitude toward the possibility of her death. If the car crashed fine, but she was not quite prepared to crash it intentionally.

These are examples of the ambivalence typically felt by suicidal adolescents. As a group they appear to lean toward life rather than death, albeit unenthusiastically. They probably hold a place along the life-death continuum somewhere short of the mid-point. This hypothesis is to be explored in the pages to follow. It is, however, an inescapable truth that teenagers, who are fully capable of killing themselves, usually fail to do so.

An understanding of the unsuccessful suicide attempt is of critical importance. Often the realization of nonlethal intent leads, through ignorance, to a denigration and trivialization of the act and of the person. This is a dangerous mistake. While recognizing the prevalence of the low-lethality suicide attempt among adolescents and especially among adolescent females, it will be the purpose of this chapter and this book to emphasize the seriousness of the act as a statement of psychological crisis.

While it is a fact that most suicidal adolescents do not kill themselves and that suicide attempts outnumber committed suicides 200 or 300 to 1 in this age group, is it, therefore, also true that teenagers who attempt suicide have absolutely no wish to die? Either a yes or no response to this question would be wrong. The matter is more complex, both in terms of the age group as a whole and for each individual case. However, most evaluators, most suicidal adolescents and most groups of lay persons with whom I have spoken and questioned feel that most adolescent suicide attempters are not compelled by a strong wish to die. There is a good deal of research and clinical experience to support this position. There is also a noteworthy disagreement between suicidal adolescents and their evaluators over the perceived level of lethal intent.

Most of the studies are based on interviews with adolescents in the emergency rooms of hospitals. They are generally of two types. One type features assessments of lethal intent made solely by clinical assessors of one form or another (physicians, psychiatrists, psychologists). Another type solicits comments from the victims themselves on the level or existence of a wish to die in their suicide attempt. A few studies utilize both methods together in an effort to compare and contrast beliefs. These are the most helpful and revealing studies. A third type utilizes brief case vignettes describing a suicidal person by age, sex, and the background precipitant to the act. Evaluators respond to these vignettes and indicate beliefs, diagnostic assessments, attitudes, or treatment plans.

As an example of this third type, Hawton et al. (1981) reported that none of the 40 psychiatrists evaluating the female teenager in the case study believed she had acutally wanted to die as a result of her suicide attempt. Hawton et al. (1978) solicited the views of nonpsychotic in- and out-patient adult psychiatric patients concerning reasons for adolescent (among others) suicide attempts. "Wish to die" was not ranked as an important factor by these respondents for adolescent suicide attempts.

Curran (1984) in a study of adolescents' beliefs and attitudes concerning adolescent suicide asked 150 teenagers to rank order by importance and frequency a list of 10 reasons for adolescent suicide attempts. The reason "wanted to die" was ranked ninth by the 131 nonsuicide attempters among this group. However, a group of teenagers within the study group who had themselves at one time attempted suicide ranked "wanted to die" second. Only 2 percent of the nonattempter teenagers in the study chose "wanted to die" as the number one reason for adolescent suicide attempts. Sixteen percent of the suicide attempters in the study chose it as the number one reason. Forty-seven percent of the suicide attempters ranked it among the top three reasons chosen as compared to only 18 percent of the nonattempter adolescents in the study.

"Wanted to die"	Attempters (%)	Nonattempters (%)
First choice	16	2
One of several choices	47	18

A few studies base their findings of lethal intent on reports from the attempters themselves. Bancroft, Skrimshire, and Simkins (1976) in a study of psychiatrists' and nurses' beliefs concerning reasons for suicide attempts reported that 42 percent of the suicide attempters in the study stated that they had not intended to die. This was not a specifically teenage population; however, the adolescents in the group were said to have had a higher percentage of those stating no "wish to die." Unfortunately no percentage was given. McIntire et al. (1980) reported that only 12 percent of a group of 1,103 adolescent suicide attempters responding in emergency room interviews said that they had wished to die as a result of their action.

Hawton et al. (1982a) produced a very valuable study in which the views of 50 clinical assessors were compared to those of 50 adolescent suicide attempters on a variety of matters pertaining to suicide. In evaluating the wish to die among the adolescent patients the adult assessors believed that only 14 percent had wished to die. Another 18 percent were believed to be ambivalent while 69 percent were felt to have had no wish to die. The adolescent suicide attempters themselves, on the other hand, saw things quite differently, as did the group in Curran's study. Thirty-four percent stated that they had wished to die with 42 percent feeling mixed and only 24 percent stating no wish to die. Further, there was very little agreement between the views of the two groups on individual cases, especially where "wish to die" is concerned. In only 5 of 17 cases did the attempter and the assessor agree that there was present a wish to die.

	Selected by adolescents (N = 50)	Selected by clinical assessors (N = 50)	No. of times clinical assessors agreed with adolescents N (% of agreement)
Wanted to die	17 (34)	7 (14)	5 (29)
Indifferent	21 (42)	9 (18)	6 (29)
Did not want to die	12 (24)	34 (68)	12 (100)

Note. Numbers in parentheses are percentages.

Studies which rely upon the suicide attempter himself (usually herself) for information on lethal intent, report incidences and levels of a wish to die generally higher than those assigned by outside evaluators. Adolescent suicidal behavior should be viewed within the context of a continuum of suicidal intent, rather than on an all-or-none basis. In attempting to gain an understanding of the meaning of adolescent suicidal behavior it is not enough to simply ask "did the person want to die or did they not?" In most cases ambivalence and ambiguity reign. It is better and more appropriate to ask, *how much* did the person wish to live or die. The question has been examined in this manner empirically (Curran, 1984) and nonempirically with interesting results. Using a 7-point rating scale, a 1 indicating no wish to die, 7 indicating a definite wish to die and 4 indicating a 50/50 level of ambivalence, 131 nonsuicidal teenagers and 19 teenagers who had attempted suicide were asked to indicate by circling a number from 1 to 7, "Do you think teenagers who attempt suicide really want to die?" Circling a higher number (above 4) would reflect a belief in a strong wish to die on the part of the adolescent attempter, whereas a low number (below 4) would indicate the opposing belief. Average response for the nonsuicide attempter group was 3.3; for the suicide attempter group it was 3.8. Though this difference did not prove to be statistically significant, a larger and significant difference in lethality level ratings was found between the nonsuicide attempter adolescent females (3.17) and the suicide attempter females (3.9). Research therefore suggests that while the level of lethal intent involved in adolescent suicide attempts may be relatively low in comparison with older age groups, it may be higher than is generally thought to be the case.

Limbacher and Domino (1986) reported the same pattern of beliefs in a study of adult attitudes stating that "suicide attempters tend to see their behavior as a serious wish to die, while most nonattempters see the suicide attempt as manipulative behavior" (p. 332). Underestimating and misinterpreting lethal intent can prove to be a misunderstanding with grave implications. The available research reveals what may be both a distinctive truth about adolescent suicide attempts as well as a serious misunderstanding. All groups appear to share the opinion that adolescent suicide attempts (especially among females) are generally low lethality affairs. However, the level of lethal intent may be dangerously underestimated. They may, in fact, have a greater wish to die than others think. While disagreement appears to exist among teenagers who have or have not attempted suicide concerning the level of lethal intent within adolescent suicide attempts, the gap appears to be even greater between adults and teenage suicide attempters. The already cited literature bears this out. Experience speaking to groups of teenagers and adults on the topic tends to validate it.

Adult groups with whom I have spoken, consistently express the belief that teenagers who attempt suicide have a very low level wish to die. Teenagers on the other hand seem to view the level of wish to die as being higher, though still relatively low. It is not entirely possible to say who is right. Often the level of lethal intent in a particular suicide attempt cannot be ascertained. Sometimes it can be understood only after months of counseling. It is, however, important to note that teenagers and especially teenage suicide attempters seem to view the act as more deadly and perhaps more serious than do adults or persons who have never made a suicide attempt.

Adolescents indicate in other ways the level of lethal intent invested within their self-destructive acts. The method of attempt, location and circumstances of the act all carry messages of hoped for results and hints as to the meaning of the act.

Self-poisoning is by far the most common mode of suicide attempt among the young and the female and the mode of choice in unsuccessful suicide attempts in general (Peck, 1986; Weiner, 1970; Weissman, 1974). Self-poisoning is rarely of high lethality (McIntire et al., 1980; McKenry, Tishler, & Kelley, 1986). Kessel (1965) concluded that at least 80 percent of self-poisonings are supported by the secure belief that death will not occur. Weissman (1974) compared suicide attempters who used pills and those who used more violent means for the level of lethal intent. "It was found that the pill users had the least suicidal intent and were using the attempt to obtain help and establish communication" (p. 743). However, it proved also true that the pill users suffered the most serious medical effects and more frequently required medical hospitalization (Robbins, & Alessi, 1985). Again, the level of lethal intent is not easily gauged, even by the degree of physical harm perpetrated upon the victim.

The location and circumstances of a suicide attempt can reveal clues as to the level or presence of lethal intent. An adolescent who seeks out a place of seclusion where he or she is unlikely to be seen, found, or interrupted and proceeds to use a firearm to inflict a mortal head wound would clearly appear intent upon seeking a goal of death. An attempt of this type will almost certainly succeed. Regardless of its success, the level of lethal intent would obviously need to be rated extremely high. Unsuccessful adolescent suicide attempts are rarely of such deadly character. Hawton et al. (1982a) studied the circumstances related to 50 adolescent suicide attempts by means of overdoses. The results are listed below:

1. Evidence of any planning for the overdose   *10 (20%)*
2. Left a suicide note   *6 (12%)*
3. Precautions taken to prevent discovery and intervention by other people   *3 (6%)*
4. Overdose timed so that intervention was very likely   *39 (78%)*
5. Someone present or nearby (e.g. in the next room)   *43 (86%)*
6. Notified potential helper after the overdose   *43 (86%)*

As the data and clinical experience makes clearly evident, rarely do the circumstances surrounding the overdose imply a predominant intent to die. Other needs clearly pertain.

In my own clinical experience, Hawton's empirical description of the typical adolescent suicide attempt is confirmed. In fact, I could think of few attempts which did not take place at home with other family members present. One exception involved a girl who was at the time living in a group home residence and who slashed her forearm in full view of several staff members and other residents. While Hawton reports that only 20 percent gave evidence of any planning for their overdose, it would appear that, on the contrary, at least unconsciously many teenagers attempt to arrange for their preservation. They often leave open the opportunity to be discovered, or may actively seek to change the course of events by alerting others, though often not a family member.

Leigh's attempt is a case in point. Prior to her nightime ingestion of approximately 20 Tylenol in her bedroom in her parent's house, she left a number of clues as to her intentions and stayed in close contact with her parents and a friend throughout the episode. Her mother observed the first of these clues immediately upon returning home from work at about 3:30 pm. As she entered the kitchen of her normally pristine home, she could not fail to notice a rather ominous array of cutlery strewn about the counter top. As Leigh had arrived home from school only a short time before, it was clear that she had left the mess of unused knives. No mention was made of it and the knives were put away by Leigh's mother. Later Mrs. M observed her daughter lying in her room with her door open (it was normally closed when she was in there alone) reading through a book on prescription and non-prescription medications. Still nothing was said. Leigh had seemed depressed that afternoon and evening but not extraordinarily so. However, at about 9:00 pm she took the Tylenol. Before her ingestion of the medication Leigh had been silent, distant, and had kept pretty much to her room. After 9:00 however, she became inseparable from her parents, even watching T.V. with them on their bed. She spoke on the phone at length with a friend. She kept *away* from her bedroom. Finally, she began to get sick and gratefully accepted the comfort of her mother, but at no time revealed to her parents the nature of her illness or her suicidal behavior of the evening.

REASONS AND MOTIVES

As with determining the level of lethal intent, the reasons behind adolescent suicide attempts can yield findings which vary considerably depending on who is asked and who is responding. Adult evaluators' beliefs about the reasons for adolescent suicide attempts are quite different from those usually given by the adolescent attempters themselves. Several different groups of adults have been studied, including psychiatrists (Hawton et al. 1981), physicians, and nurses (Hawton et al. 1981; Ramon, Bancroft, & Skrimshire, 1975), clinical assessors (Hawton, 1982a), and adolescent and adult in- and out-patient psychiatric patients (Hawton et al. 1978). Nonsuicide attempter teenagers' beliefs have been studied as well (Curran, 1984). Much similarity exists among the adult evaluators in these studies. Adults, including those in the mental health professions, tend to view adolescent suicide attempts as manipulative and hostile acts designed to punish and/or control significant others in their environment. The acts are often viewed as insincere because they are believed to be of very low lethality and are, therefore, not at all what they seem. The psychiatrists, physicians, and nurses in Hawton et al.'s (1981) study were offered a list of 13 motives for attempted suicide:

1. Seek help from someone
2. Escape for a while from an impossible situation

3. Get relief from a terrible state of mind
4. Try to influence some particular person or get them to change their mind
5. Show how much the person loved someone
6. Make things easier for others
7. Make people sorry for the way they have treated the person
8. Frighten or get their own way back on someone
9. Make people understand how desperate the person was feeling
10. Find out whether someone really loved the person or not
11. The situation was so unbearable that the person had to do something and did not know what else to do
12. The person seemed to lose control of himself and had no idea why he behaved that way
13. Wanted to die

(This list has been used in other studies of suicide motives including Curran, 1984; and Ramon, Bancroft, & Skrimshire, 1975).

From this list the following motives were ranked by the psychiatrists as the most likely reasons for an adolescent suicide attempt:

1. Make people sorry for the way they have treated you.
2. Try to influence some particular person or get them to change their mind.
3. (tied with 2 above) Find out whether someone really loved the person or not.

The physicians and nurses in the study demonstrated very similar beliefs with the only difference being the deletion of "find out if loved" and the inclusion of the reason "frighten or get their own way back on someone." The reasons associated with the adolescent suicide attempt were ascribed to the adult attempters in the study with far less frequency if at all.

Ramon et al. (1975) studied the beliefs of physicians and nurses attending to an emergency room population and gathered results strikingly similar to those of the psychiatrists in Hawton's study and exactly the same as the physicians and nurses in that study. Other nonattempter groups basically concur with these beliefs. Psychiatric patients ranked "influence persons to change their mind" first, with adult patients ascribing to young attempters more hostile manipulative motives than did adolescent patients (Hawton et al., 1978).

Sifneos (1966) expressed the belief that 65 percent of young suicide attempters seek to manipulate and control others by means of their act. These acts were felt to reflect "individual attempts to control another person or persons in order to get from them what he wishes" (p. 527). Sale (1975) reported that this belief may be shared by the lay public especially if they have had some familiarity with attempted suicide.

Adolescent suicide attempters view their acts differently, although there appears to be strong agreement among all, that adolescent suicidal behavior generally occurs within an interpersonal context as a means of communicating inner needs and as a means of escape. Bancroft et al. (1976) reported that the leading reasons given by the 26 adolescents in his study were to "seek help" and to "escape situation." These reasons were given much less frequently by the older suicide attempters in the study. Studies which compare reasons given by suicide attempters and their evaluators reflect quite clearly how different are the interpretations of the meanings of adolescent suicide. In Hawton et al.'s (1982a) study of the comparative views of clinical assessors and adolescent suicide attempters the divergence is strikingly apparent. The adolescents cited more benign motivations featuring intolerable internal distress, a need to escape, and a need to convey to others one's desperation. While the adult evaluators often saw in their behavior the hostile, manipulative motivations of the desire to make others feel sorry and scared and the desire to coerce others into a change of behavior and attitude toward them.

The beliefs of teenage suicide attempters and nonattempters have been studied and compared with results that support the bulk of the research and clinical evidence in this area (Curran, 1984). Unlike those studies comparing the beliefs of adult nonattempters with adolescent attempters, teenagers, whether formerly suicidal or not have been largely in agreement as to likely reasons for attempted suicide. Both groups chose overwhelmingly, "seek help or attention" as the most likely and common reason. Other benign reasons such as intolerable internal distress and need to escape were cited with some frequency as well. The angry, manipulative reasons so often cited by others were rarely given.

Evidently then, the reasons behind adolescent attempted suicide can seem to be a matter of opinion. It is apparent, however, that adults view it differently from teenagers, and attempters view it differently from nonsuicide attempters. It seems also to be apparent that older persons are more likely to regard the suicidal behavior of young persons as more often fueled by hostile coercive and manipulative intent. Adult evaluators are less likely to view adult suicidal behavior in this manner. Further, when the level of lethal intent is believed to be quite low, hostile and manipulative motivations are more apt to be ascribed. Adults and nonsuicidal adolescents appear to believe that adolescent suicide attempts are typically of very low lethality; lower, in fact, than is reported by the suicide attempters themselves.

Clinical experience and an impressive and growing body of literature compel one to view adolescent suicidal behavior in terms of the dynamics so often expressed by the victims themselves. Adolescent suicide is distinctive in so many ways, many of which have been already cited. More than with older persons, adolescent suicidal behavior is often not solely an effort to end one's life, but rather to perhaps ameliorate it. This reality, however, should in no way minimize the seriousness of the act. While acknowledging the relatively low lethality of this behavior it is essential not to dismiss it. Teenage suicide does indeed appear to occur within an interpersonal context and may contain efforts at attention seeking manipulation. However, rather than the angry, consciously, and purposefully coercive quality so often attributed to them, the teenage suicide attempter seems to be expressing more inner directed anger and a desperate and confused need to elicit caring from either specific individuals or from the human environment at large, to call in some stabilizing force to take control of their chaotic world. As such, it is often a communicative gesture, though one of dubious value or effectiveness. Often suicidal behavior is an attempt to escape or relieve intolerable affects or tensions existing within people and/or stresses imposed upon them from without. These individuals tend to have minimally effective means of coping with their problems and have exceeded the limits of whatever coping skills they may have.

It is simplistic, condescending, and usually erroneous to interpret an adolescent suicide attempt as solely manipulative chicanery or hostile coercion. The behavior is more complex, less purposeful, and probably far more damaging in actuality and intent to the attempter than to any significant other. While technically fitting the definition of attempted suicide, many adolescent suicide attempts are at the same time less and more than what they seem. The English have taken to calling low lethality suicide attempts "parasuicide" as if to convey the idea that acts of this type are not quite a suicidal act. Shneidman (1981) has developed a 4 point rating scale for assessing the level of suicidal intentionality. Others are being developed all the time. These efforts are important in that they help to clarify a critical area of suicidal motivation, that being the level of intent to die. However, at the same time, they may encourage adult evaluators to miss the point. When dealing with adolescent suicide attempts, it can be presumed in the majority of cases that the wish to die was not the strongest motivating factor. The level of lethal intent will often be rather low. However, this is not where the story should end, but rather where it should begin. Adults appear to project much of their anger over having been "tricked" onto the adolescent and thereby read malice in their intentions. They feel manipulated and thereby impart to the teenager manipulative intent. A clearer, more empathetic and more serious evaluation of the reasons behind adolescent suicidal behavior is warranted. The persisting misunderstanding of the meaning of these acts limits our ability to effectively respond to or prevent acts of adolescent suicidal behavior.

Sue attempted suicide by swallowing only 10 Tylenol. She was, however, a very thin, practically skeletal individual who ate only occasionally and for whom one Tylenol could be the source of drowsiness and fatigue. Sue took the Tylenol in the bedroom of her home at 10 pm, unable to tolerate any longer the isolation she was experiencing, the by-product of having been "grounded" three days before. Later that night, feeling queasy and frightened, she reported her behavior to her father. He asked her why she did it. She replied that she could not stand being grounded. At that point her father became furious, accusing her of simply using the behavior as a way to get out of a justified punishment and threatening a longer period of restriction, sent her back to her room.

Sue was unable to articulate anything of the larger meaning of her suicidal behavior beyond the most superficial precipitant. In fact, Sue was a severely depressed 15-year-old who was rapidly failing in school, a serious substance abuser, including the daily use of pot, and was emmeshed in a highly conflictual and self-destructive boyfriend relationship. She kept all of this from her parents whom, she believed, could not have handled it or helped her. What was so intolerable about being grounded, what is generally intolerable about being grounded for depressed teenagers, is that it prevents access to the desperately needed defences against depressive feelings. Denied opportunities to interact (party, in her case) with her peers, Sue was left without her primary means of distracting herself from her depression. Being held inactive, unable to avoid her feelings and unprepared, through lack of practice, to cope with them, she began to panic. She felt hemmed in by her unwelcome and intensifying feelings and sought escape once more, but this time through a suicidal act.

Sue's behavior, viewed from her father's perspective and given her terribly simplistic explanation of its dynamics, was almost inevitably destined to become misunderstood, trivialized, and as such responded to with anger and resentment, as is normal when one feels they are being blackmailed or used. It is a common course of events in the lower lethality suicide attempt.

ASCERTAINING MOTIVES

A final ingredient of caution needs to be added to the already bubbling mix of uncertainty in evaluating or understanding the motives behind adolescent suicide attempts. In individual cases, one cannot always take at face value what the suicide attempter gives as his or her reason for having attempted suicide. The actual motivation may not even be conscious to the adolescent. Bancroft et al. (1976) have suggested that the "wish to die" response may be given by suicide attempters more as a way of gaining social acceptance after the fact than as a true statement of suicidal intent. A study of nurses' and doctors' attitudes to self-poisoning reported that "wish to die" was the most acceptable motive, especially for physicians, who discriminated against the more manipulative motives (Ramon et al., 1975).

On the other hand, adolescents, imbued with a strong potential for the use of denial as a defense mechanism and an age appropriate inclination to use it, often deny a wish to die immediately after the act. This is sometimes the case even when a high level of lethal intent is obvious. There appears to exist in these cases a need to deflect attention in service of temporary withdrawal as well as a desire to deny along with the event, the feelings which precipitated it in the first place. Clinicians and hospital staff have often seen these dynamics at work. Perhaps then, these factors come close to balancing each other out. At any rate, while it is true that adolescents (and others) will not always be accurate in describing their motives, there is no other source of evidence about the suicide attempter's state of mind. Their feelings and reasons need to be gathered and attended to.

In conclusion, neither the spontaneous or solicited remarks by adolescent suicide attempters, nor the briefly stated codified motives assigned to them by evaluators can effectively convey the deeper sense of sadness, loneliness, and felt lack of love and caring from which even the low lethality adolescent suicide attempt emanates. Reasons such as "seek help and attention" and certainly ones such as "influence others" or "make others feel frightened or sorry," seem shallow and somehow frivolous in that they lack a quality of depth and history. As such, they merely scratch the surface in explaining adolescent suicidal behavior. Peck (1968) would appear to share this impression:

> We then have a picture, not of an attention-seeking, manipulating adolescent, but rather of an unhappy, helpless, hopeless youngster who desperately wants to change something in his life and is apparently unable to do so in more constructive ways. (p. 115)

4

Antecedents
of Adolescent Suicidal Behavior

Adolescent suicidal behavior has, in the past, often been viewed as an impulsive act, devoid of deep historical roots, perpetrated at times by relatively normal adolescents and prompted solely by precipitants that would appear to be rather trivial. All too often adolescent suicide attempts are perceived, from a temporal perspective, as shallow events, lacking in a developmental component and not necessarily suggestive of long-standing or serious psychological or environmental dysfunction. Rather, these acts are believed by many professionals and lay persons alike to be spontaneous occurrences that somehow appear fully grown and with the implicit necessity of a period of germination, ripening or growth (Gould, 1965; Schneer & Kay, 1961).

This chapter shall rely heavily on the work of Jacobs and Teicher (Jacobs & Teicher, 1966; Jacobs, 1971; Teicher, 1973; Teicher & Jacobs, 1966a, 1966b) as well as others, in formulating a conceptual outline of adolescent suicidal behavior, which acknowledges with Jacobziner the seriousness of every adolescent suicide attempt, regardless of the level of lethal intent, the importance of significant, numerous, and long-standing problems as the typical antecedents to the adolescent suicide attempt and, finally, the presumption of significant psychological disturbance in the adolescent who attempts suicide. Frequently, adolescent suicide attempters are dismissed as attention seeking malcontents. The level of their emotional distress is often underestimated. The presence of emotional distress is often completely undetected. While the psychotic or schizophrenic suicidal adolescent is relatively rare (Greuling & DeBlassie, 1980; Hudgens, 1974; Miles, 1977), it is wrong to suppose that adolescent suicide attempters are not seriously troubled individuals. Identifying and "naming" their disturbance has, however, proven to be a troublesome task for many evaluators and researchers. It is apparent that misunderstanding and ignorance prevail in the following two areas: first, the importance of historical factors in the development of the suicidal behavior of adolescents, and second, the level of emotional disturbance, depression, and aberration in the suicidal adolescent. These are major contributors to the misconceptions and myths widely held and subscribed to by the general public, educators, mental health professionals, and the medical community.

The adolescent suicide occurs, not as an isolated act against a backdrop of relative placidity, contentment, and well being, but as a culmination of experiences, feelings, and events which can only be described as negative, certainly at least from the perspective of the victim. It is an act understood best within a contextual setting, as an episode of overdetermined behavior. While it appears to be clear that most adolescents who attempt suicide (especially if they are female) are depressed, it is also true that most depressed teenagers do not attempt suicide. Depression is cited as an example of a typical component in the dynamics of suicide that cannot fully account for the act. The suicidal adolescent demands more comprehensive scrutiny and a holistic approach toward understanding his or her current status as a suicidal individual in process.

Jerry Jacobs, in his very important book called *Adolescent Suicide* (1971), based on comparative research between suicidal and nonsuicidal adolescents, described the adolescent suicide attempt as the culmination of a four stage process involving the following progression of experiences (Jacobs, 1971, p. 64):

1. A long standing history of problems from childhood to the onset of adolescence.
2. A period of escalation of problems since the onset of adolescence and in excess of those normally associated with adolescence.
3. Progressive failure of available adaptive techniques for coping with old and increasingly new problems leading to a progressive social isolation from meaningful social relationships.
4. Chain reaction dissolution of remaining meaningful social relationships immediately prior to the suicide attempt.

There has, of course, been a great deal of study into the etiology and historical antecedents of adolescent suicide. Most research has, however, consisted of correlational studies or the study of singular factors or groups of factors with an eye toward assessing their association with suicidal behavior. For example there has been much attention devoted to "broken homes" as a factor in the development of the adolescent suicide attempt (Barter, Swaback, & Todd, 1968; Jacobziner, 1968; Rohn et al., 1967; Walker, 1980). Other factors studied include parental psychiatric disturbance, including problem drinking (Hudgens, 1974; Jacobs, 1971; Shafii, Carrigan, Whittinghill, & Derrick, 1985), physical and sexual abuse by parents (Deykin et al., 1985; Green, 1978), modeling of suicidal behavior by other family members (Kerfoot, 1979; Shafii et al., 1985), poor physical health prior to the attempt (Hawton, O'Grady, Osborne, & Cole, 1982b; Jacobs, 1971; White, 1974, & Walker, 1980), and school problems (Berman & Carroll, 1984; Mattsson, Seese, & Hawkins, 1969; Otto, 1972; Rohn et al., 1977). However, the common denominator to the life histories of adolescent suicide attempters seems not to be found in a singular event or even a group of events alone. The cumulative experience and the adolescent's perception of events as well as the events themselves are critical factors in the development of a progressive social isolation and eventual rumination upon a suicidal act. As an example, 40 percent of the adolescent suicide attempters in Jacobs' (1971) study had a stepparent. *All* of these adolescents perceived this stepparent as an "unwanted" member of the family. Such was not the case with a majority of the control group of nonsuicidal, nonpsychiatrically disturbed adolescents, a similar percentage of whom had stepparents.

A distinguishing characteristic, then, of the lives of suicidal adolescents was found not only in the presence of particular events, but in the perceptions these adolescents had of the events, and in the qualitative differences in experience which may have helped to form their impressions. Many events found occurring with similar frequency in the early lives of both the suicide attempters and controls, including divorce, moves, and school changes, were viewed differently by the two groups, the suicide attempters holding more unhappy, negative views of these events. Another distinguishing characteristic of these histories of suicidal adolescents is that the noxious events and upheavals, usually beginning early in their lives, do not seem to abate. They multiply in quantity and intensity in a way which evades notice by many studies that focus on singular causal factors or narrow horizontal bands in the development strata. "The suicide attempters were generally subject to a greater number of debilitating events a greater number of times" (Jacobs, 1971, p. 66). Smith and Crawford (1986), in a study of the life events and circumstances of teenage suicide attempters, suicide planners (no attempt), those thinking of suicide but who have made no plan, and nonsuicidals, found attempters reporting the highest percentage of "unpleasant changes in their lives and, perhaps most importantly, the greatest number of changes in themselves" (p. 321). Jacobs' conceptual formulation of the progression toward social isolation will be used to describe how the "straws" of adversity accrue. The early straws seem innocuous enough. The "final straw" will seem insignificant to the outside observer. Seen in their totality, through the perspective of the carrier, the burden should seem a prodigious and cruelly pressing mass. A case study from my own practice will be presented in four parts in order to illustrate the process by which suicide may develop.

FROM CHILDHOOD TO THE ONSET
OF ADOLESCENCE

Adolescents who attempt or commit suicide typically have endured a series of childhood losses and disruptions that have arranged themselves in such a way that their lives come to be viewed as disorganized, unpredictable, and disharmonious. However, if one looks at the problematic events in the lives of these adolescents, it is difficult to distinguish them from a cohort of nonsuicidal, but psychiatrically disturbed adolescents. Indeed, Jacobs (1971) failed to find significant differences even between the preadolescent histories of a control group of nonpsychiatrically disturbed adolescents and the suicide attempter adolescents on a number of comparisons for discrete events or conditions. Both groups experienced similar rates of residence moves, school changes, repeated grades, serious illness and injuries to the adolescent or family members, parental separations and divorce, remarriage, drinking problems, deaths of close friends or family members, and attempted or committed suicide by parents or close friends. However, on an individual basis the suicidal adolescents had experienced a far greater number of these problems. They tended to come in bunches, whereas with the nonsuicidal group they tended to occur in much smaller doses.

Research by others have suggested important qualitative differences in the early lives of suicidal adolescents. First, while broken homes are an increasingly common occurrence in the lives of normal and troubled youths, and broken homes do not effectively distinguish between those who will be psychiatrically disturbed and those who will also become suicide attempters, it has been found that adolescent suicide attempters tend to experience this loss at an earlier point in their lives than do nondisturbed or disturbed adolescent comparison gropus (Stanley & Barter, 1970). Second, the feeling on the part of many suicidal adolescents of having been an unwanted child and a burden to the family from infancy (Schrut, 1964a), an expendable child (Sabbath, 1969) is supported by the contention of many that the family (intact or otherwise) environment of the individual adolescent in question features a climate of hostility, indifference, and overt rejection (McIntire & Angle, 1973). While many nonsuicidal adolescents may experience unfortunate and disruptive events (broken homes, etc.) they apparently are able to readjust and reconstitute with the aid of support systems that are more supportive, loving, and inclusive than those of their counterparts whose experience of similar "events" proved to be far more debilitating. These teenagers have experienced their losses as painful and permanent. As corroboration of this hypothesis, Jacobs (1971) reported that 94 percent of his nondisturbed adolescent control group felt that they had had a "happy childhood." Only 38 percent of the suicide attempters reported a happy childhood. The adolescent suicide attempters carry this sense of loss, loss of significant others, loss of a sense of stability and security, loss of self-esteem, and often a sense of the loss of childhood itself, into the turbulence of their adolescence. They enter this storm in an unsteady and vulnerable craft, ill prepared to meet its challenges.

Case Study: Cassandra C.

Cassandra's most serious suicide attempt occurred on her 18th birthday, at her birthday party, in fact. She made an attempt to slash her own throat with a large hunting knife. She had behaved self-destructively many times before and had been giving thought to suicide since she was 13. Cassandra is an attractive, though waif-like girl, whose pretty face and tall, thin body are usually enshrouded in long disheveled hair and voluminous coats and capes. Her drawn in shoulders and head and timid step give one the impression that Cassandra would just as soon be invisible. She is not pleased with her appearance and does everything possible to cover it up. However, among friends, and there are many, both male and female, she becomes anything but withdrawn. Cassandra's style can become rather manic, tempestuous, and volatile. She can blossom into a hilarious, ebullient, bon vivant, or alternately to rather infantile and excessive railing and abusiveness. In either instance, she is typically highly active and a social catalyst of events. She is charismatic. She typically trails, wherever she goes, a gaggle of admiring followers. She is, however, unaware of the attraction she holds for others.

Cassandra recalled her childhood as a happy one. In fact, she often mourned its loss. During our first therapy session when she was 14, she stated sadly that "I haven't had a good day since sixth grade." Cassandra has clung to her childhood tenaciously. She insisted that she believed in Santa Claus until she was 12. She played with toy soldiers until she was nearly 13. The youngest of three children with two older brothers, Jack and Fred, she appears to have been doted on during those years. However, she has never been as involved with her mother as she would have liked. "She left me to go to work when I was about 6 and then she'd come home and go to sleep. A girl needs her mother." Cassandra took it very personally. Their home life had been relatively stable. Her mother and father were together. There had been no separations or moves. She had lived her entire life in the same house. Her relationship with her parents seems to have been warm. Her father appeared to hold a place of special importance for her. She had been very much "daddy's little girl" and he had been available to nurture this bond. Mr. C was disabled with phlebitis and had been at home. Mrs. C had worked nights as an L.P.N. in a local hospital, but Cassandra felt close to her as well and could talk to her comfortably though she felt her mother always favored her brother Jack. Nevertheless, Cassandra entered adolescence deeply depressed. By the age of 14 she was complaining of chronic nervousness and unhappiness. Her self-esteem was very low. Everything about her manner and appearance connoted an attitude of self-loathing and denigration. She drank and smoked pot alone or with others, indiscriminately chosen. "It's my only relief, my only fun, the only time I'm happy." At times she would sit in the woods alone with a bottle and drink and contemplate suicide. She had come to feel like a "bad person," who had once been good. "I'm in trouble all the time now."

ESCALATION OF PROBLEMS
AT ADOLESCENCE

The childhoods of suicidal adolescents have been found to be in many ways comparable to those of their nonsuicidal peers in terms of the type if not the magnitude or quality of problem events experienced. Jacobs (1971), however, found that as the suicidal teenagers entered adolescence the course of their lives again diverged sharply from the experiential route of their peers. The problems encountered by the suicide attempters presented themselves in a continuing and mounting fashion at a time of relative defenselessness and developmental vulnerability. At this juncture in their lives, these adolescents underwent significantly more moves, school changes, and repeated grades, recurrent familial unrest in the form of broken homes, absence of *both* parents, and the necessity of living with relatives, parental drinking problems continuing on into the adolescence of the attempter (as compared with the control group for whom parental drinking problems typically had abated during childhood), and modeling of suicidal behavior by family and/or friends. McKenry, Tishler, and Kelley (1982) also reported a higher incidence of suicide attempts among the mothers of suicidal adolescents as compared with nonattempters. Many others have reported high incidences of suicidal behavior in the families of suicidal adolescents (Berman & Carroll, 1984; Curran, 1984; Kerfoot, 1979; Shafii et al., 1985; and Teicher, 1973). (The question of modeling and the effects of familiarity and imitation will be studied in Chapter 7.) Further, the suicide attempters were far more likely to undergo the isolating and wrenching experience of juvenile justice (including residential or foster home placement), hospitalization, school suspensions or dropouts, pregnancy, or the loss of a recent romance prior to the attempt. Deykin et al. (1985) reported that suicide attempters were six times more likely than nonattempters to have been involved with their state's department of social services. The feelings of isolation and alienation take a greater hold of the adolescent under these circumstances. Alienation is considered a key feature in the development of the suicidal act among teenagers (Wenz, 1979) and a natural by-product of the historical background of the teenage suicide attempter.

Research by Hawton, Osborne, O'Grady and Cole (1982c) pointed to the lethal effects of longstanding and multiple source problems in the lives of the adolescent suicide attempters who were studied. An association between a progression of multiple and persistent problems and the lethality of attempt was demonstrated. Parent/teenager relationships were of particular note in distinguishing between lower and higher lethality attempts as well as for the chronicity of attempts.

As teenagers newly landed on the shores of adolescence, the teenage suicide attempters often find themselves feeling far from home, alone, and scrambling over slippery rocks, buffeted by the elements. The desperate grasping for ways to hold on and to cope has begun.

Case Study (Part 2)

While Cassandra had perhaps once been "Daddy's *little* girl" it was clear that she was no longer Daddy's *teenage* girl. Her growing up was not a welcomed development. Her awkwardness, self-consciousness, and burgeoning sexuality were not supported or consoled. Rather, her efforts at growth were more often mocked and exploited by her father and brothers. Cassandra's "Eden" seemed to evaporate revealing a hostile and rejecting world that was difficult to understand but whose attitudes she readily embraced. She felt "hated" by her family and was in full agreement with them. Her efforts to escape through drugs and alcohol produced far more guilt than "fun," confirming with every episode her perception of herself as an incorrigible bad girl. Cassandra rued her mother's absence due to her job. She longed for someone to talk to. She felt increasingly trapped in a hostile land at home with her father and brothers and was compelled with increasing desperation to seek the company of her peers and the drug and alcohol abuse that came to be associated with them.

Cassandra had never been an exemplary student. School had always been a struggle. While her brothers were rather bright and fairly successful in school, Cassandra had been retained in grade one and as a teenager struggled to pass. Anxieties related to school performance became a serious drain on her energy level.

As Cassandra progressed into adolescence, simmering family problems became more apparent and were largely played out upon her. Cassandra's older brother Jack, aged 21, had become an alcoholic and cocaine abuser and a constant source of tension and conflict at home and a source of fear and abuse to Cassandra. Her mother and father were at odds as to how to deal with Jack. Mrs. C. tended to deny her son's obvious and worsening problems. Working nights and sleeping days allowed her a certain blindness as to the problems he was creating. To Cassandra, it seemed that she was simply favoring him again and at the family's and her expense. Mr. C wanted Jack out of the house. However, the mother and father rarely argued about this. Nor did they often confront "the monster" as Cassandra called Jack. Instead much of the frustration, tension, and anger which thickened the air in the home found a repository in Cassandra. She became the family's scapegoat. Her failings in school, her missed curfews and stumbling early adolescence itself, elicited what seemed to her a constant harangue from the family. Again, she tended to join in with her own internal self-flagellation. God too, it seemed, considered her to be "a rotten kid" in her view, for allowing this to happen. Feelings of hopelessness steadily accrued. "Things won't get better."

As Cassandra approached 16, her first serious boyfriend relationship developed with a 20-year-old fellow from her neighborhood whom she had known all her life. Bruce had problems of his own. Cassandra's perceived inadequacies were clearly reflected in her choice of a boyfriend. Bruce was a sometime factory worker and full-time alcoholic and drug abuser. He had been arrested several times for a variety of offenses including disorderly conduct, driving under the influence of alcohol and drugs, and assault. Bruce was considered unattractive both physically and characterologically by Cassandra's peers. However, he was also to Cassandra, "the only person who is nice to me." Thus began a stormy and mutually unsatisfying relationship which did nothing to improve Cassandra's self-esteem or minimize her growing problems with substance abuse. Cassandra had come to expect nothing better and saw Bruce everyday, their relationship developing into more of a death grip than anything else. They often discussed suicide pacts.

By the age of 16 and entering the 10th grade Cassandra had deteriorated noticeably. She had lost 15 pounds during the past year and looked gaunt and haggard. She was cutting classes for the first time and with growing regularity. Fights, often physical, with Bruce had become more frequent. The situation at home had worsened. Jack was worse than ever and Cassandra's father had become, to her, even more critical and disapproving. Her mother remained maddeningly uninvolved. Cassandra was finding it impossible to sleep without a few drinks or a joint before bed. Regardless of the amount of sleep, she never felt rested. Problems, when they arose, proved too much for her to cope with. She would become explosive, disorganized, confused, and prone to panic. Finally, confined to her room at night "grounded indefinitely" without recourse to her friends or her drugs and unable to sleep, Cassandra attempted suicide by taking 10-12 aspirin on two successive nights, alone and undetected. Her stated reason for the attempt, given many days later, included her wish "to get some sleep and not wake up" and "I can't stand being alone, being grounded." More to the point, Cassandra appeared to be attempting to escape from an intolerable state of mind. Her depression and anxiety had proved more than she could handle or avoid. A deeply devalued sense of self and a conviction that her troubles would continue interminably joined with her perception of herself as a burden to her family ("I cause them nothing but trouble. They had enough with my brother Jack. I shouldn't be giving them more."), in helping to produce her self-destructive behavior.

As Cassandra's adolescence progressed she was more often appearing to regress. Daily pot use mixed at times with hallucinogens such as mescaline became the norm and was not deterred by days of school. She was high nearly every day during her abbreviated 11th grade year. Cassandra quit school in January after having failed all her courses during the first semester largely due to absenteeism. She was often suspended for class cutting which, of course produced more absenteeism. Her relationship with Bruce continued and, if anything, became wilder. Their dates were often riotous affairs culminating in literally knock-down, drag-out fights. His personality, mirroring her own in many ways, created a scenario of chaos, violence, unpredictability, and mutual dependence that became the center of their lives and which neither were close to being strong enough to cope with or elevate to a more mature plane. Clearly, they could not live with or without each other. Knowledge of the sexual aspect of their relationship earned her the epithet of "whore" from her father on many occasions. As a nonstudent, Cassandra entered the world of work and went through several jobs in the space of 6 months. They all failed for the same reason. They caused her to feel conspicuous, pressured, disorganized, anxious, and incompetent, the same way she felt at home and in the classroom.

Within her family, pressures were continuing to mount and conditions continued to deteriorate. During the spring, it was discovered that Mrs. C. had uterine cancer which had spread already to several organs and was believed to be terminal. Jack was hospitalized for severe cocaine addiction, which was producing psychotic symptoms and paranoia. Cassandra's status as an unemployed dropout, with a "loser" boyfriend was often brought forth by her father as a problem the family and her mother did not need.

Cassandra too, had turned to harder drugs. She called me once crying, frightened, and panicked that she had just snorted a line of crushed Motrin because it at least had looked white and powdery like the drug she craved, cocaine. She persistently refused any referral to a drug treatment program. Age 17, therefore, saw Cassandra having utterly failed the course of adolescence, floundering desperately and dangerously, without solid supports or adequate internal resources.

PROGRESSIVE SOCIAL ISOLATION

Parent-Adolescent Relationship

For the adolescent suicide attempter the adaptive techniques utilized at home, perhaps in school and sometimes in the community, manifest themselves as behavioral problems that bring neither reward nor respite. It is suggested that while these adolescents may consider their problem behavior to be a device for communicating discontent and a need for caring and consideration directed at significant adults, the adults invariably view them simply as behavior problems that warrant eradication.

The pattern of interaction between suicidal adolescents and others (especially parents) is characteristically one of profound failure in communication and understanding. These adolescents seem to have lost or perhaps never developed a capacity for clearly expressing in words, their most troubling feelings. Instead, they tend to resort to behavioral manifestations that are all too often regarded as baffling and annoying to their recipients. The parents of suicidal adolescents, on the other hand, seem equally inept in responding appropriately to the behavioral vicissitudes of their young. Jacobs (1971) reported that while 70 percent of the suicide attempters in his study made their attempt in the home, only 20 percent reported the attempt to their parents first, if at all, often instead calling a friend at some distance while their parents sat in the very next room, the message being ultimately relayed to them by the alerted friend. Hawton et al.'s (1982a) research findings are very similar. These findings are certainly consistent with my own experience and speak not only to the familial context in which adolescent suicide often occurs but of a communication breakdown of absurd proportions. Lisa's suicide attempt described in Chapter 2 is merely one of many examples from my own work. Abraham (1977), in attempting to define the "suicidogenic family," reported that "the family of the adolescent suicide attempter constitutes a pathological system in which communication of self-revealing information, responsiveness to the needs of others, and awareness of familial patterns of communication are more restricted" (p. 4559 B). Capacities in these areas were more limited than in either of the two comparison groups, one being a control, the other being families of psychiatrically disturbed but nonsuicidal adolescents.

Disciplining, not surprisingly, often becomes an inconsistent, haphazard, and ineffective exercise that fails to reach the heart of the matter or the key behaviors. Since the young person and the adult hold differing views as to the nature of the problem, its reasons, and cause, they are in effect very much out of touch and become even more so. Most parents and teenagers feel this way to varying degrees. The parents of suicidal adolescents appear, however, to be distinctive in this respect. In Jacobs' study the parents of the suicide attempters manifested their confusion by using 40 percent more disciplining techniques than did the parents of the control group adolescents. Further, twice as many parents of attempters resorted to criticizing, yelling, beating, withholding of approval, and "nagging" (defined as "unfair discipline and rejection"). Nagging appeared to be at the top of their list. Conflict was chronic. These findings are supported by others. McKenry et al. (1983) describe parents of suicidal teens as using unhealthy and self-destructive means of coping. Hawton (1982) describes the parent/teenager relationship of adolescent suicide attempters as being fraught with more "rows" than those of the comparison groups. Francis (1976) reported that adolescent suicide attempters viewed their parents as more rejecting than did a group of disturbed nonsuicidal adolescents. Topol and Reznikoff (1984) found that adolescent suicide attempters felt more "unhappy" in their homes than hospitalized disturbed adolescents. They felt that they had no one to talk to at home.

McKenry et al. (1982), in a study of family cohesiveness, conflict, and parental maladaptive behaviors within the households of adolescent suicide attempters, demonstrated that the perceptions of parents of attempters as well as attempters themselves, reflect an impression of poor communication, unhappiness, and discontent. In a comparison with nondisturbed adolescents, the attempter adolescents were less likely to view the time spent with their parents as enjoyable. They viewed their parents' marriage as less well adjusted (when both parents were present) and felt that their mothers were significantly less interested in them. The suicide attempters also reported feeling greater parental pressure to do well in school. Smith and Crawford (1986) have described the homes of adolescent suicide attempters as chaotic environments and summarized their adolescents' perceptions of their parents as "very unhappy, arguing individuals, who could hardly be models of loving, hopeful, coping adults" (p. 317).

These beliefs and perceptions by the teenagers were largely corroborated by data from their parents. Both mothers and fathers of attempters felt that the time spent with their familes was significantly less enjoyable than did the parents of the adolescent nonattempters. Fathers of attempters tested lower on measures of marital adjustment than did the fathers in the comparison group. At the same time these fathers rated their wives' parenting more negatively than did the fathers of nonattempters.

The attempters' parents also evidenced more maladaptive behaviors than did the parents of the adolescent nonattempters. Fathers again were spotlighted being more depressed while the mothers were more anxious and suicidal than were the parents of nonattempters. Higher incidences of psychiatric disturbance in the parents of adolescent suicide attempters than in the parents of adolescent nonattempters have been reported by several writers (Berman & Carroll, 1984; Hudgens, 1974; Shafii et al., 1985). Problems with alcohol and drug abuse have been noted as well.

Role of the Father

A review of the literature of parents and parenting of adolescent suicide attempters indicates a need for devoting some special attention to the role of the father in the constellation of factors which appear to be instrumental in the slide of the troubled adolescent toward a suicidal act. The father's impact is implicit of course by his absence from the home as indicated by the high percentage of father-absent broken homes. The paternal influence, however, has also been demonstrated in his continuing relationship with the children and, in particular, the suicidal adolescent daughter.

White (1974) has gone so far as to characterize the father in the families of adolescent suicide attempters as "most often the nuclear problem" (p. 31). Two patterns of fathering styles were described. The first involved fathers who were rigid, strict, and uncompromising disciplinarians, displaying "marked hostility toward their children" (p. 31). Rules were laid down which were so coercive and inconsistent with normative community standards as to invite rebellion and intensified conflict and recriminations. Haldane and Halder (1962) described a similar parental style in the majority of fathers of the adolescent suicide attempters they studied. The second pattern observed by White was of fathers who were largely inadequate and ineffectual. These men were irresponsible, often alcoholic individuals who were "basically indifferent to family needs" (p. 587). They tended to be a drain on the emotional reserves of their wives and gave little support to family life. Porot et al. (1968) reporting on French female adolescent suicide attempters observed a similar style of paternal functioning.

Several studies have noted poor father-daughter communication as being a distinctive feature in the family life of the adolescent suicide attempter. Hawton et al. (1982b) reported that of a group of 13–15-year-old primarily female suicide attempters (90 percent female), 89 percent had difficulty communicating with their fathers while 48 percent had similar difficulty with their mothers. Only 9.5 percent of the adolescents in the nonsuicidal control group expressed difficulty in communicating with their parents. This dynamic has also been described by Walker (1980) and Hawton et al. (1982 c), whose classification of suicidal adolescents included the observation that regardless of the adolescent suicide attempter's group classification, their relationships with their fathers were universally reported as poor (i.e. "never able to discuss problems"). Problems of paternal communication were most severe among the most dangerously suicidal adolescents. The adolescent group was 90 percent female. All the adolescents had regular contact with their fathers.

Angle et al. (1983) reported that 0 percent of the female adolescent suicide attempters he studied felt that they had a satisfactory relationship with their father, while 28 percent felt that their relationship with their mother was satisfactory. Interestingly, in follow-up interviews, nine years later, those former suicide attempters questioned cited "moving away from home" as the leading contributor to their "increased satisfaction with life." This was far and away the number one choice of those whose status was felt to have improved from their troubled teenage years.

Jacobs' concept of the progression of events, circumstances, and feelings which lead to the adolescent suicide attempt emphasized in Stage 3 a "progressive social isolation from meaningful social relationships" and the impact of broken romances and ruptured peer relationships as leading contributors and precipitants to the attempt.

The father seems to play a key role in the development of both the normal and the suicidal adolescent female's capacity to fashion and maintain meaningful and satisfying heterosexual relationships. Lozoff (1974) cites the father-daughter relationship as being crucial in the development of women who are successful in heterosexual relations and a career. Hetherington (1972) has reported that girls from father-absent, as compared to father-present homes, are more likely to have difficulties with long-term heterosexual relationships. Biller (1974c) concurred with these results and also found the same problems in heterosexual relations to be pursuant upon females from father-present but father-unsupportive families. Fisher (1973) demonstrated that the father-daughter relationship was more important than the mother-daughter relationship in the development of an orgasmic capacity in females. Fathers who were involved, caring, and conveyed well-defined expectations and methods of enforcement were seen as being able to create a father-daughter relationship most conducive to the development of a normal orgasmic capacity in the daughter. In summary then, Lamb (1981) proposes that inadequate fathering, more than inadequate mothering makes the female more vulnerable to difficulties in sex role and sexual development, but it is of course only one of many factors. These findings are not offered in order to negate the influence of the mother or to simplify the complex familial dynamics pertaining to the family life of the adolescent suicide attempter. Rather, they are offered for the purposes of directing attention toward the often neglected paternal family member, and as a call for further research into the relatively barren field of knowledge concerning fathering, at a time when more and more children are growing up without the experience of a father in the home.

Process of Adaptive Strategies

A finding of major importance in terms of its value in refuting the notion of the "impulsive," ahistorical suicide attempt is Jacobs' description of the process by which the troubled adolescent acts out his needs in a sequential fashion which ends rather than begins with the suicide attempt. The vast majority of the 31 adolescent suicide attempters in his study went through a four stage process of attempts at less drastic adaptive behavioral strategies before the suicide attempt. The four stages were as follows:

1. Rebelling—behavior seen as normative in that controls were nearly equal to the suicide attempters in their use of this age appropriate behavior.
2. Withdrawal into oneself—used less frequently by control adolescents.
3. Running away from home.
4. Attempting suicide.

In only rare cases did a suicide attempter not employ a variety of coping strategies prior to the suicidal act. Only four suicide attempters used "rebelling" only, prior to their attempt. Only two suicide attempters used "withdrawal" exclusively prior to their attempt, and only one used running away as the only harbinger of their suicide attempt. Only one adolescent attempted suicide without first manifesting one of the less drastic forms of behavior. In this case the boy was responding to conditions associated with serious health problems which would not in any case have been ameliorated by utilization of any of the three prior stages. Jacobs believes these are significant findings: "It indicates the general reluctance of the suicide attempters and control adolescents to resort initially or exclusively to more drastic forms of adaptation before first having tried less drastic ones" (p. 81). In fact, the suicide attempters initially responded as did the control group, i.e., least to most drastic. However, the less drastic responses proved unsuccessful to the more problem ridden attempters causing them to consider and desperately take on whatever techniques remained.

More recently, Novick (1984) described the adolescent's "suicide sequence." He studied seven adolescents who made suicide attempts while in psychoanalytic therapy. He concluded that suicide was the end point to a pathological regression, rather than an impulsive act. The attempt was seen as having occurred within the context of "severe long-standing disturbance." Weiner (1970) offers an effective critique to the traditionally held view of adolescent (female) suicide attempts as purely and simply impulsive acts. He points out that this notion is based upon the idea that adolescent females, denied other socially approved outlets for aggression, tend to be more impulsive and histrionic following puberty and that this is manifested in hastily conceived low lethality attempts. "However appealing these for-mulations may be they do not stand up well to close examination" (p. 182). It is often written that girls are more likely than boys to direct self-destruc-tive aggression along nonsuicidal channels such as school failure, sexual delinquency, and neurotic ill health. The fact that males outnumber females 4 to 1 in committed suicides in adolescence, supports the reality of the more intensely suicidal tendencies of males who do have available to them socially accepted means of discharging aggression. Second, Weiner proposes that lower lethality attempts or faulty planning are most likely not due to the impul-sivity of the act but rather to nonlethal intentions on the part of the perpetrator.

We see then in Stage 3, the progressive development of conflict and anomie within the family and social life of the suicidal adolescent so that the human environment becomes one of hostility and rejection. Lacking adequate support systems and channels of effective communication the adolescent is likely to enter a process of failed adaptive techniques leading to more drastic and desperate measures. Ironically, their parents appear ill-equipped to deal with even normal adolescent peccadillos. As conflict increases and communication deteriorates, the adolescent actually renders himself less likely to acquire the familial support required even as his efforts to acquire it intensify. The pattern of ineffectual and rejecting disciplining can soon become an all-consuming feature of the relationship between the suicide attempter and his parents. It *becomes* the relationship until there is no room for anything else in the relationship except the increasingly frustrating downward spiral of conflict, followed by rejection, followed by alienation which sits at the bottom of the spiral, intransigent, and dark. Wenz (1979), in his study of alienation in suicidal adolescents, associates this condition most closely with conflict with parents and poor communication. As if attesting to the coldness of this alienation, Corder, Shorr and Corder (1974) cited a felt lack of parental warmth as among the most highly correlated factors in adolescent suicide attempts.

Case Study (Part 3)

Cassandra's repertoire of adaptive strategies for use in dealing with the myriad of stresses with which she had to contend was extremely limited. Her early involvement in drug and alcohol use, quickly turned to abuse, was actually normative behavior within her particular peer group and neighborhood. Consequently, substance abuse became her *only* coping strategy. In this respect she essentially wasted her adolescence in the sense that adolescence, being a time of relatively strong trials and tribulations, is a time where one is supposed to develop and hone the coping skills which will carry one successfully into and through adult life. Substance abuse stops development along these lines and often halts most aspects of maturation altogether if it becomes, as in the case of Cassandra, the only way to cope. Cassandra, therefore, continued to struggle with mounting difficulties with little of the maturity, versatility or strength necessary. Most teenagers change a great deal during these years. Cassandra, I feel, changed very little. She remained very much the high-strung, highly reactive and sensitive 14-year-old. Of course, there appeared not to be available to her within her family system a wealth of healthy strategies to learn from. Her brother Jack was addicted to both alcohol and cocaine. Her oldest brother Fred was considerably older and had left home prior to Cassandra's adolescence. Mrs. C. was usually away. Mr. C., like Cassandra, tended to rely on denial and avoidance of reality or stress as his way to cope. He was an inconsistent, impulsive, and harshly critical disciplinarian who sought, above all else, minimal stress in his life, and woe to the person who upset him, especially if it was Cassandra, because she was an easy mark, incapable of retaliation of any kind. Conflict resolution in this family consisted essentially of "just do it like I say," "cut it out," and "forget it," power stances which avoid the work and thought of compromise or consideration. Disciplining involved stinging insults, nagging, usually including the bringing up of past and irrelevant issues, and little else. Grounding, when it was tried, never lasted beyond a couple of days, since the family lacked the energy to maintain it. Hostility and weakness might characterize the system or lack of system. Virtually all disciplining was handled by the father.

Communication, which might have addressed the failures and tensions inherent here, was nonexistent in any mature or meaningful sense. Cassandra tried to speak with her mother, who, when she was not too ill or was not too tired, was an empathetic listener. However, she lacked the strength and courage and perhaps the will to intercede against her husband. Cassandra felt let down and abandoned by this. As for her father, she simply did not trust him and was utterly convinced that he was incapable of change, or understanding any other person's point of view or feelings if they differed from his own. Certainly, she did not expect him to understand the needs of a teenage girl. They were deeply alienated from one another. His attitude toward her depression was one of annoyed disdain. "Knock off this depression business and grow up!" was a frequent refrain.

Ultimately, Cassandra could no longer bear up under the strain. She had warded off her depression and suicidal inclinations as long as she could, medicating herself with drugs that served a tranquillizing function. Other commonly used adaptive strategies, such as rebelling and running from home, were impossible for her due to overwhelming fear. Withdrawal into herself was intolerable in that it only heightened her depression and kept her from her main defense, activity. She was left with attempted suicide, which, though hastily enacted and impulsively carried out by a highly impulsive individual, was clearly *not* without its deep historical roots.

CHAIN REACTION DISSOLUTION OF SOCIAL RELATIONSHIPS

A number of studies have sought to explain the cause of adolescent suicidal behavior by assessing the "precipitant" of the act. The precipitant is usually ascertained from the spontaneous comments of the adolescents offered either verbally or by means of a note. What are often elicited are responses dealing with immediate problems of great emotional impact or salience to the adolescent immediately prior to the act; what touched it off or what was the "final straw." These reasons can often seem trivial to the adult assessor. Precipitants as innocuous as a bad hair cut, a poor test mark, being "grounded," or an argument with a parent, lover, or friend, have been noted. Research of this type offers far less to an understanding of adolescent suicide than it purports. More importantly, it can often give the false impression to those insufficiently experienced or knowledgeable concerning adolescents and adolescent suicidal behavior, that adolescent suicide attempts are trifling, precipitous acts, devoid of deep meaning or deep roots. To base one's understanding of the cause of adolescent suicide attempts on simply the "precipitants" is very much like basing your understanding of the origins of World War I on the mere fact that Gavrilo Princip assassinated Archduke Franz Ferdinand in Sarajevo in 1914.

Studies of precipitants are important and helpful, however, in alerting us as to points of special sensitivity experienced by the adolescent and educating us about the likely warning signs to an imminent suicidal act. The precipitants most often cited involve arguments or disagreements between the adolescent and some very significant other (White, 1974). Parental conflict is often cited (Hawton et al., 1982b; Jacobziner, 1965; Walker, 1980; Weiner, 1970). Very often it involves an argument or conflict with a boy or girl friend. (Hawton et al. 1982b; Jacobs, 1971; Jacobziner,

1965; Walker, 1980). Walch (1976) and Topol and Reznikoff (1984) have reported the inordinate extent to which suicidal adolescents, especially females, rely on sources of support outside the home. For these adolescents, the perceived rupture of a valued peer relationship, same sex or heterosexual, can be devastating, but only within the context of all that exists elsewhere in their lives and all that has transpired before. This event then, despite its apparent importance as a precipitant, cannot stand alone. It gains its salience from the context both current and historical in which it exists.

The concept of a "chain reaction" is an important one in that it speaks to the problems with reality testing, vulnerability, and meager coping mechanisms associated with the personality of the adolescent suicide attempter. Under conditions of stress these adolescents are apt to become hypersensitive to slights both real and imagined. Further, they are ill-equipped to mediate effectively the feelings which these interpersonal events may provoke. As overwhelming feelings of guilt, sadness, and anger mount, teenagers are hard pressed to stabilize themselves by means of effective coping mechanisms or to prevent a worsening of this intrapsychic and interpersonal condition. Rather, the problematic relationship and condition is apt to become more so. These realizations and attendent feelings are then easily generalizable to all people and all relationships, thus putting into process the chain reaction dissolution of remaining relationships spoken of by Jacobs and seen with great frequency by those whose clinical or professional work involves adolescents. Combined with events of an inter-personal nature, are often traumatic events of other sorts. Losses, failures, and misfortunes in other areas frequently embed themselves in their lives with corrosive and destabilizing results.

Case Study (Part 4)

The toothpick structure that was the life and really the personality of Cassandra, crumbled in upon itself in June, on her eighteenth birthday, a date of ruined potential. When Cassandra quit school in January of that year, the possibility of selling the life-long family home emerged. With three kids all grown and now out of school it seemed a reasonable thing to do. Mr. and Mrs. C. envisioned the purchase of a house trailer in Florida. Soon after Mrs. C's cancer was discovered, plans for the selling of the house were finalized. It was decided that when Cassandra turned 18 the house would be sold. Cassandra was undaunted by these tragic developments at the time, and made plans to marry her long-time boyfriend, Bruce, that summer. Despite the obvious tragedy of her mother's imminent death, she could feel, with an engagement ring newly on her finger, that she at least would have a home, though her family of origin was scattering beneath her.

However, in the few days before her eighteenth birthday, things began to slip rapidly out of place. Her mother was moved out of the hospital to a unit for dying patients, and was not expected to last the week. The house had been sold and the family had to vacate by the Monday following Cassandra's Saturday birthday. Her father had rented an apartment out of town and would be moving later that week. Meanwhile, things with Bruce, predictable to all but Cassandra, had become tenuous at best. Nothing in their relationship had improved. The engagement ring had covered a goodly distance through the air during the past few months, having been bounced off walls in a number of bitter encounters. In the aftermath of another big alcohol-steeped fight on Friday night, the engagement, wedding, and plans to move in with each other and get an apartment were all called off. Saturday night, the birthday night, an attempt at reconciliation collapsed.

It was supposed to be a party for Cassandra given by friends at a friend's house. Quite a few people were there. However, there could not ever have been a worse day for her. The bottom had fallen out of her world; critical attachments kicked out from underneath her in quick succession. She was to lose, in her mind, her mother, father, home, boyfriend, and husband, all in the space of a few days and it was all coming to a head here and now during her party. Enraged, quite drunk, shaking and crying, she tore out of the friend's house, rushed to her car, ripped open the glove compartment, and hauled out a large hunting knife. It took her several seconds to get it out of its leather case. She had turned toward the house and had slashed it (lightly) at her throat when stronger arms, having followed her out of the house, arrested the act. Cassandra was subdued, bleeding, after a brief, but energetic struggle. She was brought to the hospital, where the wound was found to be superficial, not even requiring stitches. Cassandra was held for two nights and discharged, temporarily, due to a lack of space, to the care of her out-patient therapist, with the stipulation that she return to be readmitted in four days; a stipulation she willingly agreed to. During the interim she was to live with her father.

In Cassandra's case the progression to suicide was both lengthy and complex. Though none of her suicidal behavior yielded a serious medical emergency, each emanated from profound psychological distress. Problems escalated throughout her adolescence, a period of her life that she apparently was ill-prepared to enter. Devoid of healthy or effective coping skills, exhausting all available adaptive strategies, she was easily overwhelmed by events, having had far more than her share of stressful conditions and events to deal with. In fact, an irony is that, while Cassandra, more than probably any adolescent with whom I have worked, needed calm and stability, she lived a life of chronic and almost unremitting stimulation and agitation. She would cope with this only through drugs and alcohol, ultimately never learning to cope at all. By age 18, the "last straw" had arrived as a bundle, under which her will to live collapsed.

INTERNAL PROCESS

The internal process by which the adolescent becomes actively suicidal deserves more attention. While much of this chapter and book has and will focus on external factors and processes, certain elemental internal dynamics and conditions need to be discussed since, as in the case of their suicidality as a whole, adolescents manifest distinctive qualities in their psychological condition which set them apart from adults and adult suicidals.

There is considerable evidence to suggest that the essential dynamic of adolescent suicidal behavior is a constellation of feelings of guilt, abandonment, and helplessness that the adolescent feels cannot be effectively ameliorated or communicated by other methods. Adolescent suicide attempters attribute their behaviors to a variety of anxiety-provoking or frustrating circumstances other than particular depressive complaints. Actions preceding the suicidal behavior include acting-out behavior, including delinquent acts, and neurotic symptom formation, as well as mounting depression. However, depressive themes are almost invariably central to the underlying dynamic core of suicidal behavior.

Although depression, more than any other psychiatric disorder, is usually associated with adolescent suicidal behavior, its manifestations are often multifarious and difficult to identify. All of the adaptive behaviors observed by Jacobs (1971): Rebelling, withdrawing, and running away from home, preliminary to the suicide attempt itself, have been identified as common depressive equivalents. It is a distinctive quality of adolescent depression, unlike the forms that adult depression usually take, that classic depressive symptoms are often not seen or are in some way obscured. Toolan (1971) has stated that "especially in the adolescent we seldom see a clear picture of depression" (p. 407). While some adolescents will certainly evidence some of the symptoms listed above, they may lie beneath a layer of depressive equivalents which mask the underlying dynamic. This is especially true with boys for whom the need to hide their true feelings exists, particularly the softer, tender, "weaker" sentiments. Girls too, will often find these feelings unacceptable, especially when associated with dependency issues and will be avoided at all cost. Adolescents frequently desire and are able to "mask" or avoid depressive affects for a variety of reasons, among which are the following.

1. *Capacity for denial.* Young persons appear able to deny the reality of painful conditions or affects with greater effectiveness than adults. First of all, it is very unattractive for the teenager, of all people, to be depressed.

Living as they do in the high powered, fast-paced intensity of a peer group which prizes, above all other social attributes, gaiety, liveliness, spontaneity, humor, and the capacity to have and be fun, it is social suicide to be depressed, morose, lethargic, and very unfun. Adolescents feel, therefore, compelled to deal with depression in a very different way.

2. *Tendency to act out feelings.* The energy and impulsivity characteristic of adolescence allows for a greater likelihood that feelings will find expression in action rather than simply internal thought and mood. Teenagers often resort to acting out behaviors as temporary tension reducers, unable to gratify or calm themselves through fantasy alone.

3. *Avoidance of dependence and helplessness.* It is an age appropriate condition of adolescence that the adolescent desires to feel independent, strong, and able to take control of his/her life and problems. They do not want to feel dependent and needy of adults or at the mercy of events or feelings. To be seriously depressed, is to be in a way, incapacitated, rendered weak and immobile, unable to effectively control one's thoughts or moods to the degree one would expect. This state of affairs is anathema to the teenager. It is emasculating at a time when personal potency is desperately sought.

Adolescents are somewhat predisposed then, to seek alternative forms of dealing with depression. These different symptoms for the same disorder serve the purpose of allowing the adolescent to discharge and seek relief for his feelings while at the same time avoiding a recognition of his problems and feelings. Activity of this type in its many forms distracts the teenager from thinking of his problems and facing the unpleasant image he holds of himself and his life. Examples of these behaviors and their dynamics follow:

a) *Running away.* Running away from family home, foster home, or some other residential setting sometimes occurs in depressed teenagers as a means of actively dealing with overwhelming tension and the painful awakening of intolerable depressive feelings that often have their origins in intrafamilial relations. Running provides a temporary release of tension, an escape, and the feeling that one is in control. Again, the action in and of itself provides relief and a distraction from internal feelings and external realities. It serves as a denial of unhappy interpersonal and intrapsychic conditions.

b) *Sexual acting out.* The urgent necessity to ward off underlying feelings of being unloved and unwanted can push the adolescent toward promiscuous sexual behavior in which close physical contact with another person who expresses interest and affection for whatever reason, provides the major gratification. For a female, however, this means of attempting to meet one's needs is probably the most profoundly self-destructive and corrosive strategy that a girl could devise.

c) *Boredom and restlessness.* Depressed adolescents often manifest their condition by swinging from states of short-lived but unbounded energy, frenetic activity, and enthusiasm, to periods of intolerable boredom, listlessness, and generalized disinterest bordering on, and including, classic depressive symptomatology. It is to avoid coming any closer to an awareness of depressive feelings that the cycle of excited activity and restlessness is again renewed. "I'm bored" is often an unconscious code phrase for "I'm depressed" in adolescence.

d) *Disturbance of concentration.* Often this is the earliest, most frequently cited symptom which presents itself in the depressed adolescent and the only one with which he or she is aware. Again, there is a defensive quality to these concentration problems. As the mind seeks to avoid awareness of painfully sad thoughts and feelings, it may skip actively from thought to thought unable to stay still long for fear of being caught by the waiting depressive alternative. The effect on school performance can, of course, be devastating regardless of one's level of intelligence.

From my experience it would seem to be a major ingredient in chronic truancy and class-cutting. Depressed teenagers often find the classroom to be the most frightening of places. In class, the adolescent is usually denied favored vehicles for avoidance such as activity and social interaction. Concentration for these teenagers is very difficult, and so involvement with the curriculum of the class becomes impossible. Their minds are left to wander. They soon begin to feel anxious and at the mercy of their thoughts and feelings, fearful of a crying spell or noticeable agitation, with no means available for coping with them or defending against them. It may soon occur to them not to put themselves in this position again. Sometimes dropping out of school altogether becomes the result. With those less chronically afflicted, intermittent truancy and class-cutting may occur. Those who quit often find the job experience, which takes the place of school, to be much easier to deal with, at least at first. Work is apt to be active, social interaction possible, and the level of concentration needed is much less. Work is often a respite and an escape for these teenagers. It typically requires little of the ego strength of school.

A case in point regards Suzanne (the same Suzanne of Chapter 3), who at the time was an 18-year-old second semester senior who dropped out of school. Suzanne was from a rejecting, grossly unsupportive, multiproblem family. She was probably an alcoholic, had had an abortion, two prior suicide attempts, and was chronically depressed and given to suicidal thoughts. Most of this was not known to the staff at her school, though her unkempt appearance, moodiness, and lack of friends caused her to stand out quite easily as a kid with problems. Still, it came as a shock when she quit school in March of her senior year. It was hard for the adults and students alike to understand how a student with two months of school left, could give up. For Suzanne, however, the number to be struggled with was not "2" but "240" as she explained to me, because that was the number of class periods left for her between late March and the end of May. Two hundred and forty experiences which she could no longer tolerate.

e) *Aggressive behavior and delinquency.* Angry and destructive behavior, including vandalism, can sometimes be expressed by depressed adolescents, especially boys, in lieu of the depressive feelings. These actions may be designed to counteract the poor self-image and feelings of helplessness by artificially inflating the youngster's self-image as a strong, fearless, and clever person.

Dan was a 16-year-old who attempted suicide by trying to asphyxiate himself with carbon monoxide in the family car, in the family garage. He was also a firesetter with two convictions and a vandal of prolific proportions. For Dan, firesetting and other forms of expression of his angry and destructive urges, served as an outlet for powerful tensions which often welled up within him. Usually his anger found an external direction, though his tendency to get caught in his deeds suggests a self-punishing bent. Still, he found some immediate gratification and sense of power from these episodes and an escape from tension, depression, and loneliness. At times, however, his anger would swing back upon himself and he would become overtly depressed and suicidal. Though prevalent in males, this mode of dealing with depression appears to be finding favor with increasing numbers of females who are discovering the purging qualities of violence and destruction. Anyone who has had the distinct pleasure of comparing the physical condition of girls' and boys' rooms in a high school can attest to the often much more dilapidated and graffitti festooned character of girls' rooms. Teachers remark at the higher incidence of female fights as compared to male fights in high schools. Furthermore, the girls' fights are often described as more savage and unrelenting.

Masked depression and their depressive equivalents in the form of various acting out and delinquent behaviors are dangerous and unhealthy in that they obscure from the teenager and significant adults the nature and extent of the individual's distress. These behaviors are in some cases very self-destructive, especially for females in the case of sexual acting out. Finally, they forgo mastering of important issues and jeopardize normal adolescent development in favor of temporary but ineffectual relief. Blos (1963) states that "acting out by its very nature has forfeited the capacity for mastery and turned it into an act of avoidance" (p. 269).

Depressed adolescents may manifest their feelings through any number of expressive channels including attempted or committed suicide. These modes are not mutually exclusive. In fact, it is quite common to see episodes of running away, sexual acting out, drug abuse, etc., within the behavioral repertoire of the adolescent suicide attempter.

It is safe to say that while not all depressed adolescents are actively suicidal, most suicidal adolescents are depressed. However, as has been demonstrated with regard to the reasons, level of lethality, and historical antecedents behind adolescent suicidal behavior, the disturbance of the internal process is often underestimated, misdiagnosed, misunderstood, or disregarded altogether. It is indeed ironic that adolescent suicide attempters can be so needy of understanding while at the same time being so proficient at rendering themselves so misunderstood.

5

Postattempt:
Human Environment
and the Teenage
Suicide Attempter

Since Farberow and Shneidman (1961) wrote of the adolescent suicide attempt as being a "cry for help," teenage suicidal behavior has been thought of as often instrumental with motivations that are predominantly nonlethal. While committed suicides among adolescents are sharply on the rise, attempted suicides outnumber them by probably 200 to 300:1. Certainly, the research on the motivations, reasons, methods, circumstances, and precipitants of adolescent suicidal behavior is consistent in reporting sublethal intentionality in most adolescent suicide attempts. Though it appears that adult and adolescent assessors may slightly underestimate the intensity of the "wish to die" in adolescent suicide attempts, they seem to be correct in describing the behavior as intended in most cases to ameliorate rather than end lives. The reasons ascribed to these suicide attempts by both the surviving attempters and their evaluators depict the attempt as being carried out as a nonverbal communicative gesture within an interpersonal context. Often the interpersonal context is quite specific, that is, the behavior is directed toward a certain individual or individuals, parents, family members, a boy or girl friend, or some designated significant other. At times the behavior is intended for a larger audience of nonspecific persons, to the human environment at large. Nearly always it is an attempt to solicit some evidence of caring from other people, if not help (in terms of professional psychological intervention). These adolescents have come to feel intolerably alone and unattended. It is said by many researchers, adolescent suicide attempters, and their peers, that the teenage suicide attempter is seeking "attention."

Attention in this case is a misnomer. It gives the impression of shallow, manipulative, self-aggrandizement, and greed. Adolescent suicide attempters are typically needy individuals. A close inspection of their histories will often illuminate the etiology and development of their perhaps inordinate neediness. However, what they appear to crave is not attention, but caring and nurturing in a manner far deeper than can be conveyed by the word "attention." Sadly, they will, all too often, practice self-deceit and settle for transient attention instead, since it is far easier to acquire, though all too briefly satisfying.

Adolescents then, by virtue of their survival rate from suicide attempts, the relatively low lethality of their methods, and the highly interpersonal context within which their attempts take place, constitute a distinctive subgroup within the population of suicidal persons. They appear to rely more than older age groups on their human environment for support and are most sensitive to its response to their act. They are, furthermore, the age group most likely to be around to experience that response.

At the same time research strongly suggests that adolescent suicidal behavior elicits a distinctive and distinctly less favorable response than does the suicidal behavior of older persons. The youth of the attempters, the low-lethality of attempts and, what to many adult assessors appears to be hostile and manipulative motivations, combine to produce more unfavorable attitudinal responses from medical professionals and others to the adolescent attempt than to those of older persons (Hawton et al., 1981; Ramon et al., 1975).

Suicidal behavior in any form by persons of any age is considered in many societies, and certainly in ours, to be taboo. It has been censured by religion and state. It is often considered to be an affront to humanity, indicting of the group and thus tends to bring about defensive retribution in the form of condemnation and scorn.

Haim (1974) has written that this is most painfully and intensively felt by those surrounding the suicidal act of a young person, an adolescent. The suicidal adolescent defames for the adult, the meaning of life, the glorified image of youth and health, maligns the image of his caretakers, and holds aloft the fearful specter of death. These are unpleasant and unwelcome realizations. Anger, resentment, and fear typically follow.

It is into this atmosphere of misunderstanding, uncertainty, anxiety, and at times, rebuke, that the surviving adolescent suicide attempter emerges, postattempt. Hoping for embrace, he or she appears more likely to experience a cruel irony. The research is nearly unanimous in failing to demonstrate positive attitudes toward suicide attempters, especially when the attempter is an adolescent. Most studies of attitudes toward suicide attempts reveal emphatically negative feelings toward those who attempt to take their lives and fail. Though small consolation to those involved, committed suicides elicit more positive attitudes than attempted suicides, the victims appearing more sincere, more justifiably lacking in hope, and more unbearably afflicted. (Linehan, 1971; Selby & Calhoun, 1975).

ATTITUDES TOWARD SUICIDAL BEHAVIOR

Formal research into the attitudes of people toward suicidal behavior has been a relatively recent endeavor. The first studies into the issue were conducted in the early 1970's. In 1971, Ginsburg surveyed a large number of adults in Reno, Nevada, on a variety of questions dealing with beliefs and attitudes toward suicide without, however, specifying the type of suicidal behavior or considering the age of the suicidals in question. Other early studies of adult attitudes toward adult suicidal behavior give indications as to the factors influencing suicide attitudes which have important implications for adolescent attitude studies. In 1973, Nicol reported that predominantly negative attitudes were held by adult respondents toward adult suicide attempters. The attitudes elicited were found to have been especially negative when the level of stress the suicide attempter was under was judged to be relatively low. Male attempters under perceived low stress conditions were judged most harshly by the male and female respondents. Adolescent attempts, particularly when judged solely by their precipitants (i.e., argument with parent or lover), which often seem trivial out of context, are frequently judged to have occurred under low stress circumstances by adults who view the teenage years as "the best years of your life" and relatively unstressful when compared with the strains of adult life.

Sale et al. (1975) found that among the adult women studied, negative attitudes were held toward suicide attempts. Attempts were regarded by these women as "manipulative" and not due to mental illness. Lower lethality attempts elicited the most negative attitudinal responses. Bell (1978), in a study of the suicide attitudes of undergraduate psychology majors, reported negative attitudes toward peer suicide attempters especially if the behavior was chronic. Those who merely thought about suicide were regarded more positively. The suicide attempters were described as "cowardly," "sick," "bad," "unpleasant," "disreputable," "cruel," and "unfair."

Much research has focused on the attitudes, level of sympathy/antipathy and the degree of readiness to help of the medical and mental health professions toward the suicidal behavior of adults and adolescents. The research is consistent in its findings that the medical profession is often ill-disposed toward the suicidal patient. Writing in a leading medical journal Patel (1975) states,

Viewed as attempts at self-destruction, many of these episodes appear to be half-hearted or histrionic and the medical staff who have to deal with them sometimes feel a sense of irritation which they find difficult to conceal. (p. 426)

Bernard (1974) writes from a large London teaching hospital,

Attempted suicide is of course the most unpopular of all complaints with the medical profession, and even the most angelic nurses can turn quite waspy at the sight of a living attempt. (p. 27)

Murray (1974) echoes these acidic sentiments. "The fashion is to treat them with contempt and discharge them as soon as possible."

The bulk of the literature in this area, while lacking some of the vitriol of the preceding comments, supports the notion that suicide attempters especially when young, will not be well received by those who may be called upon to treat them first, postattempt. This is understandable since by training and perhaps by temperament, medical personnel are better prepared to treat organic rather than emotional dysfunctions. Barber et al. (1975) have suggested that the training process itself may account for some of the negativity of attitudes on the part of physicians. He demonstrated a difference in attitudes between fourth and final year British medical students. While the attitudes of all were predominantly negative, the final year students had become significantly more so. All the medical students considered that the attitudes of the medical profession as a whole were harshly negative toward suicide attempts and much more positive when dealing with the patient with organic ailments. Barber refers to

an apparent decline that takes place in students "humanism" as undergraduate training progresses and to the preference that students seem to show for the organic rather than the psychological aspects of medicine (p. 433).

He further states that "it appears that attitudes to emotive conditions harden as the student approaches graduation." The social work students who served as a comparison group did not show this pattern or the same degree of negativity of attitudes.

Negative attitudes held by physicians and nurses toward suicide attempters have been reported by others as well (Ansel & McGee, 1971; Ghodse, 1970; Hawton et al., 1981, 1982a; Patel, 1975; Ramon et al., 1975). Ansel and McGee (1971) found that professional staff (psychiatry residents, psychiatric nurses, emergency room personnel, suicide prevention center personnel, and police) assigned the task of dealing with the suicide attempter held no less negative attitudes than the general lay public. Ghodse (1978) reported negative attitudes on the part of ambulance as well as casualty staff (physicians and nurses) which deepened with increased experience.

More recent research (Domino and Swain, 1986; Swain and Domino, 1985) strongly supports the presence of a correlation between judgments of level of lethality of attempt, and attitudes. These studies found that among mental health professionals those having lower levels of knowledge as to signs of suicide, judged suicide attempts to be of lower lethality than those professionals with more knowledge in this area. Further, less knowledge was associated with beliefs that attempted suicide was an act of "manipulation" provoked by a "self-destructive drive" which was out of control, whereas more knowledgeable evaluators more often cited a "cry for help" in the face of negative "external environmental aspects" as the primary dynamic.

Research directed at studying attitudes towards adolescent attempters reveals a generally higher level of negativity. Ramon et al. (1975) found that while negative attitudes and a reduced "readiness to help" existed among physicians and nurses toward all attempters, the adolescent attempter elicited the greatest amount of "antipathy" and the least degree of "readiness to help." This response was associated with the belief on the part of the professional respondents that the adolescent's attempt was more "manipulative" than the other adult attempters with far less intent upon dying. Hawton et al. (1981), in a replication of Ramon's study, confirmed both the overriding negativity of physicians and nurses as well as psychiatrists and its association with perceived lowest lethality and "manipulative" and "hostile" motivations. Hawton's study is extremely valuable for its analysis of some of the elements of negative attitudes. Adolescents' suicide attempts were attributed by the professionals to reasons which they deemed "least favorable" based on their ranking of 11 possible reasons for a suicide attempt. The leading reasons ascribed to the adolescents' suicide attempts included "make people sorry for the way they have treated the person," "try to influence some particular person or get them to change their mind," "frighten or get their own way back on someone," and "find out whether someone really loved the person or not." While the psychiatrists proved to be slightly more "ready to help" than either the physicians or the nurses, they showed the same pattern of declining readiness and sympathy as the lethality of the attempt seemed lower and the reasons for the attempt less favorable. Hawton cautions against extrapolating research findings to actual clinical practice while citing, however, the recurrent findings which suggest that,

*For many physicians, overdose patients are regarded as a nuisance
and less deserving of medical care than patients with physical illness.
(p. 346)*

Only Ansel and McGee (1971), and Dressler, Prusoff, Mark, and Shapiro
(1975) have reported more positive attitudes toward the lower lethality
attempter. While the age of the attempter was not a variable in either study
and thus no ages were reported, psychiatric residents in both studies were
found to feel "less anxious" and less "angry" toward less chronic and less
dangerously suicidal patients.

It has been amply demonstrated that peer relationsips are an important
source of support to the adolescent suicide attempter (Mishara, 1982; Topol
& Reznikoff, 1984; Walch, 1977). Problems in these relationships are often
a critical ingredient in the precipitation of the suicidal act itself (Jacobs,
1971; Rohn et al. 1977; Teicher, 1973; Tischler et al. 1981; Walch, 1978;
Wenz, 1979). Adolescent suicide attempts often follow the perceived rupture
of a close friendship or romantic relationship. These relationships are
frequently very highly valued. They are supercharged with the emotional
investment drained off from what are often empty and frustrated familial
relationships. It is therefore important to inquire into the attitudes held by
the peers of teenaged suicide attempters since this population often constitutes both the primary reference group and last visible source of support to
the troubled, suicidal adolescent. To date little research has been devoted
to adolescent attitudes toward adolescent suicide. What exists is very recent
(Boldt, 1982; Curran, 1984; Stillion, McDowell, & May, 1984; Stillion,
McDowell, & Shamblin, 1984).

Curran found that, much like the adult groups studied, adolescents too,
held predominantly negative attitudes toward adolescent suicidal behavior,
especially if it was chronic or repetitive within the same person. However,
there were reported important sex influences upon these attitudes. Female
adolescents were found to hold significantly less negative attitudes than males
toward peer attempters. Both male and female adolescents felt more negatively toward male suicide attempters. Both sexes were most negative in their
attitudinal responses toward chronic attempters. Stillion et al. (1984) in an
expanded treatment of adolescent attitudes toward suicide, reported results
which closely parallel Curran's. Females were found to be more "sympathetic" to suicidal individuals than were male teenagers, especially if the
attempter was female. However, the older and brighter (based on I.Q. score)
adolescent respondents were less likely to hold more sympathetic and
agreeable attitudes. The hypothesis is put forth that the higher rate of female
adolescent suicide attempts may be a reflection of expectations on the part
of females of a warmer human response, whereas males may accurately assess

the level of acceptance for nonlethal suicidal behavior on their part to be low. Males may then opt more often for committed suicide, expecting rebuke in some form if they should fail to die. Nicol (1975) also reported that females (adults) tend to hold more positive attitudes toward suicidal behavior than do males and that females also elicit more favorable responses. Ramon et al. (1975) found physicians' (primarily male) attitudes toward suicidals to be more negative than nurses' (primarily female) attitudes. Profession was not controlled for, however, since sex was not an intended variable in the study. Others (Ansel & McGee, 1971; Linehan, 1971; Kalish et al. 1974; and Bell, 1978) found no significant main or interactive effects for the variable of sex on attitudes in their studies of adult attitudes toward adult suicidals.

Research into the attitudes of adolescents toward adolescent suicidal behavior has proven fruitful in identifying a group (adolescent suicide attempters) that do not appear to hold negative attitudes toward suicide attempters and in its suggestion that adolescents as a group may hold generally more favorable attitudes toward suicide than do adults.

Female adolescent suicide attempters were found to hold more neutral, perhaps slightly positive, attitudes toward nonchronic peer suicide attempters (Curran, 1984). These attitudes were joined by a belief on the part of the suicide attempters of a higher level lethal intent associated with adolescent suicidal behavior as compared with the beliefs of the nonsuicide attempter adolescent respondents. Hawton et al. (1978) also have reported relatively less negative attitudes held by adolescent suicide attempters toward attempted suicide in general, and adolescent suicide attempts, in particular. While the psychiatric patients and drug overdosers in his study were found to hold largely negative attitudes toward suicide attempters and as a group responded with the least "sympathy" toward the adolescent suicide attempt, the subgroup of adolescent psychiatric patients who had also had a history of suicide attempts themselves clearly deviated from the group's overall response. Limbacher and Domino (1986) compared attitudes of undergraduate attempters and nonattempters finding that nonsuicide attempters tended to believe that adolescent suicide attempts did not involve "a serious wish to die" and were viewed as "manipulative behavior."

Adolescents as a group may, in fact, feel generally less negatively about suicide than adults. Certainly, adolescents have often distinguished themselves from adults in their acceptance of different values, attitudes and "deviant" behaviors in the areas of sexuality, drug use, and certain forms of delinquent behavior. Evidence for differing attitudes between adults and adolescents toward suicide is, however, scanty. Boldt (1982) compared the attitudes and beliefs of adolescents and their parents concerning suicide with interesting results. The adolescents were found to be significantly more accepting of suicidal behavior than their parents. They considered it less "shameful," less "stigmatizing," and were less 'judgmental" in their responses.

While one would certainly assume that the attitudinal response of the adolescent's peer environment is of great importance, it is widely accepted that the likely root of the suicidal adolescent's self-destructive wishes lie within his familial relationships as documented in Chapter 3. With this in mind, the reactive attitudes and feelings of the families of adolescent suicide attempters have been studied, though not extensively or often in an empirical manner. Rosenbaum and Richman (1970) observed that family members and other relatives expressed "an overwhelming degree of anger" toward the suicide attempter. Wenz (1978) stated that families (as well as peers) tended to "label" the adolescent attempter in their midst as "suicidal," whereby they were "treated as suicidal." This consisted of a relationship postattempt that was contaminated by "the search for [suicidal] signs," "suspicion" and "exclusion." More research is needed on the reactive style of families to the unsuccessful suicide attempts of their adolescent sons and daughters. That few studies exist should not be surprising given the sensitive status of such a family, postattempt. Powerful feelings of guilt, shame, and anger would likely present a formidable obstacle to any intrepid researcher.

THE MENTAL HEALTH SYSTEM

Attitudes toward suicide attempters may impact significantly and negatively on the successful engagement of the attempter in psychotherapeutic treatment. The mental health and medical professions appear, often, to be failing to meet the needs of the suicide attempter, postattempt. Dorpat and Ripley (1967), and Weissman (1974) have reported that suicide attempters are at greatest risk for a repeat attempt during the first two years after the act. Goldacre and Hawton (1985) reported that adolescent self-poisoners are at highest risk of repetition during the first few months after an overdose. This finding is similar to those of Bancroft and Marsack (1977). However, adolescent suicide attempters are often not referred for mental health services after the attempt is discovered. This suggests a lack of serious regard for the meaning and importance of the lower lethality attempt on the part of the referral agents as well as a reduced readiness to help. Sifneos (1966) reported that 23 percent of suicide attempter emergency room admissions at Massachusetts General Hospital in Boston were not referred for mental health services of any kind. Weissman (1974), reporting on the renowned New Haven Study on adolescent suicide, wrote that only 38 percent of the suicide attempters were referred for treatment, and of those, only half showed up for their first appointment. Bancroft et al. (1976) presented the interesting finding that only 50 percent of those adolescent suicide attempters (emergency room admissions) who stated that they had not intended to die were referred for counseling, while 70 percent of those stating a "definite wish to die" were referred. White (1974) reported that 30 percent of the suicide attempters in his study were not recommended for psychological services, as did Hawton et al. (1982). Hawton's group of suicide attempters were classified into three groups based on the severity and chronicity of behavioral problems. Among the group considered to have experienced, in the view of the clinical assessors, the most recent onset of problems, 70 percent were not referred for counseling.

Toolan (1975) and Weiner (1970) have urged that every adolescent suicide attempter be referred for psychological services. With greater awareness and knowledge among referring agents, perhaps this is beginning to happen. Tishler et al. (1981) reported findings on emergency room admissions in Columbus, Ohio, that 100 percent of adolescent suicide attempters were referred for treatment, 85 percent out-patient and 15 percent in-patient.

The reasons for the high percentages of nonreferrals is likely due to ignorance of the deeper meanings of adolescent suicide attempts and misunderstanding and underestimates of the degree of personality disturbance typically associated with it. Crumley (1982) and White (1974) have written of the pervasive "underdiagnosis" of adolescent suicide attempters. Often not apparent is the extent or presence of depression and long-standing problems of self-esteem and suicidogenic family dynamics. Emergency room personnel and other clinical assessors are often fooled by the apparently low lethality of the attempt as indicated in the method, circumstances, and stated intent. They often attach too much importance to the stated precipitant of the act which may, thereby, seem so trivial and the act so impulsive. By this process they may fail to see the precipitant (i.e., argument with parents or friends) as the last straw, but rather as the only straw. Further, the frightened, embarrassed, and ashamed adolescent may well mask and deny the feelings and experiences from which his/her behavior evolved, putting on a good face and insisting the whole thing was a terrible and foolish mistake, an attitude which many adults appear all too willing to embrace.

Considerable research suggests that negative attitudes toward adolescent suicide attempts serve to create feelings of hostility, antipathy, and a diminished readiness to help on the part of medical staff most likely to attend to and refer for psychological services. It may be that attempts perceived to be manipulative and hostile are not readily indulged. It would appear that both beliefs and negative feelings combined influence the decision to refer (or not to refer) in these cases.

Once the suicidal person is referred for therapy, however, no-show and premature drop out rates are very high (Berman & Carroll, 1984; Leese, 1969;

Walker, 1980; Weissman, 1974). White (1974) and Litt, Cuskey, and Rudd (1983), both reported that 37 percent of adolescents referred for counseling services failed to comply. Hawton's (1982) opinion is that adolescents do not make the attempt with the hope of obtaining professional help. The adolescent is more likely to have specific, known individuals in mind as providers of caring and support or a more vague wish for a warm, caring embrace from the human environment, in general, rather than the mental health profession, in particular. Further, the adolescent's wish to quickly restabilize, pass the crisis and deny and avoid their suicidality and associated conflicts and feelings, may yield an apparent diffidence in accepting an initial offer of help from the clinical staff. This is, of course, most likely to be true when the staff is viewed by the adolescent as being negative, unaccepting, unsympathetic or hostile. Hawton's comments on the apparent disinterest of adolescents in obtaining professional help postattempt, is contradicted by other research of his own (Hawton et al., 1982c) which tells quite a different story and suggests strongly the powerful impact of sensitive, attentive medical intervention on successful connection to therapy. In the latter study, only 8 percent of 50 adolescent suicide attempters, identified by emergency room admission, refused out-patient counseling. This very low refusal rate may have been an artifact of the attempters having been a part of a research project, entailing several one to one interviews with concerned and interested researchers who considered their attempts to be matters of importance and worthy of considerable attention. This approach may have connoted to these adolescents a positive regard which caused them to have greater faith and investment in their referral to counseling.

It may very well be that professional help is not the goal of the adolescent suicide attempter. However, their typically high rate of failure to comply with referrals may not be due entirely to any inherent unwillingness or lack of a capacity to engage in therapy. Berman and Carroll (1984) cite parental pathology and denial as impediments to providing psychological services to the suicidal adolescent. Weissman (1974), however, voiced the feelings of many clinicians in citing "difficulty in engaging the more mild attempters in out-patient treatment" (p. 743). The implication is that failure in treatment is the fault of the adolescent alone, rather than a more complex phenomenon involving the adolescent's defensive response to his experience, the attitudes of his family, and perhaps the negative attitudes of the referring party.

Problems with the mental health profession do not cease for the suicidal individual with their compliance with the recommendation for therapy. Again, feelings and attitudes on the part of mental health professionals toward suicidal clients may result in premature termination or failure of the therapy which may be more due to the professional than the client. Clinicians have been shown to hold negative attitudes toward attempted suicide and a reduced readiness to help. Among therapists, feelings of anger (Litman, 1968) and anxiety (Mintz, 1968) toward suicidal clients have been described. Frederick (1971) has shown that the suicide "taboo" is strong among mental health professionals, though it may be below the level of awareness, denied, inadmissible and intellectualized and, therefore, dangerously contributory to countertransference problems. Reubin (1973), in a review of the literature, reported that suicidal patients were the ones most likely to be seriously mismanaged and rejected by therapists and that mental health professionals tended to be unwilling or reluctant to treat suicidal clients. Yalom (1975) recommends that they not be considered for group therapy because of the anxiety and pressures of responsibility they place on other group members.

An understanding of the adolescent suicide attempters' capacity or readiness for engagement in psychotherapy must include a study of the role of attitudes toward these attempters on the part of the medical and mental health personnel most likely to be in the position of introducing the idea of referral to therapy or actually carrying it out. It is wrong to assume that this population does not want or cannot handle it. The professionals' response needs to be sensitive and attentive from the start in order to facilitate a necessary referral and involvement of the adolescent and his or her family in counseling services. Attitudes do not necessarily equal behavior, however. The behavioral implications of negative attitudes need to be empirically validated. Attitudes may, at the least, serve as predispositions to behavior

> *The action tendency component of an attitude includes all the behavioral readiness associated with an attitude. If an individual holds a positive attitude toward a given object he will be disposed to help, reward or support the object: if he holds a negative attitude he will be disposed to harm, diminish or destroy the object. (Krech and Crutchfield, 1962, p. 139.)*

It would seem safe to say that suicide attempts are not well received behaviors by our society. Negative attitudes prevail which may render unlikely the possibility of the attempter actually gaining, by the act, a reasonable measure of what he or she had wanted, needed, or expected. Indeed, the teenage suicide attempter is more likely to be responded to with rejection, censure, or neglect. They are likely to experience in some way a greater distance from people than they had felt before. Even the relatively less negative attitudes of their peers often fall far short of the actively positive response which the adolescent suicide attempter may crave and anticipate.

6

The Wish and the Reality:
Effect of Negative Attitudes
on the Adolescent
Suicide Attempter

The fact that adolescent suicide attempters survive their attempts with greater frequency than do suicidal individuals in any other age group is usually not due to mere chance, but rather to a conscious or unconscious wish to survive the attempt. There is implicit in the methods, circumstances, and reasons for the adolescent attempt the hope on the part of the attempter that the act might elicit a human response that could serve to gratify or in some way seek to address the profound needs of the suicidal teenager. As is suggested in attitude research in this area, the suicidal adolescent is apt to become bitterly disappointed by that response. The adolescent has in many instances offered up the act of attempted suicide in anticipation of reactions to it. Research and clinical experience strongly indicate that the assumptions held by the teenage suicide attempter concerning the likely response of others are very wrong.

Other adolescents appear to share a view similar to suicide attempters as to the reasons for attempts (seeking of help or attention). While acknowledging the feelings of teenage attempters their attitudes indicate that they do not condone the manner of expression, the method of communicating these feelings.

When I give talks to adolescent groups on the subject of adolescent suicidal behavior, I always at some point explore the attitudes of the group, both for my own purposes and in an effort to demonstrate to them their attitudes toward suicide and their likely behavioral response to a suicidal peer. I ask them to imagine themselves, individually, in a situation in which they are late for lunch at the school cafeteria. They arrive to find all seats taken except for two that are in different areas of the lunch room. They do not really know any of the people sitting next to either of the empty seats, but next to one empty seat is a same sex peer who they know has made a suicide attempt recently. Other than that, the person is unknown to them. Next to the other empty seat is a similar grouping of students also unknown except for the fact that, as far as is known, none of them has made a suicide attempt. They must sit in one of these empty seats, either next to the "suicidal person" or one who is not. Among the groups who have responded to the question "Where will you sit?," about eighty percent choose to sit with the nonsuicidal peer rather than the suicide attempter. When asked why, they say things like "I wouldn't know what to say"; "he (or she) might be weird"; or "what if we got talking and I said the wrong thing." In short, adolescents, a population often of critical importance to the support of adolescent suicide attempters, are apt to distance themselves from peer suicide attempters. Though they may not overtly castigate the individual they, nonetheless, appear ill-disposed to providing the embracing response which may have been wished for. Instead, they shrink back in uncertainty and fear. If the attempter is a friend, the response may include actual and active disapproval and criticism. The act will not adequately communicate the complexity or depth of feeling that instigated it and will, therefore, not be taken as seriously as the attempter would have liked and needed. Teenagers, in my experience, often do not understand the need for caring involved in the suicide attempt. They are apt to respond, as may adults, with anger, impatience, and resentment at what they perceive to be attention seeking behavior. They seem to feel that while seeking attention may be an acceptable desire, the means used is both manipulative of others and unfair. On the other hand, I have witnessed episodes of extraordinary compassion and tenderness on the part of teenagers toward their troubled peer, behavior which has done much to prevent or forestall suicidal acts, or support the friend after the attempt.

Parents and family members also have a great deal of difficulty productively dealing with the adolescent postattempt. Wenz (1978) has described the highly negative "labelling" that takes place within the family and its alienating effect on the attempter. This dynamic is brilliantly portrayed in the 1980 film "Ordinary People" in which a family struggles to reintegrate a teenage son into the home following his hospitalization for a suicide attempt. It would seem that the adolescent suicide attempter may sometimes be in greater jeopardy after the attempt, than before it. Failing to ameliorate in a significant way, one's life, the suicide attempter is at greater risk for further problems, including another attempt.

The feeling at Alana's house was that Alana had put her parents through a very difficult time during her tumultuous fifteenth year. A bright, talented, diminutive individual, she had become increasingly depressed over the course of the past two years. Her having been adopted (at the age of two months) was growing in importance as were self-deprecating questions concerning why her biological parents had given her up. As a burgeoning adolescent she had grown increasingly dissatisfied with her physique and overall physical and health status. Alana was only 4'7" and due to a medical condition would not grow any taller. She had developed a kidney problem which had required surgery once and threatened to necessitate it again. Allergies, both severe and chronic, bedevilled her. The cumulative effects of these various maladies left her feeling defective, inadequate, and insecure. Depression was hindering her efforts at school. Alana was of superior intelligence but was beginning to struggle with C's. A school change, from one private school to another, did not help. Friends seemed to come and go. She latched onto a particular boyfriend relationship with great intensity and saw herself precipitously and painfully abandoned.

The summer she turned fifteen was a very bad one. She had lost her boyfriend, she had lost most of her school friends because, as is the case with many private school kids, vacations bring separations as students return to different towns or different states or to vacation trips. She had the feeling she had lost a good deal of her health and physical integrity with the kidney surgery having just taken place and more, perhaps, on the way. Further, her sense of loss for her biological parents as well as her roots intensified as her sensitivity to adoption increased. Finally, as an adolescent she was feeling the loss of her adoptive parents from whom she felt more and more estranged, misunderstood, and perhaps, misplaced.

Late in July that year, she overdosed on valium, taken in her bedroom with her parents present in the home. Alerted to her vomiting they rushed her to the hospital where the suicide attempt was revealed and a two week in-patient stay commenced. Alana's parents visited her regularly, but found it very difficult to speak to her. They could not understand her behavior or her feelings. They could see no reason for depression. Naturally, as their only child, she was more than provided for. They were permissive with rules and curfews, accepting of her friends. They could not discern the emptiness and fear Alana felt, and on her part, Alana could not or would not begin to articulate it. Very few friends visited, and those who did visit came only once. Relatives were angry with her for frightening and upsetting her well-intentioned parents. Nonetheless, referred to an out-patient therapist, Alana was released to her still anxious, distant, and uncomprehending parents. By September she was on the verge of suicide again and it was at this point that I became involved. Her therapist was away on vacation for most of August and I began to see her in the interim. The interim, as it turned out, lasted more than a year as I became the new therapist. Among her first statements

to me during our first session was that she felt very suicidal and thought
she needed the hospital again. After hearing more I fully agreed, called her
parents and made arrangements for her return, this time for a three week
stay.

Work with the parents then commenced in earnest. Alana's parents
were a middle-aged couple who maintained a cordial but rather cold and
distant relationship with each other. Her father understood depression having
experienced it himself. His brother had experienced severe depression.
Though empathetic, he was underinvolved in Alana's parenting and in her
life. His work and his apparent desire to be away from home kept them apart
most of the time. He slept a good deal of the time when at home. Alana's
mother was a full-time mother and housewife; an intelligent and sociable
woman who had apparently gone to extraordinary lengths for many years
to steel herself against ever feeling depression, unhappiness, or negative
thoughts. She was maddeningly pleasant. During our first session together,
discussing Alana's suicide attempt and the danger of another, she never lost
her smile even while speaking of the saddest and most terrifying prospects
such as the potential death of an only child. She herself had been a foster
child during much of her adolescence, had been the primary caretaker of
her younger brothers and sisters due to the loss of their mother, and obviously had to be tough, responsible, self-reliant and independent in order
to survive and she did. She had also suffered a previous divorce. Now,
however, she appeared incapable of seeing in her daughter any of the sadness,
loss, fear, any of the feelings she had struggled to repress during her youth.
This essentially shut her off from Alana. Further, it angered her that Alana
threatened to provoke these feelings in her, and shake her hard won and
rigid equilibrium at this point in her life. Both parents politely and pleas-
antly blamed each other for Alana's problems, though never sure what her
problems were.

Meanwhile, Alana struggled to survive her loneliness, alienation, and
depression. The support of close new friends was of critical importance as
was her heavy reliance on her therapist. However, Alana attempted suicide
again in the spring; again by means of self-poisoning (allergy medication).
Her attempt and the true nature of the sickness it produced were kept secret
from her parents and reported initially to me the following day. She was
not hospitalized this time. The parents were called in to meet with Alana
and myself. They were given the following note to read, which Alana had
written the night before

*I feel like a balloon with too much air in it. Everything has been
bottled up inside of me for so long. All I ever wanted was a family.
I guess I never got it. Everything I ever loved I've lost. I lost my*

natural parents. I love them so intensely. I wonder if they'd love me too. I love my daddy, but somehow along the way I lost him too. I loved Matt and Tom, but I guess they outgrew me. I loved Pat, Donald, and Tracy, but they left. me. I loved Margaret, but she had too many other things to worry about. I loved Mary, but she was taken away from me. I love Jay, but I lost him once, and things aren't the same. I love Lisa, but she won't let me into her life anymore. I loved Debbie and Becki and Sue, but they're gone now too. This isn't to say that I don't love my mother. I really do. But somehow I don't think I ever had her. I know everyone will be mad at me for doing this. But I just can't take it anymore. I can't stand feeling worthless. I'm sick of pretending I'm happy so that I won't aggravate people anymore. I'm sick of people asking me what's wrong without even caring about the answer. I'm sick of trying to prove I'm okay to everyone else when I don't believe it myself. I'm tired of being lonely. I'm tired of being by myself. I'm tired of being walked on. I'm sick of talking to people who don't hear me. I never wanted to hurt anybody. I'm sorry for it and for being such a let down to everybody.

Weeks later Alana's mother was speaking to me of what she considered to be Alana's improved condition. She said, "You know, other than that thing that occurred a while back, she hasn't seemed at all depressed for months." I did not know what she was talking about in referring to "that thing" and I could not agree that recently missing two or three days a week from school, home in bed, was not a sign of continuing depression. I asked her what this "thing" was. She replied, "You know, when she took those pills." She could not say suicide. Nor could she accept its reality, its dynamics, or its meaning within their family.

Alana's task, among other things, has been to give up suicide as a way to cope and communicate. Certainly, in her family, it could not work. Her father was concerned but remained unavailable. Her mother could not, for Alana's sake, change. Alana believed that they loved her very much, but had to accept that they could not help a suicidal person. Further, she had to learn that her parents, and particularly her mother, were the way they were for reasons which were every bit as legitimate as her own reasons to be depressed. More importantly, it was not because of her. Her anger toward and alienation from her parents lessened as she began to understand and accept them more. It perhaps should have been the other way around with the parents doing the understanding, accepting and changing, but since that could not happen, Alana had to and she did. As a less depressed, less suicidal daughter, she became an easier and more enjoyable daughter and one her parents could feel close to, less threatened by and much more comfortable with. But they never were able to deal with suicide in their midst. The more suicidal Alana got, the further away they went from her. Suicide had to go away before they could return. When Alana understood this she could begin to regain her parents.

INCIDENCE OF REPEAT SUICIDAL BEHAVIOR

Very little research exists which deals with the postattempt status and life course of the adolescent suicide attempter. Though some data exists concerning the incidence of further attempts or eventual committed suicide among former suicide attempters, few studies look at adolescents as a distinct group. Further, there is almost no existing research that investigates the causes of repeat attempts among adolescents and their relationship to the response the individual received to his initial attempt.

It is clear, however, that persons who have attempted suicide once are at much greater risk for a repeat attempt or committed suicide. Herjanic and Welner (1980) reported that 10-15 percent of suicide attempters later commit suicide, and that 25 percent of committers had made a prior attempt. Billings (1974) also reported mortality rates among suicide attempters to be about 10 percent. Dorpat and Ripley (1067) cite higher levels on both counts, reporting a 22 percent rate of eventual committed suicide in a long follow-up study and the finding of prior suicide attempts in up to 62 percent of eventual suicide committers. Shafii et al.'s (1985) study of the psychological autopsies of twenty adolescents who had committed suicide, found that 40 percent had made at least one prior suicide attempt.

Weissman (1974) has reported that the suicide rate among former suicide attempters is about one percent per year, with a peak during the first three months postattempt and a plateau effect thereafter. Dorpat and Ripley (1967), and Herjanic and Welner (1980) cite a critical period of up to two years after the attempt, while Stengel (1972) has stated that the risk of eventual death by suicide does not ever appreciably diminish after a suicide attempt.

But what of adolescents? Few studies deal specifically with adolescents or distinguish between the individual whose first attempt occurred during adolescence as opposed to the person whose first attempt occurred later in life. In fact, little information is available about the repetition of suicide attempts in adolescents. Some have reported high rates of repeat attempts among adolescents. Weissman (1974) reported that 50 percent of the adolescents studied had made repeated attempts. These adolescents had been hospitalized psychiatrically following their initial attempt and might, therefore, not be representative of adolescent suicide attempters as a whole. Crumley (1982) reported that 42 percent of adolescent attempters repeat the attempt. McIntire and Angle (1980) report rates ranging from 26 percent to 52 percent with the more lethal attempters being most likely to repeat. Hawton (1982) reported that 10 percent repeat within one to five years. Repeat attempters in his study were described as having long-standing problems, disturbed behavior, were far more likely to have been living away from family or relatives, and to be having poor relationships with their peers, as well as being involved in drug and alcohol abuse. A replication study by Goldacre and Hawton (1983) found 9.5 percent repeating a suicide attempt within 2.8 years of the initial attempt. The average annual death rate in this cohort was four times the national average with suicide being the leading cause of death.

Otto (1972) conducted a 10–20 year follow-up of a large group of Swedish adolescent suicide attempters. Comparison with a general population control group demonstrated that attempters had a higher death rate (mainly due to suicide), a higher crime rate, lower marriage and higher divorce rates, more physical illness, and a higher rate of emigration. The risk of suicide among this group was greatest during the two years after an attempt. Among females, those most likely to later kill themselves were those who were young teenagers at the time of the initial attempt and those who had initially attempted suicide by more violent means. Otto's study is based on data obtained in the late 1950s and, therefore, this type of study needs to be replicated.

High rates of repeated attempts reported among adolescents by Crumley and Weissman raise a question as to whether adolescents are more prone to multiple attempts or chronic suicide attempts than are older persons. Since adolescents sometimes use suicidal behavior as a form of acting out, which may be repetitive like running away or other symptomatic behaviors, it may be that adolescent suicidal behavior, given its many distinctive qualities and instrumental character, is apt to be repeated more often than the suicidal behavior of older persons whose acts are often motivated by different intentions. Given the woefully inadequate data on the incidence of attempts in general, it is not possible to do more than speculate upon many aspects of this troubling phenomenon.

NEGATIVE RESPONSE AND REPEAT SUICIDE ATTEMPTS

Clinicians and others working with adolescent suicide attempters have long been sensitive to the enormous importance of the human response to the young person's suicide attempt. It is clear that the adolescent, postattempt, remains in a highly vulnerable condition in reference to his reactivity to the attitudinal and behavioral response of others. Powers (1954) warned potential responders of the dangers to the suicidal adolescent of a hostile response

> *To react with scorn and rejection to such a person, particularly the young individual, is merely to force him further into isolation. (p. 1002)*

Weiner (1970) described this heightened sensitivity in stating that

> *The suicidal adolescent has typically arrived at his self-destructive resolve through a progressively increasing conviction that he is cut off from the affection, nurturance, and support of others. He is thus exceedingly sensitive to indications that his suicidal behavior has earned him even more condemnation and rejection than he was already feeling. (p. 196)*

The response of others to a person's suicide attempt may in fact play a decisive role in the development of repeated suicidal acts. This may be especially true in the case of adolescent suicidal behavior. Ansel and McGee (1971) implicated the role of negative attitudes in contributing to repeat attempts in stating that,

> *it may be these negative attitudes which cause attempters to perform further suicidal acts, since these attitudes may stand in the way of changes desired by attempters, or be experienced as further rejections. (p. 27)*

Ramon et al. (1978) and Bancroft et al. (1976) both spoke of the powerful influence which the response of "significant others" can have on chronic suicidality. Bancroft et al. (1979) again emphasized that this relationship is of "crucial importance" in influencing possible recurrence.

Bloom (1967) offered some empirical validation of the impact of human response on further suicidality, focusing on mental health professionals as the studied responders. In a retrospective analysis of 32 successful suicides by persons in therapy, partly because of a previous suicide attempt, he found that in each case, the suicide was preceded by rejecting behavior on the part of the therapist. Interviews with the therapists revealed strong countertransference reactions in the form of denied, repressed, or suppressed hostility toward the patient.

Wenz (1978) has investigated the nature and extent of labelling of the suicide attempter as a "suicidal person" by the individual's family and peers.

His findings suggest that labelling behavior does exist, defined as "search for signs," "suspiciousness," and "exclusion from social circles"; and that the greater the degree of labelling behavior the greater the likelihood of repeat suicide attempts. Family members were reported to have engaged in the highest degree of labelling followed by peers

> *There is a direct relationship between labelling and repeat. Interaction and treatment by family and friends is an important variable in understanding multiple suicide attempts. (Wenz, 1978, p. 9)*

Adolescents would appear to be particularly likely to both experience and suffer the effects of labelling. More so than older suicide attempters, they are apt to be living at home, with their families or with some family. Further, they often rely on supportive accepting peer relationships to a greater extent than older persons, while being less able to escape or avoid a negative or unsatisfying peer relationship experience. Any adolescent attending school is trapped in an intense social environment from which it is virtually impossible to hide. The suicidal adolescent, therefore, is more likely to be labelled, less able to escape it, and perhaps, most adversely affected by it. These adolescents remain at serious risk for a repeat attempt. It has been solidly documented that the risk of committed suicide increases with each attempt as subsequent attempts become more lethal in nature (Dorpat & Ripley, 1967; Kreitman, 1977; Stengel, 1972; Weissman, 1974). Robbins and Alessi (1985) found a strong association between increased chronicity and lethality of suicide attempts in adolescents

> *The association between the number of instances of self-destructive behavior and the medical lethality of the most recent behavior is noteworthy. All of those who made very serious attempts (SADS medical lethality rating of 4 or more) had made previous less medically serious attempts. This association with previous attempts judged to be more communicative than serious has been observed in adults. . . and suggests that those who make nonlethal attention-seeking attempts may be at higher risk for more serious attempts. (p. 591)*

NEGATIVE ATTITUDES AND THE CHRONIC ATTEMPTER

Persons who make one suicide attempt are more likely than nonattempters to make a suicide attempt at some point in the future. Adolescents in particular seem to study keenly the attitudinal and behavioral responses of others to their attempt. Often the response is a negative one. Even benign neglect or neutrality, falling far short as it does of the hoped for response, may be perceived by the adolescent suicide attempter as overt rejection. Feeling labelled, more isolated and rejected and possessing ineffective strategies for coping with the associated feelings, the adolescent is at high risk for making another attempt. Research strongly suggests that individuals who are known to have attempted suicide (unsuccessfully) more than once, elicit highly negative attitudinal responses from their peers (Bell, 1978; Curran, 1984). Attitudes were found to be significantly more negative toward chronic attempters than first time attempters. Curran, in studying adolescents' attitudes toward peer suicide attempters found that both male and female adolescents held strongly negative attitudes toward chronic adolescent attempters. Males were more negative in their attitudes than females, while both were more negative to chronic attempters than first time attempters. Even the adolescent respondents who had themselves attempted suicide held strongly negative attitudes toward the repeat suicide attempter. This is a particularly noteworthy finding in light of the mildly positive attitudes held by the adolescent suicide attempters toward first time peer attempters.

Adolescents who repeat their suicide attempts risk a serious deepening of their crisis, as well as an intensification of the rejection and sense of isolation they experience. Wenz (1978) reported that labelling, already implicated as possibly contributing to repeat attempts, is more likely to occur in the case of the chronic attempter. Given the heightened lethality often seen in repeat attempts, the suicidal adolescent would appear to have ventured to the edge of an ominous and potentially deadly whirlpool.

EFFECT OF POSITIVE ATTITUDES
ON REPEAT ATTEMPTS

There exists in the literature some dispute over the question of how the human environment should respond to the unsuccessful suicide attempt. In the preceeding pages it has been stated that predominately negative attitudes exist toward the act of attempted suicide. This appears to be particularly so when the attempter is young and the attempt is perceived as being of low lethality, enacted under conditions of minimal stress and intended for manipulative and hostile purposes. Further, negative attitudes and responses have been implicated as having a potent effect on the likelihood of repeat suicide attempts. Neutrality and benign neglect have also been considered as dangerously insufficient responses. Not all writers in this area agree with this line of thinking. Sifneos (1966) seems to take the position that "manipulative" suicide attempts are more apt to be repeated if the acts are successful in producing change in others

Patients who manipulate, effectively or otherwise, are prone to make future suicide attempts because they seem to discover the power that suicide commands as a weapon in social maneuvers. (p. 533)

Ignoring deviant behavior as a means of exterminating it has long been advocated by mental health, behavioral and educational specialists, and accepted as a reliable strategy by many among the lay public. Parents, teachers, and child care workers are encouraged not to respond to negative behaviors in order not to reward it. Research by Boldt (1982) demonstrates that adolescents are more accepting of and sympathetic to suicidal behavior than are adults. In his findings, he further suggests that more accepting attitudes may not only coexist with, but actually contribute to the rising rate of adolescent suicidal behavior

In other words, consideration must be given to the possibility that the rising suicide rates among youth today may be, in part, attributable to the fact that, as a sub-cultural group, they are more tolerant of suicide and less fearful of the consequences. Hence, in a crisis, the act is more "available" to them than it is to the parental generation. (p. 154)

Sale et al. (1975), however, report conflicting findings from Tasmania, Australia. A survey of community attitudes and beliefs concerning suicidal behavior in which women from two suburbs differing widely in their rates of suicide attempts was reported. Sympathetic attitudes to suicidal behavior and to those who engage in it were significantly more prevalent in the low-risk area of the community. Positive attitudes were, therefore, correlated with reduced suicidality, rather than the other way around, as hypothesized by Boldt (1982). Stillion et al. (1984) pointed out that while more accepting attitudes on the part of adolescent females toward female suicide attempters may contribute to their higher rate of attempted suicide (than males), it may also contribute to a lower (than males) death rate. Adolescent males may perceive more negative attitudes toward male attempted suicide and may, therefore, more frequently opt not to survive their attempt; they use more lethal means and die.

While it is unclear what effect attitudes have on suicidal behavior, I, along with most writers in the field, favor a positive, responsive, concerned attitude toward the suicide attempter, postattempt. It is felt by most that the greater danger lies not in "indulging" the adolescent attempter but in ignoring or rejecting him. Weiner (1970) expresses this view superbly

The more a suicidal adolescent's parents and others have rallied to his cause and been willing to reassess the events and attitudes that led to the attempt, the greater the possibility for some favorable resolution of the adolescent's distress. On the other hand, if there is neither positive parental concern nor any change in family patterns the danger of further suicide attempts is enhanced. (p. 194)

Weiner goes on to say that:

It is the youngster who achieves no gratification, whose message remains unheard or unheeded, that requires the greatest clinical surveillance and is most likely to meet with subsequent tragedy. (p. 194)

It must be stated that a suicide attempt should never be condoned or accepted as a viable form of communication. To do so would be not only irresponsible, but erroneous, since the suicidal act has been proven to be an extremely ineffective form of expressing the depth and complexity of feelings which produce adolescent suicidal behavior. Adolescent suicidal behavior is usually misunderstood, undervalued, misdiagnosed, and misperceived by the human environment, including those closest to the suicidal individual. Consequently, the act must be discouraged, but the person must never be. The feelings need to be acknowledged and responded to while the person is helped to find better ways of communicating and discharging his feelings. This is very old advice, but especially important under these circumstances.

THE SPIRAL OF ISOLATION

For some adolescents, the threat of suicide and the troubles that give rise to it will subside with adolescence. As teenagers age and enter adulthood, move out of the house, escape the pressures of school and the highly judgmental and intense social environment of adolescence, they are sometimes able to shed a fair share of their problems and move on. Much of the research reviewed in this chapter, however, suggests that the historically troubled, multiproblem adolescent suicide attempter remains both at risk for further suicidal acts and likely to be burdened with significant and debilitating problems of living even as adolescence passes. Weissman's (1974) finding that only 20 percent of a group of adolescent suicide attempters considered themselves "better off" one to four years after their initial attempt is instructive. Dorpat and Ripley (1967) and Herjanic and Welner (1980) reported that adolescent suicide attempters who eventually commit suicide manifest a peak in incidence during their early twenties. Otto's (1972) massive longitudinal study of Swedish adolescent suicide attempters found that 10 to 20 years later they were more likely than the comparison group of nonattempter adolescents to have experienced serious problems with criminal behavior, family life, and physical health. These findings would seem to support the idea that adolescents who engage in suicidal behavior are a significantly and chronically disturbed population with a history and perhaps a future of problems if left untreated.

Negative attitudes and responses to this deviant, dangerous, and ineffectual form of communication and expression probably contribute to the worsening alienation and isolation often experienced by the adolescent postattempt. This and a deepening sense of hopelessness elevates the likelihood of repeat acts of suicide and the subsequent intensification of rejection and hostility from the human environment. Adolescents, who by their chronicity of suicidal behavior, demonstrate a lack of adaptability or flexibility in style of coping, discharging feelings, and efforts at conflict resolution present an extreme danger in terms of worsening pathology and risk for eventual committed suicide. Suicidal adolescents must learn through education, counseling and/or caring lay persons and friends, other forms of expression, and problem solving while their pain and the reasons for the attempt are acknoweldged and accepted. Ignoring or denigrating the attempter would seem to seriously worsen their condition and, in fact, jeopardize their lives.

Familiarity, Modeling, and Imitation: Suicide in the Experience of the Adolescent

Adolescents are generally considered to be highly susceptible to the influence of their peers. Public concern over negative peer pressure in regard to drug and alcohol use, sexual behavior, and academic achievement are longstanding. More recently, "epidemics" of adolescent suicidal behavior in communities around the United States have raised serious questions among the scientific and lay community as to the possible contagion effect of suicidal acts among adolescent populations. In 1984, the Atlanta Center for Disease Control contracted with the National Institute of Mental Health to begin a large scale study of this question and many others within the area of adolescent suicidal behavior.

At this time, little research exists which deals specifically with the extent to which adolescents are familiar with or influenced by suicidal behavior. Some excellent and compelling studies have been carried out considering the influence of suggestion and imitation on suicide. These studies have analyzed the effect of publicized suicides on the rate of suicide in the affected area following the dissemination of the story. These studies do not, however, focus on an adolescent population and it is not known whether the findings can be generalized to teenagers.

It is obvious, however, that with continuously rising rates of attempted and committed suicide, adolescents are likely to become increasingly familiar with suicidal behavior. Recent research strongly suggests that most adolescents know someone who has attempted or committed suicide. In the majority of cases it is a person well known to the teenager, a friend, relative, or immediate family member.

Curran (1984) reported that 71 percent of the (150) adolescents questioned had some familiarity with suicidal behavior. Females reported the greatest degree of familiarity with 87 percent stating that they knew someone who had attempted or committed suicide. In most cases (40 percent), the person known to have attempted or committed suicide was a "friend." Fifty five percent of the female adolescents reported close familiarity with suicidal behavior, meaning that the person known to them who had attempted or committed suicide was either a friend, close relative, sibling, parent, or self. Among the males questioned, comparatively fewer indicated familiarity with suicidal behavior (57 percent) and of these 29 percent reported close familiarity.

The sex difference seems due to the higher rate of suicide attempts among adolescent females. Twice as many female respondents reported knowledge of a friend's suicidal behavior as did the male respondents. Female teenagers are more likely to learn of the suicide attempt of a same sex peer. It has often been reported in the literature that adolescent attempters are most likely to alert a friend first, and perhaps exclusively, about their attempt. Studies surveying familiarity with suicidal behavior among college students have also reported that a majority of students knew someone who had attempted or committed suicide (McIntosh, Hubbard, & Santos, 1985; Mishara, 1982). These findings compare rather closely with those of Ginsburg (1971) whose pioneering study of suicide familiarity and beliefs revealed that, among adults, 79 percent knew someone who had committed or attempted suicide, with 37 percent having had close familiarity.

Any possible causal relationship between familiarity and actual suicidal behavior, while theoretically plausible, remains speculative, particularly in individual cases. Corder et al. (1974), however, found that a group of adolescent suicide attempters were more likely to have had close familiarity with suicide than nonsuicidal peers. Shafii et al. (1985) reported highly significant differences in the level and type of suicide familiarity between adolescents who had committed suicide and a matched group of nonsuicidal teenagers. Sixty percent of the suicide victims had been exposed to the suicide of a sibling or friend as compared to only 12 percent of the control group. Smith and Crawford (1986) reported similar findings.

As the rate of attempted or committed suicide increases among American adolescents, the level of familiarity is likely to increase. Corder et al. have stated the opinion that exposure to suicide, as a form of acting out or expressing one's inner needs and concerns, increases the likelihood of that behavior being internalized as a viable mode of expression. Whatever the cause/effect relationship, it is evident that suicidal behavior is apt to be an increasing part of the experience of adolescents.

Modeling of suicidal behavior within the family has often been cited as a factor positively correlated with suicidal behavior in the adolescent. Teicher (1973) found that 20 percent of the adolescents he studied had a parent with a history of suicidal behavior which was known to the adolescent. Kerfoot (1979) found a high incidence not only of parental, but sibling histories of suicidal behavior in the families of suicidal adolescents. Paulson and Stone (1974) reported that 50 percent of the group of adolescent suicidals studied had relatives who had attempted or committed suicide. Shafii et al. (1985) found that 30 percent of the adolescent suicide victims studied had experienced suicidal behavior on the part of a parent or close adult relative, while only 12 percent of the comparison group of nonsuicidal teenagers had been similarly exposed. Curran (1984) reported only a 7 percent frequency of suicide in the families of a group of 131 nonsuicidal adolescents with only .06 percent being parental suicide.

Certainly, behaviors and coping styles modeled within a family exert a powerful influence upon the developing behavioral repertoire of the young person. Genetic effects need also to be considered for their contribution to the origins of mental illness in general, depression, sensitivity, and reactivity to stress and perhaps to a predisposition toward suicide itself.

Research dealing with the effects of suggestion and imitation on suicidal behavior has yielded findings which make a consistently strong case in support of the notion that knowledge of another person's suicidal behavior may cause certain others to emulate the act. Newspaper coverage of notable suicides have long been considered as a contributing factor in later suicides, as the following passage confirms

> *Some plan for discontinuing by common consent the detailed dramatic tales of suicide, murder and bloodshed in the newspapers is well worth the attention of their editors. No fact is better established in science than that suicide (and murder may perhaps be added) is often committed from imitation. A single paragraph may suggest suicide to 20 persons; some particular chance, but apt, expression seizes the imagination and the disposition to repeat the act in a moment of morbid excitement proves irresistible. Do the advantages of publicity counter-balance the evils attendant on one such death? Why should cases of suicide be recorded at length in public papers any more than cases of fever? (W. Farr, 1841)*

More recently, after the highly publicized suicide of Marilyn Monroe in 1962, the U.S. suicide rate rose 12 percent. The Japanese author, Yukio

Mishima, who killed himself amid great international publicity on November 24, 1970 is another outstanding example. His death by suicide has been associated with increased suicide rates by implication, based on a highly significant rise in fatal auto accidents, in the area studied, immediately following his death (Phillips, 1979). Increases in suicide rates occurring briefly following publicity given to the suicides of famous people have been documented by Hewitt and Milner (1974) and Phillips (1974). There is evidence of time clustering of suicides at Beachy Head, Sussex, England, a famous cliff 600 feet high (Surtees, Taylor, & Cooper, 1976). Prisoners in Finnish jails kill themselves more often than expected in the 48 hours after a fellow inmate commits suicide (Niemi, 1975). The recent suicide (April,, 1986) of a highly popular 18-year-old Japanese pop singer, Yukiko Okada, has triggered a series of apparently imitative suicides among Japanese teens. The toll at one point had reached 33 young people in the 17 days following Okada's suicide. Many of the victims jumped to their death from tall buildings as had the pop singer.

Acting in the belief that knowledge of suicide begets suicide, the American Academy of Medicine in 1911 and the British Medical Association in 1948, proposed bans on press reporting of suicide inquests. The *Lancet,* in 1969, proposed a recommendation for less sensationalism. Durkhiem 1897), the renowned sociologist, however, advocated a differing position on the effect of imitation stating that imitation could not explain incidences of suicidal behavior, nor could suppressing newspaper accounts prevent suicide. It was his view that societal factors alone were to blame for suicide, epidemic or otherwise.

The power of suggestion, modeling and imitation as a force in influencing behavior is, however, fully accepted by many others. In 1985, the U.S. advertising industry spent more than $96.5 billion (McCann-Erikson, Inc. and *Advertising Age*) on the working assumption that commercial behavior is influenced by suggestion, modeling, and imitation. The literature on this topic had been estimated to include at least 5,000 articles and books, ten years ago (Jacoby, 1976). The effects of imitation, suggestion, and modeling on violent behavior has been extensively studied by psychologists and others concerned primarily with the effects of media and T.V. violence on children and youths. It is right, therefore, to consider the effects of imitation, suggestion, and modeling on another form of violence, violence against the self. Several studies deserve close scrutiny in addressing this issue.

Research by Barraclough, Shepherd, and Jennings (1977), Phillips (1974, 1979), and Bollen and Phillips (1982) have effectively countered earlier research by Motto (1967, 1970) that had not found significant effects for media (newspaper) publicity on suicide rates in the geographic area of the publication.

Barraclough et al. (1977) reported convincing evidence of a statistical association between newspaper reports of suicide inquests in a local paper and the subsequent rise in suicide rates of men under age 45. He takes the strong position that "there seems to be no doubt that suicide is contagious" (p. 531). Other research, while not finding men under 45 so particularly affected, have nonetheless documented very strong associations between knowledge of suicidal behavior and suicide rates.

Phillips (1974), in a study of major importance, demonstrated that, (a) the national level of suicides increases significantly for a brief period after a suicide story is nationally publicized by newspapers; (b) this increase in suicides occurs only *after* the suicide story is published; (c) the more publicity given to the story, the more the national level of suicides increases; (d) the increase in suicides occurs only in the geographic areas where the suicide story is published. These increases are significant even after accounting for the effects of seasonal, yearly, or random fluctuations of the suicide level.

In 1979, Phillips reported on the effects of newspaper coverage of suicides and the rise in single person, single car fatal automobile accidents. It has been conjectured that some motor vehicle accidents have a suicidal component (Holinger, 1979). Phillips was able to show that motor vehicle accident fatalities increase markedly just *after* publicized suicide stories and increase proportionate to the amount of publicity given the suicide story. The increase in fatal accidents was found to occur predominantly in the area where the suicide story was publicized and that single person, single vehicle crashes increased more than other types of accidents. Further, suicide stories involving young persons tended to be followed by single vehicle crashes involving more young drivers, while stories about older persons tended to be followed by fatal crashes involving older drivers. This suggests, of course, the process of identification. Finally, stories about murder-suicide tended to produce increases in the incidence of multiple car fatalities, whereas the suicide stories saw increases only in the single vehicle, single driver fatal accidents. Though not a focus of the study, it is interesting to note that the suicide story which was followed by the greatest increase in fatalities was the publicized suicide of a psychologist.

Bollen and Phillips (1982) expanded the inquiry into the question of suggestion, modeling and imitation with an investigation of the association between T.V. news stories dealing with suicide and suicide rates. All earlier findings relative to newspaper stories of suicides were supported. New findings concerning a time factor influencing subsequent suicides were reported. Suicide stories appear to affect mortality for a period of ten days with two peaks occurring, first from 0-1 days followed by a second peak at 6-7 days. This is an especially important finding in that it bears implications for, among other things, crisis intervention in schools after a suicide occurs. High schools and colleges may need to act very quickly after a tragedy such as suicide occurs within their midst. This may prove effective in minimizing a spread or contagion effect among peers.

Judging from a consensus of the research, it appears very likely that a significant imitation effect exists

> *Taken together, all of these findings support the hypothesis that publicized suicides trigger imitative behavior; sometimes this behavior is overt (in the form of an explicit suicide) and sometimes covert (in the form of automobile or airplane accidents). (Bollen and Phillips, 1982, p. 807)*

It would appear that not only is suicide influenced by suggestion, modeling, and imitation, but perhaps the method of committing or attempting suicide is affected as well. Ashton and Donnan (1981) studied this question in the form of an inquiry into the increase in suicide by self-immolation after a widely publicized burning suicide. Self-burning as a form of suicide, while common in parts of Asia and Africa, was and is quite rare in the West. However, a dramatic increase has been seen since the famous political self-immolation of the Vietnamese Buddhist monk, Thick Quang Duc, in 1963. For instance, Crosby, Rhee, and Holland (1977) studied all accounts of suicide by burning appearing in the *Times* (London) and the *New York Times* from 1790 to 1971. A total of only 133 cases were reported in the 181 year period. All but 38 of these occurred *after* 1962.

Ashton and Donnan focused on the suicide of Lynette Phillips, a 24-year-old Austrian heiress who on October 2, 1978, burned herself to death in front of the Palais de Nations in Geneva, Switzerland. She was a member of an antipolitical religious sect who committed the act as a demonstration against world corruption and injustice as proclaimed in a statement released immediately after her death.

Following her death a dramatic rise in suicides by self-burning was seen over a one year period in England among white, native born Englishmen, and women. None of the deaths were associated with political, social, or religious protest. From a total of 24 suicides by burning in 1977, an increase to 82 suicides by means of self-burning was documented from October, 1978 through September, 1979.

The population of self-immolators has been found to be a significantly more psychiatrically disturbed one as compared to those choosing other methods of suicide. Andreason and Noyes (1975) have reported on the high rate of psychosis among self-immolators.

Not all suicides are of equal weight, however, in their capacity to influence imitative responses. Of critical importance is the extent to which the suicide victim is one with whom people can readily and strongly identify. Kessler and Stipp (1984), for example, found that fictional T.V. suicides appeared to have no effect on suicide rates or single vehicle auto deaths in the community. Apparently real living people are more intensely identified with and perhaps emulated.

Wasserman (1984), in elaborating on Phillips' research, investigates the types of individual suicides which correlated most powerfully with increased suicide rates and found that celebrity suicides were most likely to exert a significant effect. Marilyn Monroe and Japan's Yukiko Okada would serve as examples of this phenomenon. It would appear that it is not only publicity or the proliferation of knowledge of suicide, but the type of person who is the object of that publicity which determines the strength of the impact of the event on others.

"EPIDEMIC" SUICIDAL BEHAVIOR:
IS IT CONTAGIOUS?

It has been demonstrated by well structured empirical research that publicized suicide and the awareness of the suicidal option thus promoted, is associated with significant increases in suicide among the population touched by the publicity. It has further been suggested that males may be more affected by the publicity than females and that males under 45 years of age are most particularly affected (Barroclough et al., 1977). Others, however, have failed to report sex or age as factors influencing one's susceptibility to the suggestion of suicidal behavior. It is not known, for instance, whether adolescents, male or female, are more or less affected by the suggestion of suicide or prone to imitative suicidal behavior. It has been found by several researchers that adolescents who have attempted suicide or committed suicide have had greater familiarity with the behavior than nonsuicidal peers. Some have gone on to suggest that familiarity with suicidal behavior increases the likelihood of suicidal behavior in teenagers.

Recent spectacular and highly publicized suicide "clusters" among adolescents in various parts of the United States such as Leominster, Massachusetts, a town of 35,000 where at least 6 teenagers died by suicide in two years; Clear Lake and Plano,Texas; and Westchester County, New York, provide powerful impetus to the notion of a strong contagion effect in adolescent suicidal behavior though it has as yet never been studied nor validated. It remains, therefore, a compelling question and issue.

It is generally assumed that adolescents are greatly influenced by their peers in ways that determine much of their physical appearance, manner of dress, speech, and other behaviors. What must be considered, however, is that unlike many aspects of teenage appearance and behavior, including sex, and drug and alcohol use, suicidal behavior is not normative and is decidedly pathological. This is not only the judgment of adult professionals, but adolescents themselves. Those who attempt suicide are often regarded by other teenagers as mentally ill, demonstrating "sick" behavior (Bell, 1977; Curran, 1984; Hood, 1973); or at the very least, acting in a manipulative manner which is disapproved of (Limacher & Domino, 1986).

It is possible, however, that some adolescents may misread societal or peer values and attitudes regarding suicidal behavior due perhaps to faulty reality testing or a romanticized image of what suicide is apt to mean to one's self and others. Boldt (1982) has reported that adolescents in general are relatively more accepting of suicidal behavior than are adults. They stigmatize the behavior less and appear to view the suicidal individual as less "bad" than adults do. This is not to say, however, that they support the behavior as an acceptable coping strategy or consider the suicidal person to be "normal." Boldt's research offers another important and disturbing finding, however, concerning the adolescent's perceptions of death. Among the adolescents studied, 42.5 percent believed that all suicides would go to some sort of a "heaven" as compared with only 22.5 percent of the older generation sharing the same belief. Conversely, only 22.5 percent of the adolescents believed that all suicides would go to some sort of "hell," compared to 52.5 percent of adults sharing this belief.

The question remains, however, as to whether adolescents constitute a group especially susceptible to imitative suicide. Obviously, certain adolescents will be far more affected by the suggestion, modeling, and imitation of suicidal behavior than others. However, we must return to earlier chapters and the work of Crumley (1982), Jacobs (1971), Weiner (1970), and others to remind us that suicidal adolescents do not represent a normal, well-functioning population of teenagers. Shafii et al. (1985) conclude:

> *Exposure to suicide or suicidal behavior of relatives and friends appears to be a significant factor in influencing a* vulnerable *[italics added] young person to commit suicide. Other factors that contribute to vulnerability are history of antisocial behavior, inhibited personality, frequent use of drugs or alcohol, history of emotional problems in parents or self, and parental absence or physical or emotional abusiveness. (p. 1064)*

The concept of contagion is, therefore, a poor one in that it implies, at least to the lay public, a sense of indiscriminate alarm for their adolescents. It conveys the notion that all teenagers are nearly equally at risk, as with the flu. It tends to diminish the importance of readiness and predisposing factors.

One does not "catch" suicidal behavior as one catches a cold. Unlike colds and the flu, suicidal behavior, while familiar to most adolescents, harms a very few. Those few are exceptional individuals usually with atypical backgrounds for whom the suggestion of suicide carries far greater compulsion than it does for the "normal" adolescent.

Durkhiem (1897) believed that imitation played no significant role in the rate of suicide. His belief was that, though a brief rise in incidence may occur after a well-publicized suicide, these suicides would probably have occurred eventually anyway and that over the long run, the publicity would have no effect on suicide rates. The work of Phillips (1974, 1979), and Bollen and Phillips (1982), as well as others clearly indicates the immediate impact of suggestion on suicide. It should not imply, however, that suggestion *caused* people, who were not already at risk, to become suicidal or that it led to suicides which would not otherwise have eventually occurred.

A suicide is an event which unquestionably reverberates in powerful waves through the social community in which it occurs. Those closest to the event will feel its effects most. Those who feel closest to the person will be rocked most forcefully. Those who are most unsteady will be at greatest risk for being themselves toppled over. Adolescents tend to feel an especially close kinship with one another as brothers in arms against the seemingly hostile world of adults and amidst the confusing and insecure passage of adolescence. They are greatly affected by events among their peers to the extent that the life of the peer group has become the center of their world. Thus, suicide or attempted suicide with the adolescent's peer group is apt to be an especially powerful event. In my experience, however, I have seen great variety in adolescents' responses. Some are drawn to the act as a model for suicidal thinking, plans, or actual behavior of their own. Others are repulsed by the act, impressed and frightened by the permanence and finality of death in the case of committed suicide, or reject the futility of the attempted suicide. Wasserman's research (1984) suggests that contagion depends as much on the type of person modeling the suicidal behavior as on the type of person exposed to it. Generally, I have seen great resistance on the part of the vast majority of teenagers to emulating suicidal behavior. Working as I do in a public high school and consulting to others, I have had numerous opportunities to observe both individuals and large groups respond to suicide, and clearly the power of the drive and will to live is nearly always prominent. Nonetheless, the committed or attempted suicide of a close friend, relative, or family member is a destabilizing experience for the adolescent, though one which most will recover from with support. Those who are particularly vulnerable and without adequate supports or effective means of coping may become dangerously at risk as they collide with the experience of suicide.

The roles of suggestion, modeling, and imitation, as well as familiarity relative to suicidal behavior are important and interesting areas of inquiry. They deserve much further research. At this point it remains unclear what impact these factors have upon adolescent suicidal behavior. Those responsible for evaluating and interviewing adolescents after their attempts should include questions dealing with the individual's familiarity with suicide and where they got the idea. Their concept of death should be evaluated. Beck, Schuyler, and Herman's (1974) Suicide Intent Scale addresses both of these questions. Test batteries should, when possible, include assessments of the suggestibility of the suicidal person. Research is lacking on the effect of attempted as opposed to committed suicide on the suicidal behavior of others.

In any case, recent events (cluster suicides) and preliminary findings indicate the possibility of an imitative component for some teenagers. Vigorous intervention needs to be forthcoming, therefore, in any community where an adolescent commits suicide or makes a well publicized attempt. Students must be given an opportunity to ventilate their feelings and thoughts after such an event and have available educational and counseling resources to help them understand suicide and its aftermath. This issue deserves greater attention and will be pursued in greater detail in Chapter 10.

8

Judging the likelihood of suicidal behavior is perhaps the most difficult and unnerving responsibility that rests before the mental health professional (health care provider, custodial adult, educator). While it is a well accepted fact that future behavior cannot be predicted with any certainty, we are still routinely asked to make predictions in the matter of suicide. The task is often a very difficult one and can be particularly so when responsibility is heightened by the youth of the person at risk. Young people *are* the responsibility of adults. Because of this, acknowledgment of an adolescent's suicidal behavior can be hard and the assessment of suicidality in adolescence or childhood is all the more difficult. Nontheless, this is our task and so it should be.

Adolescents present special challenges to make the process of evaluation quite complex. Factors such as the highly equivocal nature of their suicidal acts, difficulty in ascertaining motives, often questionable level of lethal intent, impulsivity of the act, apparent absence of a clear and understandable precipitant, difficulties in gathering a history, and possible influence of imitation, all serve to obscure a clear understanding of the meaning of an adolescent's suicidal intentions or behavior. As adults we are often in a position to know very little about critical aspects of the lives of teenagers which are of great importance in being able to assess the quality of their lives and the likelihood or origins of a suicidal act. Areas of their lives such as substance use and abuse, and the quality of their love and sexual relations, which are of great diagnostic importance, are often closed to us. Knowledge of family life, family history, the mental health and parenting status of parents, is essential to the assessor of adolescent suicidality but extremely hard to come by. Parents are not always able to provide adequate help due to their lack of objectivity and their own ignorance of the often secret lives of their children. Suicidal adolescents themselves may be of little help (at least initially) due to their possible lack of trust in adults as well as their own confusion and lack of awareness about the actual nature and history of their problems. In short, assessors of adolescent suicidality sometimes work with minimum information from which critical judgments must be made. However, approached with adequate knowledge, preparation, and care the suicidal adolescent will rarely remain entirely indiscernible or incomprehensible.

Assessment can be divided into three areas. First, the conditions under which the suicidal episode or risk has developed need to be assessed. A study of the past, present, and future circumstances of the individuals' lives, under which they live and attempt to maintain themselves should be carried out. Knowledge of the backgrounds, lifestyles, and life problems associated with suicide attempters and committers helps to spotlight the presence of similar circumstances or conditions in the lives of the individual being assessed. A comparison may then be formed as one means of evaluating the level of risk.

Second, the individual's state of mind must be evaluated along a number of lines. The focus here is more, but not exclusively, on the present. How is the person responding to and coping with the circumstances and conditions of his or her life which cause stress?

Finally, the assessment of suicide and suicide risk will include some differences in focus and areas of evaluation, depending on whether the adolescent has very recently made a suicide attempt or is being considered for suicide potential. The primary difference, of course, involves the assessment of the suicide attempt itself. The diagnostic implications of the method used and the circumstances surrounding it (i.e., presence of others, efforts to prevent detection, etc.) will be discussed in the section titled Assessment of the Atempt. Assessment should also include recommendations for treatment and at times the very tricky process of referral. Given the magnitude of time and effort involved, it is no wonder, then, that some health care providers feel the overpowering need to run screaming into the distance at the sight of the suicidal adolescent, and that even more carry out the task with clearly evident traces of frustration, impatience, and anger.

CONDITIONS AND CIRCUMSTANCES
OF THE SUICIDAL EPISODE

Regardless of whether the adolescent being evaluated is being assessed for suicidal intent prior to an actual act of suicide or after the attempt has occurred, level of risk for future self-injurious behavior is a primary focus of evaluation. Therefore, assessment should always include a consideration of all the areas to be discussed in this section. Although these items are presented separately they must, in reality, be considered in combination.

Sex and Age

The younger the teenager the lower is the likelihood of committed or attempted suicide especially if the person is female. This is a general rule and does not, of course, apply to each individual case. However, there are a number of good reasons why this is generally true. Younger adolescents may not yet have experienced their problems as chronic and never ending in a way which only time can bring. They are less likely to have lost hope or exhausted all their available resources for adaptation and coping. The number of traumas and failures may not have had time to accrue with their typically cumulative and intensifying effect. Females, as has often been stated, commit suicide far less often than males and this is especially so in adolescence. Males tend to use more lethal and violent methods, may expect a less accepting, more negative response to an attempted suicide, are more reluctant to reach out for life-sustaining help and support, and may, according to some, be more disturbed than female suicidal adolescents. For whatever reason, the suicidal male is generally considered to be at greater risk for more lethal suicidal acts, although the adolescent female is far more likely to attempt suicide.

Health Status

Poor health is a major factor to be considered in the suicides of older individuals. This is far less often the case with adolescents, of course, whose health is usually quite good, despite their often unrelenting abuse of their bodies. The reason, in fact, for suicide being ranked so high as a cause of death in adolescence is not because suicide is all that common, but rather, because they are too healthy to be dying in larger numbers from natural causes such as heart disease and cancer. Violent and accidental deaths are about all that is left. Still, problematic health histories and conditions play a decisive role in some adolescents' suicide attempts as has been the case in a few with whom I have been involved. Adolescents tend to cope poorly with debilitating physical conditions or physical defects. Normal adolescent self-consciousness and self-deprecation are, of course, heightened to intolerable levels for some adolescents experiencing physical anomalies, such as diabetes, various severe allergic conditions, visible physical defects, bed-wetting, or other problems. Self-esteem in adolescence is inextricably related to physical adequacy. Teenagers will probably never care as much or be so psychologically burdened by their particular health or physical problem as they will be as an adolescent, but that is of no consolation to the vulnerable teenager for whom physical adequacy is of paramount importance.

Incidence of Runaway, Abuse, Incest, and Foster Care

It is safe to say that most adolescents become suicidal, at least in part, within a context of family dysfunction that impacts upon them in a deleterious fashion. At times the problems are quiet and subtle, not noticeable to the casual observer or even to family members. Quite often, however, glaring dysfunction and disharmony exist and are even on record with courts, schools, or social service agencies. A high incidence of suicidal behavior has been reported in association with teenagers who have been sexually or physically abused or are victims of incest. Adolescent suicide attempters are more likely to have been in foster care than nonsuicidal teens. A study of suicidal thinking among adolescents living in a shelter for runaways found that 70 percent were actively considering suicide (NETwork News, April, 1986). Frequently an adolescent experiencing one of these traumas will have actually experienced them all. All are exceeding noxious experiences. All convey a deep sense of loss, abandonment, and rejection. The runaway may have left home initially as a way to cope with intolerable and chronic family conditions. Finding out, as most teens do, that running away provides little in the way of solutions or support, the lonely adolescent's sense of hopelessness is apt to increase to dangerous levels. Many runaways, of course, are throw aways, who have not adopted the act as an adaptive strategy. Rather, they have been victimized by their family with ostracism or have been compelled to flee situations which they perceived as too threatening to continue to endure, such as sexual and physical abuse.

History of Prior Suicide Attempts

Whether the person being evaluated has just made a suicide attempt or is believed to be considering one, it is essential that information on prior attempts be gathered. The best predictor of future behavior is past behavior and this concept applies to suicidal behavior as well. Persons who have already attempted suicide at least once are far more likely to attempt it again than people who have not as yet attempted suicide. Again, this is a general rule and will not apply to all individual cases. However, people with histories including suicide attempts, have indisputably demonstrated their capacity and disposition for the act. The more attempts the person has made, the more lethal the attempts have been and the more recently they have occurred, the greater should be the level of concern for future episodes. It is well established by research that repeat suicide attempts tend to become more lethal. It has further been demonstrated that suicidal behavior is usually, at least for adolescents, an unproductive and unrewarding means of expression and attempt to get one's needs met. If the behavior is repeated it is reasonable to suppose that healthier more effective methods of communication and coping are unavailable to the adolescent, and, therefore, they are likely to have remained in a condition of alienation and desperation. Chronic attempters quickly wear out sources of support and increase the likelihood of being left alone to deal with the problems that beset them, thus, paradoxically increasing the risk of further suicidal acts.

Presence of Other Forms of Self-Destructive Behavior

Suicidal behavior is not the only form through which self-destructive urges may find expression. There are many approximations and substitutions and one may flow or evolve into another. A history of accidents (including auto accidents), numerous injuries, disciplinary problems in school, or arrests may indicate an unconscious desire within the individual to be harmed by events and circumstances that may be consciously perceived as persecutory. Holinger (1979) has reported that the adolescent homicide and suicide rates rise and fall together and has suggested that while some adolescents express depression and self-destructive wishes overtly through suicide, others may express the same wish by unconsciously engineering their death by the hand of another. Adolescents who repeatedly place themselves in a position to be injured, disciplined, or arrested are simply not taking very good care of themselves. Sometimes it is simply because they do not care to. Some will find these experiences a needed salve to feelings of guilt. Some may need to go further and branch off to intended acts of suicide.

Substance Abuse

Drug and alcohol abuse certainly qualify as forms of self-destructive behavior but they stand apart from the others as especially strong indicators of the presence of depression and as a factor very highly correlated with suicidal behavior in adolescence as has been demonstrated recently by Robbins and Alessi (1985). Adolescents who abuse drugs and alcohol are probably demonstrating poor impulse control, poor frustration tolerance, a minimal tolerance for stress, and an impoverishment of their capacity to utilize a range of effective strategies for problem solving. In short, they are rendering themselves unable to manage the multiple stresses of adolescence except by artificial means. Hence, they remain weak, inflexible, and undeveloped in the maturational sense while creating mounting problems for themselves by their choice of a solution. Teenagers who use drugs on a nearly daily basis do not do well in school, in relationships or, usually, at home. In this way substance abuse is not only a symptom of underlying problems but a very serious problem in itself at a critical developmental juncture for the teenager. From such a scenario suicidal intentions often develop.

While knowledge of drug and alcohol use is important in assessing the conditions under which an adolescent's suicidal behavior has developed, it is also difficult to obtain. Living as they do in a drug and alcohol using culture they may easily deny the relative importance of their own habits. On the other hand they simply may not want to tell the assessor anything of their drug habits feeling that no good can come of revealing the type and amount of drugs they may have ingested that day. Parents too, may minimize or be unaware of the extent of drug involvement on the part of their teenager. Ultimately, the assessors are left to their own skill in conveying to the adolescent their genuine concern for his welfare and their need to know as much as possible about the teenager's life in order to be a help in preserving it. Confidentiality must be discussed and a rationale offered as to why this information is important and why so many apparently irrelevant (to the suspicious teenager) questions are being asked.

Status of Adaptive Strategies

In short, how well do adolescents solve problems and cope with stress? What do they do when they get upset or are faced with a difficult situation? How do they relax and organize themselves? What strategies were used prior to resorting to suicide? An assessment needs to be made of the coping history and style of the individual and whether the person really is at the end of his rope, having exhausted all available internal resources. Are there areas of strength and effectiveness in dealing with stress that are adequately functioning and that the person can be redirected to? Evaluation along these lines has the two-fold value of being both therapeutic and diagnostic at the same time. Helping teenagers to focus on the style and efficacy of their problem-solving or coping can help promote greater self-awareness about neglected or underutilized areas of strength as well as giving hope and self-confidence in dealing more effectively with the problems that remain in their lives. Adolescents can also be directed to resources and strategies that are within their reach but have not been considered, such as various relaxation techniques or counseling. Diagnostically, it is essential to know by what process the person became actively suicidal. How many and what kind of barriers does the person have in the form of adaptive strategies between him or her and suicide? The fewer and weaker the barriers the more precipitous the decline into suicidality.

It must be presumed in most cases that adolescents will return, after their suicidal episode, to conditions and circumstances similar to, if not the same as, those which begat the suicidal intentions in the first place. In any case, no adolescent can be insulated or protected from stress, though hospitalization can accomplish some of this temporarily. Consequently, it is important to know how tolerant and adaptive the adolescent can be in dealing with continuing stress or, conversely, to what extent the person feels completely overwhelmed, hopeless, and helpless in its wake.

Chronicity and Multiplicity of Problems

The strength, versatility, and resilience of adaptive strategies must be evaluated in relation to the magnitude and persistence of the forces brought to bear upon them. Some teenagers will be overwhelmed by relatively transient or short-lived problems that, although intense, have not existed in any debilitating way in their lives prior to adolescence. Many adolescents experience for the first time severe assaults on self-esteem brought on by such things as worsening grades and the painful losses in relationships which can be a part of adolescence. Confusion around identity issues and loosening ties with older support systems, such as have existed within the family, can leave the vulnerable teenager feeling lost, alone, and floundering in a condition which seemingly will not end or improve, leading to thoughts of suicide and suicidal acts.

More often seen and more serious, however, are situations involving longstanding and mutually supporting problems that predate adolescence in areas such as self-esteem, peer relations, health, family, and school. Research by Novick (1984) and Jacobs (1971) has documented the presence of chronic and multiple problems in the lives of most adolescents who make suicide attempts. Again, accurate history gathering can present serious challenges and obstacles to evaluators. However, certain outstanding circumstances may be ascertained and must be considered in judging suicide risk. Conditions such as divorce, remarriage, parental separations, death of parent, key relatives or siblings, the presence of alcoholism or drug addiction in the home, the extent of family mobility, the presence and effect on the family of psychopathology within the parents, any history of abuse, neglect, incest, or sexual abuse, history of school problems including retentions, disciplinary actions, suspensions, special education involvement, truancy, delinquent behavior, history of foster home placements, runaways and, finally and more subjectively, the quality of life in the home for the adolescent over time, all need to be addressed by evaluators for their historical and cumulative impact.

The problems that suicidal adolescents experience tend not only to have been of long duration but to be multifaceted as well. Evaluators must not think in terms of the single precipitant that may have served as only the final straw. Teenagers who become suicidal often feel virtually surrounded by a complex array of conflicts that outnumber the beleaguered individual's capacity to fend them off. Unable to concentrate on any single conflict, the person may become unable to concentrate at all. This should be of great concern to the evaluator. The more problems or conflicts, the less likely adolescents are to feel competent to organize themselves toward understanding them, and the less energy will be available to deal with them. Left in this condition for long periods of time the teenager is apt to develop dangerous levels of the feelings of hopelessness and helplessness and to seek escape through suicide and/or substance abuse or some other serious symptomatic behavior.

In general, the more serious and numerous are the conflicts the adolescent struggles to deal with and the longer the duration of their problems the more likely the adolescent is to feel overwhelmed and to be at risk for dangerous behavior as an antidote for his condition. Occasionally, seemingly singular issues such as pregnancy, fear of homosexuality, the threat of imminent punishment of some type such as criminal prosecution, physical conditions such as obesity or an especially painful loss may appear to account entirely for the suicidal intention of the teenager. One should mistrust these initial impressions. They will usually be too simplistic. When singular issues seem to exist, though they will have their various branches off that particular issue, the situation will often appear more manageable. Teenagers can more easily be helped to organize themselves to deal with their problems and see to the other side of them to some type of positive resolution. It need no longer be seen as a condition that is incomprehensible or interminable. The prognosis will usually be better, the level of suicide risk, less.

The Experience of Loss

Loss is the central issue in depression as in most cases of suicide. For suicidal adolescents loss may be experienced along a number of fronts and usually is. More seriously suicidal adolescents will usually be more seriously depressed and will have experienced more numerous and painful losses. The experience of loss may include loss of a parent by death, divorce, separation, or abandonment. The loss becomes more serious when it is interpreted as a rejection. The feeling of rejection can be carried into adolescence from early childhood and even by teenagers who never met their lost parent. It is very common for teenagers to maintain as a central figure in their lives the image of a parent who left them before their memory. They are often left in perpetual mourning for these living figures whom they believe have stayed away because they were not good or loveable enough to draw them back. Losses of parental figures become multiple through multiple divorces, separations situations with various male or female friends or mother or father. The foster care experience typically involves multiple placement and multiple losses. Young people take these losses personally as evidence of some unidentifiable but deep and profound failing within them. Younger children tend to be more vulnerable to these effects and suffer most from their repetition and are likely to carry these effects into their adolescence.

As adolescents, losses may come in more variable form. Many adolescents sense what they feel to be loss of parental love as separation progresses. Sometimes the impression is real, for others it is imagined. Loss of innocence, purity, virginity, and childhood are of great concern to many teenagers who feel themselves to have become corrupt as sex, drugs, delinquent behavior, and declining grades have entered their lives in place of Little League, the school band, and bubble gum, leaving some with a deep sense of badness and uncleanliness. Some mourn their childhoods as idealized Edens in comparison to their adolescence and they miss it. They may also miss having a close, loving relationship with their parents who seem now to be out of their lives entirely and, perhaps, from some parents' points of view, quite happy to be.

Loss of friendships and lovers can be a normal part of adolescence, but for the vulnerable teenagers who may already have had their share of losses, a great sensitivity and perhaps reactivity to loss will exist. In fact, a break up in a key relationship is most often cited as the precipitant, if not the reason, for adolescent suicide attempts. When adolescent losses form a chain-reaction, the condition becomes very serious. Alana's letter in Chapter 6 and the circumstances surrounding the suicide attempt of Cassandra in Chapter 4 bear this out. For Cassandra, loss included, either literally or symbolically, her family, her home, her boyfriend, her past, and her future, all in the space of about a week. Even these were not, it may be recalled, the limits of the problems she faced.

Among the things depressed adolescents tolerate least well is loneliness. The loss of a beloved pet on top of other losses, can be devastating. Losses of all types leave the depressed individual feeling not only diminished, but devalued and intolerably lonely. Loss of a key relationship through death or suicide can sometimes exert an especially strong pull toward suicide as a way to rejoin the lost one or as a way to gain the peace the deceased seems to have obtained.

Support Systems

Knowledge of the type, magnitude, complexity, and duration of problems in the life of a suicidal adolescent and the adaptive strategies and internal resources available to the adolescent for dealing with these problems constitute two elements in a triad of interrelated factors to consider in assessment. The third part involves the external supports available to the adolescent and his ability to use them. Unsupported teenagers will need much greater internal strengths and resources to cope with their problems. The fewer and less stable are the supports suicidal teenagers appear to have, the more suicidal they are likely to become. Supports can come from a variety of sources and at best should come from more than one. Family, extended family, school personnel, peers, clergy, and other adult friends and advisors can serve as needed sources of support not to mention counselors and therapists. Typically, the suicidal teenager is impoverished in this respect or is unable to effectively utilize available supports. Research has characterized the families of suicidal adolescents as being uncommunicative and unsupportive leaving both parents and teenager feeling distrustful, frustrated, distant, and alienated from one another. Fewer and fewer families have extended family support within reach as increased mobility has created greater physical distances among family members. Increased mobility has even made community support more difficult to establish.

Peers are the most common sources of support for teenagers. However, adolescents who become suicidal have usually experienced problems here as well. Some never felt well liked or accepted even as children. Other have found the mixing and matching of early and mid-adolescence to be a period of social failure. Many maintain numerous but superficial relationships, while another type invests everything into a single supercharged relationship, which they typically overwhelm with their neediness, driving person after person away from them. All share in common the feeling of being alone or as Alana said, "in a bubble," able to see others and have others see them, but unable to make any real or lasting contact.

School personnel, teachers, counselors, and coaches often provide an alternate source of adult support outside the family which many adolescents make good use of. Assessors need to closely analyze the presence, extent, and quality of supportive people and systems available for the suicidal teenager. They should consider areas which have as yet remained untapped or underutilized. Recommendations for school counseling, special education assistance, or alternative educational programming, psychotherapy with or without the family, and even a move away from the home to a more supportive environment can at times provide a first step toward filling a void that the adolescent felt impotent to fill. On the other hand, life circumstances or the personality of the individual at risk may have created a more persistent crisis in obtaining support. Adolescents who are not attending school, have no close friends, are deeply estranged from parents, and who find it nearly impossible to trust or confide in others are at great risk if they are also dealing with problems beyond their own unaided ability to cope. Adolescents with borderline personality disorders are often represented within this group. The assessor should question whether teenagers have ever had counseling, what their attitude is or has been toward it, and whether they seem able to make productive use of it at this time as a source of support. Finally, attention should be focussed on whether the individual relies precariously on a single or very few supports that are or are likely to be very unstable and short-lived. Assessment of the quality of these supports or individuals can sometimes be an important way of evaluating the risk of suicide for such a teenager.

Reaction of Parents and Others

How parents respond to the suicidal intent or behavior of their son or daughter may tell much about family dynamics, the relationships that exist between that teenager and his or her parents as well as something about the likelihood of future suicidal behavior. In fact, the reactions of all significant others need to be attended to. If the adolescent is not taken seriously, if he or she is responded to with anger, rejection, aloofness, helplessness, a trivialization and denigration of his or her problems, and a greater distance than had existed before the suicidal episode, the adolescent may be in greater danger for more extreme behavior. Nonetheless, these reactions are quite common, both among adults and the peers of suicidal adolescents.

STATE OF MIND

The conditions and circumstances under which suicidal behavior or intent exists provide a backdrop against which an assessor may place the adolescent in order to get a sense of the context in which the episode has occurred or is occurring. It enables the assessor to take a broad view of the life of the adolescent at risk and the chronicity and multiplicity of stressors and conflicts with which he attempts to cope. In a temporal sense the perspective is both horizontal and vertical. The assessor looks back in time as well as at a host of conditions and circumstances which exist in the present.

In assessing the state of mind of the suicidal adolescent the perspective is more temporally current and the focus more narrow. The assessor is attempting to gauge more immediate risk by developing a sense of the present capacity and willingness of the individuals to continue to cope with their lives, given the conditions and circumstances they must face. In most cases this type of evaluation differs very little from the evaluation of suicidal persons of any age. Assessors of adolescent suicidality sometimes err, however, in believing that low lethality of attempt means a low level of psychological crisis or disturbance. Further, adolescents often respond to treatment and evaluation of their suicidal behavior with strong denial, resistance, and a reversal of mood as they attempt to act and feel as far removed as possible from the behavior and feelings which provoked the self-destructive behavior.

Both adolescents and their parents may seek to minimize the importance of the event in both their emotional and intellectual responses to it. These factors among others present special challenges to evaluators of the state of mind of adolescents who have engaged in or are considering suicidal behavior. Areas to be focused on follow.

Level of Depression

Robbins and Alessi (1985), based on their research on depressed and suicidal adolescents, have reported that depression and suicidal behavior are so closely related that the DSM-III (Diagnostic and Statistical Manual of Mental Disorders) diagnostic criteria for major depressive disorders functions just as well as a diagnostic criteria for suicide. The more closely adolescents approximate the condition of major depression the more likely they are to be suicidal. The DSM-III defines major depressive disorder as comprising at least four of the symptoms listed below (DSM-III, 3rd ed., 1980, p. 214). These symptoms must have been present nearly every day for a period of at least two weeks:

1. Poor appetite or significant weight loss (when not dieting) or increased appetite or significant weight gain
2. Insomnia or hypersomnia
3. Psychomotor agitation or retardation (but not merely subjective feelings of restlessness or being slowed down)
4. Loss of interest or pleasure in usual activities, or decrease in sexual drive not limited to a period when delusional or hallucinating
5. Loss of energy; fatigue
6. Feelings of worthlessness, self-reproach, or excessive or inappropriate guilt (either may be delusional)
7. Complaints or evidence of diminished ability to think or concentrate, such as slowed thinking, or indecisiveness not associated with marked loosening of associations or incoherence
8. Recurrent thoughts of death, suicidal ideation, wishes to be dead, or suicide attempt

The adolescent, however may present the assessor with numerous pitfalls and camouflages through the use of depressive equivalents as described in Chapter

4. Nonetheless, depression is usually present in suicidal adolescents and the level of depression is a most important diagnostic indicator.

Some depressed adolescents are unaware of depressive processes within themselves or may consider them, if they are aware, to be normal and insignificant. They may be unable to recognize the signs or the association between depressed feelings and actual behavior. They may be unable to attribute any of their problems to depression. For instance, difficulty with concentration may be expressed but unattributed to depression. Sleep disturbance may be ascribed to an overly busy school, work, and social life. A frenetic pace of activity, chronic restlessness, and an intolerance of being alone may be viewed as quite normal and even laudable rather than as evidence of adolescent depression. Adolescents who are unable to function in or attend school but who can work a job may externalize the issue as a problem with school rather than as a manifestation of moderate or major depression. At any rate, evidence of a powerful and debilitating depressive condition is a very serious sign especially when associated with insomnia and substance abuse and when the condition has persisted over a number of weeks or months.

Hopelessness, Helplessness, and Attitude toward the Future

Very closely associated with depression are the feelings of hopelessness and helplessness that are critical factors in one's decision whether to prolong one's life. The more hopeless and helpless people feel is their situation concerning the conditions in their life that burden them, the more depressed they are likely to feel and vice versa. Evaluators of suicidality need to assess the strength of these feelings. Do these teenagers think that problematic circumstances and conditions in their lives absolutely cannot change? If they can change, when might that happen? Does the person derive any solace from the belief that positive change can occur? Can they stand the wait? Time is a cruel enemy in the eyes of many adolescents. We as adults look at future time as through a telescope with the future seeming to loom up at us all too near. Adolescents often view time as if looking through the wrong end of that same telescope. The future is distorted and seems far away and practically unreachable. Most teenagers cannot wait as well as most adults. They do not tolerate short separations as well. Feelings of hopelessness find fertile ground to grow here. If teenagers seem to believe that they will always feel as unhappy and alone as they do now, that changes at home (or escape from home) are impossible, that friends or lovers will be unable to effectively support them, that school offers nothing positive, and that gratification and affiliation are unavailable from any source and likely to remain so, then trouble may well be at hand.

Helplessness, on the other hand, involves individuals' sense of potency or power to either create better situations for themselves or to take advantage of ones that may exist. Depression saps energy and can render one's feeling of helplessness more severe. People feel themselves sinking (or already sunk) and feel they can do nothing about it. Hopelessness and helplessness influence each other and both are affected by faulty perception and memory that highlight, for the person, the negative aspects of conditions and circumstances and tend to devalue or ignore more positive elements within themselves and their lives. The evaluator needs to take note of adolescents' integrity of reality testing and whether they are able to see anything good, hopeful, or worthwhile in themselves and in their lives and whether they feel able to take advantage of it with help.

Openness and Effectiveness of Communication

Adolescents who become suicidal are often, regardless of how intelligent or articulate they may be, unable or unwilling to communicate to others any meaningful sense of who they are or how they feel. For them, behavior, such as suicidal behavior, takes the place of words and does so ineffectively. I have known many who would fit this description. It is a very positive sign if a suicidal adolescent is able to speak honestly and coherently about his or her feelings. Those who are able to acknowledge and share how they feel and who they are, are far more likely to establish close, meaningful, and supportive relationships, to get and make use of help, and to not be alone. Adolescents who, on the other hand, appear unaware of and/or unwilling to open up and communicate their needs to others place themselves at greater risk. Again, as with assessment of the adolescent's support systems, the adolescent's attitude toward counseling may tell much about his or her openness and desire to communicate. The degree of willingness on the part of the adolescent in accepting a referral to counseling can be an important diagnostic sign in itself. It suggests the presence of hope on the part of the teenager that counseling may help as well as a desire to open up to someone. Communication is a coping skill and when it is genuine it is a very healthy and effective one. Those who appear able to use it are generally at reduced risk for suicide provided the circumstances and conditions with which they contend are not too noxious and overwhelming.

Perturbation

One of the most critical indicators of a potentially suicidal person's immediate level of lethality is the person's level of perturbation. Level of perturbation refers to the level of panic, disorganization, and agitation that the suicidal person is manifesting. Do individuals have at that moment the capacity to formulate a way out of their problems or, more realistically, a way to *begin* that process? Are they capable of relaxing or calming themselves? To the extent that people appear to have lost control of their thoughts, emotions, and behavior, they may be considered seriously perturbed and more seriously at risk. Perturbation is monitored and assessed throughout the evaluation. The assessor needs to be aware of changes in the level of distress over time and the pattern of change. Does the person present him or herself as relatively calm and become increasingly agitated or is the pattern reversed? Does perturbation manifest itself in an irregular pattern of peaks which cannot be ascribed to or contained by external conditions? How long does it take for individuals to become more calm and composed? Are they able to achieve it themselves or do they need more or less help in doing so? The conditions which appear to effect the level of perturbation in the evaluative process need to be noted. Do adolescents seem more distressed while in the presence of their parents? Are they more relaxed in a one to one situation, as opposed to being alone or with more than one person? Easing the level of perturbation may or may not bring about improvement in the adolescent's organization of thought. Reduced perturbation may yield a deepening depression and blunting of energy devoted to consideration of the person's own suicidality or alternative adaptive strategies. A more hopeful development would see reduced perturbation yielding more organized thinking and problem solving.

Adolescents will vary greatly in how amenable they are to efforts on the part of others toward reducing perturbation in cases where they are not able to calm themselves unassisted. Adolescents who readily allow themselves to accept help in this regard and are able to make use of it offer a more positive picture. In contrast some teenagers will either remain highly resistant to or unaffected by efforts to help them compose themselves. Certainly no potentially suicidal adolescent can be released from supervision or care while in a highly perturbed state of mind. The assessor can feel more hopeful about the level of risk when the level of perturbation is relatively low, when the adolescent is able to assist in the calming process, when perturbation is more immediately responsive to palliative intervention and when reduced perturbation brings about more organized thinking and efforts at a more effective coping style.

Attitude toward Death

Beliefs and attitudes toward death can be as compelling a force toward suicide as are attitudes and beliefs about life. It is essential to know something of the meaning and attraction of death to the suicidal adolescent.

Would death mean the provision of a wonderful afterlife of some sort? Boldt (1982) found a majority of adolescents studied believed this would be true even after a suicidal death. Does death mean reunion with decedents? Is the teenager's death intended to gain relief from suffering, a never-ending sleep, an escape? Beck, Schuyler and Herman, (1974) consider the absence of contemplation on the matter of death to be a serious sign. Those who appear not to have given the meaning of death any thought at all or to have for-mulated only vague notions as to what death might entail may be highly impulsive and ultimately more dangerous to themselves. When in a state of stress they may simply act without benefit of any extensive internal dialogue. Some adolescents will speak of death as if it were a living state. They imagine being able to witness the reactions of others to their death and perhaps even speak to those people. It is as if they had planned to attend their own funeral. They may not have developed a mature concept of the permanence and irreversibility of death and its effect on survivors. Their suicidal intention is filled with life-oriented motivations.

Whenever death is understood by the adolescent on a mature level and is viewed as offering a significant improvement in condition over life, and if it is not possible for the person to conceive of ways to make life better or more tolerable, risk may be considered as serious. Adolescents who, on the other hand, do not fully understand death may make serious attempts or even kill themselves without really meaning to die in the mature sense of the word. Suicidal adolescents who give no thought to death's meaning or implications may be more dangerous still. With this in mind, evaluators of suicidal teenagers need not feel fearful or reticent about discussing death or focussing in their assessment on the adolescent's thoughts about death. Helping teenagers to think about and articulate their notions concerning their death and death in general is valuable both diagnostically and therapeutically. It is far more likely to serve a preventive function than to be a dangerously provocative issue.

One more circumstance to consider is the duration of suicidal wishes. How long has the person been thinking about suicide? How long has he been feeling that maybe he would rather not be alive? Usually the longer the per-son has been struggling with thoughts of suicide, the more serious is the risk of an eventual suicidal act. Suicidal thoughts may be chronic, nearly constant, bearing varying degrees of compulsion. The issue of prior attempts is of great importance here in helping to gauge the individual's resistance to those thoughts or urges. Those suicidal adolescents who have thought of suicide but who have not yet attempted it and those who may have attempted before but are now in the process of merely thinking about a repeat attempt need to be asked what keeps them from engaging in the act. It is essential to know the nature, stability, and strength of the life forces within a suicidal teenager.

Certain factors in an adolescent's struggle with suicidal wishes may exert a powerful and persistent counterforce. Teenagers who are holding back from suicide because they feel it is a sin, or because they fear death or Hell, do not want to hurt their parents, or perhaps want to see how their lives will turn out, may be at less risk. Teenagers who are holding back in order to give a broken love relationship one last try, or are awaiting the results of some competitive performance or an unlikely change in some chronically unfavorable life situation, or simply do not know why they have not attempted suicide may be more dangerously at the mercy of events.

The assessor must consider whether adolescents' attitudes toward their suicidal thoughts are accepting, rejecting, or ambivalent ones. Wishes for death may not always involve strong compulsions to suicide. We frequently encounter "suicidal" adolescents who appear to wish they were dead but who have very little intention or desire to kill themselves. If an assessor were to ask one of these teenagers if they wanted to kill themselves they might respond "absolutely not." However, if the question were posed another way, such as, "Do you sometimes wish you were no longer living?", the answer might be "absolutely!" The wish to die here is a much more passive one. The teenager would not mind dying, might even yearn for death, but is rejecting the idea of suicide. These adolescents may present as a significant risk, however, if their more passive wish to die involves reckless behavior which is potentially life-threatening, such as poly-drug (with alcohol) abuse, driving under the influence, or any number of stunts or deeds that place life on a precarious balance.

ASSESSMENT OF THE ATTEMPT

Individuals who have at some point in their lives attempted suicide have demonstrated conclusively that they are capable of self-intentioned harm. Whether assessing lethality pre or postattempt, the nature of a person's past suicidal behavior must be ascertained. Future risk is judged in part from the lethality of one's past behavior, especially those most recent acts. The extent to which adolescents have appeared determined to die in the recent past is of paramount value in assessing their current intentions and potential for suicide. Therefore, each episode of a person's suicidal behavior needs to be evaluated for the methods, circumstances, and thoughts related to the attempt. For those appearing to be only contemplating suicide, with no prior attempts, the details of their actual plans for suicide (if they have any) need to be discovered and assessed in considering lethal potential.

The method used in the suicide attempt is of obvious importance in gauging both lethal intent and future risk as has been discussed in previous sections of this book. Methods that are more violent allow for little or no opportunity for rescue or repair, and methods, that are more instantaneous in their effect are not only more lethal in fact, but generally signify a more lethal intention, a greater commitment to death. Methods such as a gunshot wound to the head, any effort involving a shotgun, a leap from a tall building (above 4 stories), ingestion while alone of a quick acting toxin, severe cutting causing profuse and rapid blood loss (also while alone), are examples of extremely lethal methods of attempting or, more likely, committing suicide. The level of wish to die must be considered very high. Adolescents, as has been pointed out, frequently present a much more equivocal picture of lethal intent and lethality of method. Methods chosen by adolescents, especially adolescent females, typically range from those that are virtually incapable of causing death—light overdoses of nonprescription medicines or cutting involving scratches on wrists that do not require medical attention—to suicide attempts in which death is rendered improbable due to the likelihood or even the certainty of intervention by some outside agent (person or persons). Examples of the latter type would be suicide attempts that involve more serious drug ingestions, self-poisoning, or cutting that take place in the presence of others or in the belief that the person's condition will be discovered and treated before life is in serious jeopardy. Smith, Conroy, and Ehler (1984) have compiled a very useful ranking of the various more common methods for attempting suicide ranging from the least to most lethal types. These comprise an objective suicide intent rating scale based exclusively on the method and circumstances of a person's suicide attempt.

The circumstances surrounding the suicide attempt will offer some indication as to lethal intent and the motivation behind the act. The circumstances must be interpreted in association with the method used, the person's statement as to the purpose of the act and the person's own apparent beliefs as to the lethality of the attempt. Key factors to be considered include whether the person took precautions against intervention or rescue by others. How well thought out, energetic, and complete were these precautions? These efforts may range from situations that insure complete isolation from others where vigorous effort has been spent to ward off possible rescue, to attempts that take place among several family members or friends offering the absolute certainly that the act will be interrupted. The timing of the attempt should be considered in light of the probability of intervention. Suicide attempts will sometimes take place in isolation but with the expectation or at least the probability that another person is soon to arrive and in time to effectively intervene. Deady errors in planning, however, have occurred when timing has been off or anticipated intervention has been too slow in arriving. Some adolescents will take a much more active role in placing themselves in the way of assistance in the immediate aftermath of a suicidal act. Often, potential helpers will be notified shortly after or during the attempt. Others will make contact with potential helpers after say, a drug ingestion so as not to be alone and to be accessible to help should they feel they need it, though they might not specifically alert the other person of the suicidal act. The case of Leigh described in Chapter 3 is an example of this type of precautionary behavior.

Evidence of specific planning or acts in anticipation of a suicide attempt can offer some insight into the commitment of the individual to a more or less lethal act. Reference here is to suicide notes or final statements, threats or intimations of suicidal intent either verbal or in writing, the giving away of personal possessions, final arrangements being made in the areas of relationships, obligations, or personal goals, or finally, the extensiveness of plans (if any) in support of or in preparation for a suicide attempt.

As Hawton et al. (1982a) have pointed out, adolescent suicide attempts are less likely to occur in complete isolation, beyond the aid of others, or timed so that help is impossible. Most attempts appear to have involved little conscious planning. Suicide notes are infrequently left, less so than by adults (Peck, 1986). Impulsivity is characteristic of adolescent suicidal behavior and can be an extremely dangerous quality in a highly suicidal person. Impulsivity also negates the opportunity for the suicidal adolescent to carry out very much in the way of preparatory steps and activities such as suicide notes and final arrangements. Most often the behavior occurs rather spontaneously and while serious problems may be longstanding and thoughts about suicide may have existed for some time, the actual suicidal act may occur with minimal preparation or planning. Usually, with teenagers, this phenomenon works in favor of life, supported by powerful wishes for survival. When extensive preparation appears to have taken place for the purpose of moving the suicidal individual further away from potential helpers and from life itself, more serious levels of lethal intent can be inferred.

Assessment of a suicide attempt by study of the method used and the circumstances surrounding the attempt involves objective evidence. It has the advantage of being obtainable independently from the victim himself and is therefore resistant to the effects of denial, lack of cooperation, lack of responsiveness, or changes in attitude on the part of the suicidal individual, which may cause him to either forget, hold back, or alter the thoughts and feelings associated with his suicidal behavior. Nonetheless, no assessment of the meaning of a suicide attempt or its relevance to suicide risk can be complete without some consideration of the adolescents' subjective interpretation of their motives for the act, their beliefs about the lethality of the method, their expectations and wishes about death. Objective evidence concerning method, preparation, and planning need to be checked against the teenager's own thoughts. For example, a purely objective assessment of method of attempt would lead most evaluators to consider a 10 regular strength Tylenol tablet ingestion to be indicative of a very low level of lethal intent and perhaps an equally low level of immediate risk for suicide. However, ignorance of pharmacology and physiology, coupled with the impulsive quality of many adolescent attempts, can produce situations in which intent to die is at least temporarily quite strong, though the method chosen turns out to be of low lethality. Some teenagers may believe that what are actually mild overdoses can kill and therefore objective circumstances alone may offer a grossly and even dangerously incomplete or inaccurate picture of the intention and level of risk involved. Adolescent suicidal behavior presents many such contradictions and inconsistencies. The bottom line or key determinant in attempting to understand the behavior is often the adolescents' own statements in regard to what they did and why they did it. Obtaining self-reports can be, however, as much of a challenge as interpreting them. A number of areas need to be covered.

Most suicide intent scales seek to discover, among other things, the purpose of the attempt. It is a limiting question, however, to simply ask "Why did you do it?" Adolescents tend to respond with mention of precipitants rather than "reasons." Rather, this question needs to be presented as, "What was it about your life or the way you felt that made you try to hurt yourself?" This type of question generally allows for a broader range of responses having more to do with larger issues and feelings in the adolescent's life rather than merely the most recent specifics. Responses, of course, can range from "I don't know," to "I just wanted to die." Those which appear to favor escape from unbearable feelings and life conditions rather than seeking help or caring (more interpersonal or life-oriented reasons) are suggestive of a stronger leaning toward death.

As suggested before, adolescents' expectations and beliefs about the lethality and probable outcome of the method chosen is of critical importance. Accurate knowledge, on the part of the teenagers, of the actual effects of the typical (drug) methods should never be presumed. How sure did the teenagers feel that death would result from their act? Did they consider lethality when administering to themselves the self-destructive behavior? A 15-year-old girl who had made two suicide attempts by means of drug overdoses, kept a medical reference book on prescription and nonprescription drugs in her bedroom and is known to have consulted it immediately prior to both attempts with the probable intention of insuring survival. Did the person in fact want to die and did those feelings change after the ingestion or cutting, etc.? A 15-year-old boy whom I recently evaluated in a hospital after he had been admitted for a nonlethal overdose of antibiotics responded to the question, "Did you want to die?" by saying that, yes, when he was putting the pills in his mouth he did, but that after he had swallowed them he felt very "stupid" and changed his mind completely. This is a rather common phenomenon. An 18-year-old girl who had been a client of mine in therapy and who was also diabetic, attempted suicide by purposely mismanaging her insulin treatments over a period of time. After the first week in this process she changed her mind about wishing to die and tried to make up for her self-imposed insulin deprivation by superdoses over the next couple of days, ultimately sending herself into shock and severe, life-threatening acidosis. She barely avoided a coma. Therefore, questions pertaining to the adolescent's wish to die need to keep temporal effects and situations such as these in mind.

Whether evidence is profuse or lacking with respect to planning for a suicide attempt, the adolescent must be questioned about premeditation. Attempts which leave behind no objective evidence of preparation or planning may have involved hours or even days of prior thought. How long had the person been considering the act and the method? What thoughts did the person have, if any, regarding precautions for or against discovery and rescue by others? Keep in mind, however, that no one wishes to appear to be a caller of wolf, to be an attention-seeking manipulator. Adolescents, being no different, may prefer not to cast themselves in this light by admitting they had hoped or even planned to be rescued or prevented from completing their act. They, perhaps accurately, anticipate less positive regard as a low lethality suicide attempter as compared to the more "serious" suicide attempter or committer.

Two final aspects of the adolescent's suicide attempt deserve discussion before leaving this section. They refer to the adolescent's own reaction to his or her behavior and second, the degree of involvement of alcohol in the suicide attempt. Of all the conditions, circumstances, history, feelings, and beliefs associated with the adolescent's suicide attempt, one of the most important in gauging immediate risk is the person's reaction to the attempt itself. It is very reassuring to the assessor to see that the teenager is relieved to have survived and is rejecting of the behavior. Survivors who remain highly agitated, or deeply depressed, or who regret having survived present cause for great concern and caution. Again, the reaction needs to be monitored over time as dramatic changes can occur with initial relief turning to renewed depression and hopelessness. Regret over survival, due to for instance, acute shame and embarrassment (as in "I'm so embarrassed I could just die") may just as well turn to more positive feelings, especially when the attempt is responded to with support and sincere concern.

Alcohol intake may render more serious the medical emergency involved in the suicide attempt and imply more lethal intent. Heavy usage prior to or during an attempt, when used to facilitate the mental commitment to the act and/or heighten the lethal effect of the method used is a very serious sign. The use of alcohol is frequently found in association with adolescent suicide attempts (Robbins & Alessi, 1985) and may represent another example of teenagers unwittingly overendangering their lives.

In conclusion, the three primary areas of assessment, methods, circumstances, and the adolescents' subjective impressions of their suicide attempt, must always be interpreted in combination, none being allowed to stand alone as the sole indicator of the meaning or predictive value of the act. Adolescents being assessed as potentially suicidal, prior to an actual suicide attempt, must be evaluated with appropriate aspects of this process in mind. Issues such as the presence of a suicide plan, choice of method, the reason for feeling suicidal and the incidence of suicidal communications must be considered along with the circumstances and conditions of their lives and their state of mind.

Several researchers have contributed scales for measuring and assessing the intent and lethality of suicide attempts. Among the most widely used is the Beck, Schuyler, and Herman (1974) Suicide Intent Scale which elicits from the attempter and informed sources information regarding the circumstances, intentions, beliefs, and expectations associated with the act. The scale allows the assessor to judge the purposefulness of the behavior and the extent of planning and commitment for death. The scale does not rely on a purely objective evaluation of the methods used or solely on the extent of physical danger posed by the attempt. Rather, it seeks to assess the psychological orientation toward death of the attempter. While a very helpful device, its effectiveness can be severely compromised by witholding, confused, hostile, or denying individuals who will not be able or willing to give honest consideration or response to the questions involved.

A different approach to the assessment of intention and lethality in suicide attempts has been developed by Smith, Conroy, and Ehler (1984). Their scale bypasses the self-reporting format used by Beck et al. (1974) and others (Dorpat & Boswell, 1963; Farberow & Shneidman, 1961; Freeman, Wilson, Thigpen, & McGee, 1974; Moffa, 1965; and Weissman & Worden, 1974). Instead, this scale judges lethality based strictly on the method and means of attempting suicide as well as the circumstances related to the attempt (precautions taken to prevent discovery or intervention) in an objective assessment of suicidality. Lethality is measured along an eleven point scale with 0.0 indicating the low point of lethality ("death is an impossible result of the 'suicidal' behavior") and 10.0 indicating death as a near certainty regardless of emergency intervention. Level 0.0 behavior consists of such things as light scratching of the skin not requiring sutures, ingesting mild overdoses or small foreign objects, and other "ineffective" though possibly reckless acts usually demonstrated in the presence of others. Attempts move higher up the rating scale as the medical emergency increases and circumstances are controlled to more effectively prevent rescue.

A 10.0 attempt may include severe cutting of wrists and/or neck or ingesting highly toxic substances with maximum precautions taken against rescue, jumping off a tall building (more than 4 stories), and gun shot wounds to the head.

It would be advisable to consider both scales in assessing the lethality of suicide attempts, though it is likely that most attempts by adolescents will be judged to be of relatively low lethality by any scale. Smith et al. (1984) reported on the judgments of groups of psychiatrists, psychologists, social workers, and nurses, as to the point (using the rating scale) after which an attempt was considered to be "serious." Together, the professionals indicated a point on the scale descriptive of a degree of lethality well above the level seen in much adolescent suicidal behavior. Smith and Crawford (1986) applied this scale to a group of 32 adolescent suicide attempts and found 90.6 percent of the attempts to be of "very low lethality" (mean = 1.8).

Findings and judgments such as these, while helpful in predicting future risk, can be dangerously misleading. All adolescent suicide attempts represent a psychological emergency, if not a medical one, and are a serious sign of psychological distress. It is of critical importance when dealing with the adolescent suicide attempter, postattempt, that one's understanding of an response to the attempter are not determined solely by the lethality of the attempt.

The challenges confronting assessors of adolescent suicidality, whether they be professional or nonprofessional, are enormous. Essential information regarding adolescents' histories and current functioning is often unknown, unavailable or withheld. The methods, circumstances, thoughts, and feelings associated with attempts will usually be highly equivocal, conflictual, and contradictory. Adolescents themselves are frequently of little help in offering meaning and clarity to the assessment process due to distrust, fear, shame, or confusion. The clarity of our own thinking may be distorted by our attitudes, prejudices, and misconceptions concerning adolescents and adolescent suicidal behavior. Myths and misconceptions abound about suicidal behavior in general and, I suspect, are especially abundant concerning adolescent suicide.

MYTHS, MISCONCEPTIONS, AND SUICIDAL SIGNS

The assessment of suicidal risk is not restricted to the evaluation of individuals who have either attempted suicide or have given some specific indication of thoughts of doing so. Suicide prevention for adolescents has come to involve the extensive publication and distribution of so called "signs" of potential suicidality and the active involvement of educators, parents, peers, and others in identifying those teenagers who appear to meet the criteria and are thus labelled as at risk. The media have been energetic in dispensing lists of "signs" of the adolescent suicide candidate. Certainly, the public needs to be sensitized to the existence of great unhappiness in increasing numbers of our young of which suicidal behavior is one symptom. However, the signs of suicide that are frequently offered tend to be presented in a manner that is simplistic, all-encompassing, misleading, or just plain wrong. Efforts at education about suicide for the purpose of identifying and assessing the troubled adolescent prior to a desperate act is more than laudable. It is simply much more difficult a process than it is often made to appear.

In order to address the issue and the problem of the signs of adolescent suicide, the more commonly offered warning signs are presented below and will be critiqued with recommendations as to how they might better be applied.

Threat of Suicide

Though seemingly an obvious and irrefutable sign of potential suicide, the threat of suicide is a victim of one of the more prevalent and erroneous myths regarding suicide. The belief that those who threaten suicide are less likely to do it is supported by the insinuation that threats of suicide represent attention-seeking behavior, especially among the young. Many feel that threats of this type are best ignored. To indulge them is to encourage more of the same. In fact, most adolescents who do make suicide attempts have preceded the act with some form of warning to others. It is also true, however, that the majority of adolescents who threaten suicide do not attempt it. Nonetheless, suicidal communications are very significant indicators of psychological distress. They need not be validated by an actual suicide attempt. Suicide threats have important meanings. They are often attempts to check out the level of caring and responsiveness that exists out there for them in their world. Suicide threats are not generally offered indiscriminately to insignificant persons in the adolescents' lives. Rather, they are presented to key individuals whose responses are of enormous importance. Unfortunately, adolescents who become suicidal have often come to be that way, in part, because their inability to effectively open up to or communicate with others has left them feeling hopelessly alone and unsupported. Their problems with communication often carry over to poorly and indirectly articulated suicide threats that are difficult to understand, and therefore may not be heeded or responded to, sometimes with tragic results (Ross, 1980). Some adolescents will warn no one. Some will, in fact, seem considerably less depressed, even quite happy, immediately prior to attempting suicide. In these cases, a decision to attempt suicide, to end it all, has lessened the depression by the putting into place of an active plan to gain relief. In short, one should not feel necessarily reassured that an adolescent is not yet at risk because a suicide threat has not been offered as a sign. Neither can one ever dismiss the importance of a threat if it should occur. Adolescents who make suicide threats need to be considered suicidal until proven otherwise.

One final note deserves mention. With alarm over adolescent suicidal behavior running high, high school teachers, among others, who are heavily exposed to the thoughts, verbalizations, and writing of adolescents, are often frightened by themes of death expressed by teenagers. Death becomes an important concept to adolescents as they approach maturity and become fully cognizant for the first time of their own mortality. Death then will find its way into their thinking and expression as a normative phenomenon. Thoughts of their own death become possible and common. Sometimes expression of this nature in their art, creative writing, or in conversation, is mistaken for unnatural morbidity or suicidality by adults taken by surprise or unprepared perhaps due to their own efforts to fend off such thoughts of death and mortality. Teachers and adults in such a position need guidance in sorting out suicidal communications from more developmentally normal thoughts of death. At times, however, a very fine line divides the two.

Depression

As often stated, depression is a key sign of suicidal potential. The description of major depression functions as an adequate description of the suicidal person. The more depressed a person appears to be, and the more closely this person approximates descriptions of those who have attempted or committed suicide, the greater is the potential and danger of suicidal behavior. Adolescents have particular difficulty tolerating depression. Depression in its milder forms, however, is quite commonly seen in adolescents. There is much to be depressed about. Social and academic competition, self-consciousness and self-deprecation all hit hard on the adolescent's shaky self-esteem. Most adolescents feel depressed at some point to some degree (Oldham, 1978). Depression, however, becomes of critical importance as a sign of suicide not by its mere presence, but by its severity and its persistence. Finally, it must be remembered that adolescents will not always manifest depression in easily recognizable form. Many dangerously depressed adolescents will present a picture which confounds the notion of depression as typically described. Therefore, even so unanimously accepted a sign as depression has its elusive qualities, particularly when applied to adolescents.

The following signs, often derivatives of depression, are often seen in lists of signs of suicide. They are treated separately from depression here as they are in popular usage. They are: declining grades, behavior changes, mood changes, loss of previous interests, risk-taking behavior, changes in appearance and drug or alcohol use. When I read lists such as these I feel, oftentimes, that I am reading a list of some of the descriptive qualities of adolescence in general, especially early adolescence. This is not to say that these "signs" are worthless, only that they must be considered with numerous qualifications.

Declining Grades

Declining grades appear to be a normative condition of early adolescence. I base this statement on purely nonempirical observation. As an example, I have for several years given talks to 8th graders as part of a program of orientation to their newly arrived adolescence and to the high school that they have entered (their high school enrolls grades 8-12). As a way of intro-ducing them to the idea that adolescence really does come with added stresses and distractions, I ask them to think back to their elementary school years. Were you pretty consistent students during that time? If you were a "C," "B," or "A" student in third grade, were you a "C," "B," or "A" student pretty much all the way through? Most eighth graders (and their parents) believe that this, for them, was true. Next I ask them to consider the more recent past. I ask them if they have noticed a significant drop in their overall grades recently as compared with their elementary school days. About eighty percent consistently respond that this has indeed been the case with them. Approximately 10 percent will say they have stayed about the same and another 10 percent rather sheepishly admit that their grades have gone up. For most of those struggling souls in the former and much larger group, the grade drop will be a temporary thing. As adjustment to adolescence proceeds, they settle down to adolescent life and perceive the future as closer and more real; academics may seem more relevant and meaningful and grades will go back up. For some, academics will not grow in meaning nor will interest return, but for this to be the case they need not be disturbed, depressed, or suicidal. They simply no longer view school as the path leading them to where they wish to go. Whether they are right or wrong, they are certainly not necessarily pathological. Declining grades do take on meaning as a sign of possible trouble when it occurs later in adolescence, after ninth grade, and when the decline is dramatic and precipitous. Usually though, declining grades needs to gain its meaning as a symptom from other signs, as is true for most of the symptoms to be presented.

Changes in Interests, Behavior, and Mood

It is a cliché, but nonetheless a reasonably true one, that teenagers are a rather changeable and inconstant lot. This is not to say that they are generally labile or approach pathological dimensions in this respect. It is only that in comparison to the typically more stable temperament of the latency years, adolescents appear more volatile and inconsistent in their interests, behavior, and moods. Parents are often concerned (to put it mildly) when their 14-year-old son or daughter quits sports, band, old friends, and begins to bring home lower grades. It is clear their child is changing. They fear it is for the worse and cringe at the thought of where they might be headed as they extrapolate somewhat wildly into the future. In fact, sports are often dropped because they have become much more competitive, time consuming, and require higher levels of skill. Band is often dropped as an expression of rebellion and separation since it was usually parents who initiated their child's involvement in the first place and who have maintained their continued involvement. One way for the teenager to declare his limited independence from parental authority then is to quit band.

Characteristic behaviors change as adolescents try on new ways to act and new ways to be. Younger adolescents, in particular, are keenly aware of and influenced by the prevailing mores and superficial styles of their peer group and will need to emulate as closely as possible the changing pattern of acceptable peer group behavior, the consternation of adults notwithstanding.

Changes in moods have much to do with changing physiology and changes in the adolescents' perceptions of their status in the fast-paced and highly judgmental (sometimes cruel) world of the adolescent. Again, none of these changes, if normative, should range into the clearly pathological. In other words, most should occur without upsetting the basic equilibrium of the individuals or their capacity to function effectively. If changes in these areas are associated with significant and prolonged dysfunction in peer relationships, eating, sleeping, capacity to concentrate, antisocial behavior, school attendance, or performance, to mention a few, then a more serious, if not suicidal, condition may exist. Again, marked changes in the areas of interest, behavior, and mood take on greater significance when occurring later in adolescence. If the star quarterback of a winning football team suddenly quits the team in his junior or senior year, without apparent cause, one must wonder. If the genuinely funny, well-respected bon vivant suddenly becomes morose and reclusive, concern is justifiable. If an always well-groomed, attractive, and careful dresser begins to present as unkempt, uncared for, shabby, or even dirty (and I don't mean Punk) something not very nice is probably developing.

Reckless Behavior

Reckless, potentially self-destructive behavior has been noted before as an approximation, in some cases, of suicidal behavior, with the one sometimes flowing into the other. If my own adolescence is any example, however, reckless behavior occurs with some frequency among large numbers of relatively normal adolescents. Risk-taking behavior, formerly within the province of males, is now common among male and female teenagers alike as they test themselves and their need for control, mastery, and even omnipotence against their environment. Fortunately, most survive unscathed, though usually by pure luck. Teenagers can sense, however, when one among them needs to go too far, when one is driven to lengths that no longer feel like fun. Adults are usually unaware of the distinction. They are not present at the events. These more extreme adolescents will sometimes surface as frequent accident victims or juvenile offenders. Some will not surface at all to adult view. They will remain known only to their friends who may continue to enjoy their friend's exploits while privately concerned as to their real nature.

Drug and Alcohol Use

Though drug and alcohol use are associated with depression and suicide, it is really only substance abuse that consistently signals a strong likelihood of serious problems. The prevalence of drug and alcohol use among adolescents greatly reduces the symptomatic value of the mere use of pot and alcohol. Further, abuse is not always easy for adult observers to detect since this behavior often resides within the secret realm of adolescent lives. However, teenagers who do seem to be using drugs as a kind of medication, whose capacity to work, succeed in school, or maintain relationships appears to be compromesed by a greater investment in substance abuse are demonstrating some serious problems in living. An image comes to mind as a comparison. Astronomers sometimes can detect the presence of an initially invisible but influential celestial object by the behavior of other objects around it. Though this object is the central and guiding force in the perceived activity around it, it may be the last entity to be noted. Rather, it rests in dark secret, suggested at first only by the manifestations around it. So it can be with substance abuse among adolescents. It is often a dark, closely held secret to be kept from adults and hinted at initially only by its derivatives. Orbiting problems such as worsening school performance, mood swings, or a constriction of interests may be only the more noticeable manifestations leading back to a more dangerous but indiscernable core.

Giving away Possessions

This sign of imminent suicidal behavior is rarely omitted from lists of signs and is probably just as rarely seen in cases of actual adolescent suicide or attempted suicide. This is probably true for two reasons. First, adolescent suicide behavior is so frequently invested with a powerful desire to survive. Second, the suicidal behavior is usually an impulsive act, devoid of any extensive planning. In short, adolescents do not generally take the time to make final arrangements such as the dispensing of prized possessions. Further, they may sense at some level that they will still be around after the suicide attempt and may want their record albums or other paraphernalia back. Obviously, final arrangements may be carried out even in adolescent suicide. When it does occur it is an exceedingly important nonverbal sign. Nonverbal signs, incidently, are often all we have to go on. However, one should not wait for this sign to occur before taking the threat or possibility of a teenager's suicide seriously.

Social Withdrawal

As an important aspect of depression, social withdrawal is an important sign of potential suicide. With respect to adolescents, it can be at the same time an especially powerful indication or of very limited use. This, again, has to do with the nature of adolescent depression.

The need to maintain peer involvement and social competence is, of course, very strong in adolescence. The inability to utilize energy toward that end is, therefore, an important sign of depression. This is especially apparent in cases where a normal or even greater than average level of social activity and involvement had been once present. But what about the more quiet, solitary teenagers who have never had many friends or social engagements, who have always kept pretty much to themselves? There are many nonsuicidal types within this category of high school age adolescents. It becomes very difficult to spot growing suicide potential in cases such as this using this sign.

Finally, even very depressed adolescents may not manifest noticcable changes in their pattern of social activity. Often this area of functioning will be maintained at all cost, though functioning in all other areas may suffer. Peer relations are a source of distraction from depression and a source of critical support. For a variety of reasons then, social withdrawal might not occur or may not be noticed.

Break in Key Relationship

This final item in this list of ten signs of suicide has been described in earlier chapters as a common precipitant to adolescent suicidal behavior and so it is, but it is of little value on its own. This can be said of most of the signs presented with the exception of a suicide threat, major depression (which is really many signs), substance abuse, or the giving away of prized possessions. Breaks in key peer relationships are a normal and even necessary part of adolescent development. Adolescence is a time wherein learning about how to make and keep relationships takes place. Trial and error attempts, with many trials and many errors, are to be expected as the adolescent essentially practices relationship making. Relationships, especially love relationships, are, therefore, forming, ending, and reforming all the time as teenagers evolve toward, hopefully, more stability and maturity in preparation for adulthood, marriage, and a family of their own. Nonetheless, breakups in greatly valued and relied upon adult or peer relationships are very painful to the adolescent who naturally does not view them as temporary or developmental. It can be the final unbearable loss to the vulnerable teenager who has perhaps already endured more than his or her share of losses. Teenagers, therefore, who are known to be depressed, vulnerable, overstressed, and undersupported need to be treated with the utmost care and vigilance when a significant loss appears in their lives.

Accurate knowledge about suicide is the first prerequisite to intelligent assessment and appropriate intervention. Research has indicated that knowledge about suicide is far from complete among the lay public (Ginzburg, 1971; Domino & Swain, 1985), the clergy (Domino, 1985; Swain & Domino, 1986), professional health care providers (Domino & Swain, 1986; McIntosh, Hubbard, & Santos, 1985; Swain & Domino, 1985), or college students (McIntosh et al., 1985). The research has further indicated that lack of accurate knowledge about the signs of suicide can affect attitudes in such a way as to impair one's ability to effectively assess or intervene.

Some of the more common myths and misconceptions have been addressed in the section on signs. However, a few more deserve attention. The *Network News,* a monthly newsletter devoted to the problems of adolescent runaways and suicides has compiled a list of commonly held misbeliefs about teenager suicide (March, 1986). A few items from their list will be commented on here:

1. *Nothing can be done to stop an adolescent from killing him/herself once he or she has* decided to commit suicide. It should be clear by now that few suicidal adolescents are 100 percent committed to death. Most are looking for a reason to live. Suicidal crises are usually rather brief. Much can and should be done to help the teenager through it. It may be the proof the person needs that he is cared about and that life is worth another chance.

2. *The adolescent who fails at suicide the first time will eventually succeed.* Though they are more likely to commit suicide at some point than a person who has not made a previous attempt, they are still unlikely to

eventually commit suicide. Their behavior usually has more to do with life than death. Only 1-2 percent of all survivors of suicide kill themselves within one year, only about 10 percent within ten years.

3. *Talking about suicide with depressed teens may prompt them to kill themselves.* On the contrary, talking about it is essential both for assessment and prevention. It shows you are willing to talk about their most frightening feelings. This often comes as a great, even life-saving, relief to them.

4. *There is a certain type of adolescent who commits suicide—usually from poor families or the mentally ill.* Psychosis and poverty are infrequent conditions from which adolescent suicides arise. Adolescents who become suicidal come from all kinds of backgrounds and can even appear quite normal. Profound unhappiness will be present, but usually not mental illness in the sense of severe personality, developmental, or schizophrenic disorders.

5. *People seeing a psychiatrist (psychologist, counselor) rarely commit suicide.* Unfortunately, this is not true. Therapy cannot always prevent suicide. Too much can happen to the suicidal adolescent outside of therapy that is beyond the control of the therapist. The adolescent's history cannot be changed by therapy and some are unable to use therapy effectively. Therapists have their limitations and make their mistakes too. People should not feel that "everything is taken care of" just because the suicidal adolescent has entered therapy. Therapy is only one part of what needs to be a multi-component intervention.

6. *Assessing suicidal risk is something best left to mental health professionals.* Since we do not have mental health professionals with training in suicide in every school, home, and on every street corner, we cannot leave the job entirely up to them. It is a job we all have and one which must fall as well to the parents, peers, and teachers of adolescents. Most adolescents who become suicidal are not in counseling and are virtually unknown to any mental health professional, so there is no one but the nonprofessional available to assess suicidality. The need for education in this regard, therefore, is quite essential.

I cannot leave this section without attempting to debunk what I feel to be two final myths that personally annoy me. They involve the purported effect of rock music and the nuclear threat on adolescent suicide. In my view, their combined effect is somewhere between practically none and none. In my experience and from all I have read and learned, the problems of suicidal adolescents are experienced as immediate and concrete. They are concerned with the problems of daily existence. They do not look beyond the parameters of their tangible, highly personal, felt existence. Abstract threats of world annihilation are of little interest or meaning. Existential issues concerning the value and meaning of life in a nuclear world are really much too far away and impersonal to have much effect, certainly on the adolescents I have known. They deny or ignore the atomic peril as readily as they do the chances of them becoming drug addicted or pregnant, believing that since it has not happened, it will not happen.

Rock music is now being blamed for adolescent suicide in a laughably simplistic effort on the part of some adults to blame a highly complex problem on a single external source. Also involved, I feel, is an effort to put the blame on the teenager since, after all, it is *his* music. Recently, an Indio, California man filed suit against rock singer Ozzy Osbourne and CBS Records, in the aftermath of the 1984 suicide death of his 19-year-old son. The father alleged that his son, John, was influenced to commit suicide by Ozzy's music, of which he listened to a great deal, and in particular a song entitled *Suicide Solution.* Looking past the boy's musical tastes, however, we see a picture with greater depth. John had been described as a quiet loner, who dropped out of school during the ninth grade, and had been arrested for drunken driving. His interest in heavy metal music may have been the center of an otherwise solitary life. It is unlikely that rock music created this void. Rather, it seems to have filled it, though obviously very incompletely. Art as a reflection of life will mirror all aspects of it including suicide. Literature offers far more examples of "suicide solutions" than does the brief history of rock music. *Romeo and Juliet* is one example. It is true that adolescents spend a great deal of time with rock music and are impressed with its lyrics. However, as with exposure to publicized accounts of suicide, only a very vulnerable few will find the suggestion of suicide so personally meaningful and compelling as to precipitate a suicidal act of their own. Even the death of a friend by suicide does not cause all of the friends to commit suicide. Neither can a song or story of suicide have such an effect. There are thousands of songs published and played each year in popular music. Very, very few deal with suicide. Ozzy Osbourne is not a major star and the song in question was and is not a big seller. What made this song stand out so boldly for John (if in fact it even did) was the personal relevance he gave it to his life. Kessler and Stipp (1984) have demonstrated in their research that fictional or hypothetical stories of suicide have no effect on suicide rates by way of an imitation effect. It is worse than a waste of time to look at rock music as the culprit. It is dangerously misleading since it causes us to ignore the more critical issues leading to adolescent suicide.

In concluding this section I must summarize by saying that while knowledge of suicide and its signs is an obvious essential, it does not guarantee unmitigated success. We will all be fooled, as I have, more than once. Regardless of the level of our expertise, we can never attain anything near to perfection in the assessment of suicide. The imprecision of our science shows, perhaps, most clearly here.

REFERRAL

Assessment is difficult. Referral can be even more so. Referral is, of course, a by-product and extension of the assessment process and is influenced by, not only the conclusions reached about the status of the adolescent, but by adult beliefs and attitudes about adolescents and their suicidal behavior. Research has shown that adults often fail to appreciate the magnitude or legitimacy of the psychological emergency inherent in adolescent suicidal behavior. Ignorance or feelings of hostility and avoidance engendered by an adolescent's suicide attempt will greatly affect the postassessment management of suicidal adolescents. Some teenagers will not even be referred for psychological services. It is not enough, however, to simply refer. Research has shown (see Chapter 5) that the mental health system has failed to successfully engage a significant percentage of adolescent suicide attempters. Many fail to show for initial appointments. Many others terminate prematurely. While accepting the observation of many that adolescents as a group are difficult to engage in out-patient therapy when they have not referred themselves, it nonetheless, is of great concern that adolescent suicide attempters, often acting out, at least in part, a desire for help and caring, are so often underserved by those whose role it is to respond to such legitimate needs.

The problem of referral can begin with the message of unacceptance and disapproval that the adolescent attempter may receive from adults who have been made aware of their suicide attempt. Referrals from adults responding in this way are unlikely to be trusted or accepted by the adolescent. They are not apt to be viewed as expressions of caring and concern. It will probably be supposed that the adult professional to whom they are being referred may share the attitudes of the referring adult. In believing this the adolescent might not be guilty of overgeneralization.

Effective referral then, begins with a caring appreciation of the adolescent's condition and an attempt to understand and take seriously their needs. While it is true that their method of expression needs not to be encouraged, nonetheless, it needs to be accepted for what it represents.

Referral needs to be handled carefully so as not to imply rejection, scorn, or the insinuation that the adolescent is bizarre or insane. This can sometimes be a very delicate matter when the adult who is referring is one to whom the adolescent has come willingly to report his or her thoughts or behavior; or is otherwise a trusted and important support person, parent, teacher, family physician, or other. In cases such as these the adolescent may expect this individual to be the one to care for them and alone respond to their enormous needs. A referral to another by such an adult can come as a shock to the expectant teenager.

Referrals of this type might be handled by expressing to the adolescent concern and continued availability while being careful not to extend of oneself more than one can actually provide. After hearing from the adolescents as much as possible about their feelings and thoughts about their life and their attempt, the referring person should urge him/her to seek professional help beyond what he can provide. The critical point is to convey the message that this help is *beyond* rather than *instead of* what the referrer can provide. The referral needs to be expressed as an acknowledgment of the legitimacy of the adolescent's problems and the opening of a new door toward increased support, while retaining older, trusted others.

It may be necessary at times for someone to accompany the adolescent to his or her first session. Familiarity is of great importance to any adolescent and a familiar person can provide a critical link to the unfamiliar therapist. This familiar person will often need to be someone other than a parent. It may even need to be someone who is not an adult. Often in my work I have had suicidal adolescents brought to me by their friends without whom they would not have come. The availability of competent school-based counseling services is probably the best vehicle for offering and providing services to high school age adolescents. Self-referral and word of mouth peer referral is then possible in the same way that adults seek health services. Once safely inside the therapist's office, however, a host of other complex problems arise.

9

Treatment

A great deal has been written about counseling strategies with adolescents. I will restrict my comments to those that have particular relevance to the adolescent engaging in suicidal behavior, to those dynamics most typically present in these individuals, and their impact upon the process of counseling. These need to be considered, of course, within the broader context of therapeutic principles, differing schools of thought, and varied methods of implementation. I will be writing with the idea of an individual therapy modality in mind.

It is always imperative for therapists to have a high level of self-awareness and vigilance against destructive countertransference. Countertransference refers to attitudes and feelings that the therapist holds toward the client. In working with the suicidal client, given the stakes and the typically very high level of sensitivity on their part toward any suggestion of disinterest or rejection, it is of particular importance that therapists be attuned to their own attitudes toward the client and aware of and in control of the feelings that are likely to be provoked by the implicit threat of suicide. Therapists need to be on guard against their own feelings of anxiety which may cause unbearable feelings of insecurity within the client. Suicide is a form of rejecting behavior. Therapists may feel threatened by feelings of failure as clinicians should their clients attempt suicide while in treatment. Farberow (1970) points out that one of the most important issues in dealing with a suicidal client is "the willingness and the ability to undergo the emotional strain during the period of suicidal crisis" (p. 427). However, clinicians need not to appear intimidated by the client and must accept that they are not solely responsible for the life of the client. Clients themselves bear ultimate responsibility and deal daily with forces beyond the control of the therapist, and with a history that cannot be changed.

Avoidance, withdrawal, and denial, as well as anxiety, are all normal reactions to the fact or threat of suicidal behavior. These are responses that the therapist is not permitted the luxury to indulge. Such reactions present not only a danger to the continuation of therapy, but of course, to the client as well. These reactions are constantly struggled with. If therapists are feeling manipulated by clients, or overwhelmed by feelings of responsibility, or threatened by the level of depression and sense of hopelessness evident within clients, they are at risk for responding in ways that will appear to the clients as rejecting, uncaring behavior.

Denial is a particularly strong form of avoidance in that it negates the plight of the suicidal individual by actively failing to acknowledge it. Suicidal tendencies in young people may be especially potent in provoking denial on the part of adult clinicians who either fail to take adolescents seriously enough or who, for personal reasons, simply cannot cope with the idea of death at a young age.

Naturally, problems in these areas present a serious challenge to the development of a trusting therapeutic relationship. However obvious these dangers may seem, they are nonetheless very difficult for the clinician to cope with alone. For this reason it is essential that therapists working with suicidal clients have available to them sources of professional supervision and support. Further, they should guard against overburdening themselves with more than a very few highly suicidal clients at any one time. Shneidman (1981) recommends seeing no more than one or two highly lethal clients at a time.

Clinicians need to humbly acknowledge their finite capacity for maintaining their clients alone. They should develop an awareness of their client's environment for other possible services and sources of support. Even if the family is not in therapy with the client, members of the nuclear and extended family or friends may be utilized to serve the goals of therapy and the well-being of the client. Services within the adolescent's school should always be considered if the teenager is still attending. Special education services and in-school counseling may be needed. The school can be assisted in productively coping with possible problems of truancy, failing grades, or behavior troubles in a way that allows the school to be part of the solution, rather than part of the adolescent's problem.

These comments provide a basis upon which therapist readiness should rest in preparation for the suicidal client. The therapist needs to be emotionally and intellectually ready for the formidable challenge these people present. It is difficult and dangerous to attempt to learn or adjust on the run, though we all find ourselves in that position from time to time.

There is some convergence of the psychology of suicide and the psychology of adolescence. What Tabachnick (1981) has called the "interlocking psychologies of suicide and adolescence" help to form a basis from which much of our understanding of common psychotherapeutic issues will flow. Features of suicidality that also predominate within the developmental struggle of adolescence include object loss, loneliness and alienation, hopelessness and helplessness. An understanding of the suicidal adolescent cannot be gained without a thorough knowledge and appreciation of the nature of adolescence.

Object loss for the adolescent means the leaving behind of old supports (typically parental) and the taking on of new responsibilities and relationships. This transition is accompanied by terror for some adolescents. Those who have jumped or been pushed too early away from faulty or unstable support systems stand in greatest jeopardy of failing to negotiate this developmental transition successfully. For those who become suicidal, object loss often includes, as well, the more complete or actual loss of one or more parental figures, self-esteem, a feeling of goodness, competence, health, and general well being. No new supports have appeared to effectively fill the void. Loss then is an essential feature of both adolescent development and suicide, though one that has been exacerbated within the experience of the suicidal adolescent.

Loneliness and alienation are often experienced by humans first and most intensely during adolescence, at a time when they have come to rely (or at least think they do) so thoroughly on external sources of support, validation, identity, and self-esteem. Older familial attachments have been discarded. Tabachnick speaks of a prevalence of adolescent dreams bearing images and themes of being "at sea" or "deserted." The suicidal adolescent has come to believe more fervently that his or her alienation is chronic and likely to remain so, contributing to feelings of hopelessness and helplessness.

Much adolescent hopelessness and helplessness has to do with distorted time sense as well as the relative novelty of experiencing difficulty in achieving or maintaining a level of adequacy related to sexuality, work, and interpersonal relationships. Life's problems suddenly are multitudinous. The unavailability (and eschewing) of parental support leaves adolescents often feeling helpless to cope with it all. Again suicidal adolescents, with more than their fair share of problems to deal with will experience feelings of helplessness more intensely than most.

Within the therapeutic setting and relationship, these issues and others will present themselves in a variety of forms. The manner in which they often manifest themselves and some guidelines for psychotherapeutic management are the central focus of this chapter.

COMMON THERAPEUTIC ISSUES

Therapist Activity vs. Passivity

A longstanding and widely held opinion states that therapists working with suicidal clients must put aside passive, nonintrusive attitudes and adopt a much more active role (Bellak, 1981; Farberow, 1970; Millen & Roll, 1985). It is a rule of thumb, in early sessions with adolescents, suicidal or otherwise, that the therapist not be too passive. Few adolescents will be prepared for a very passive orientation. Such an experience is likely to produce intolerable feelings of anxiety, and threaten continued treatment. With a suicidal adolescent, it threatens to imply a lack of concern, or even therapist helplessness, in the face of the teenager's problems. The therapist needs to take control of the initial sessions, to structure them and explore the reasons for the adolescent being there in the first place, and to find some common ground for continued work. Suicidal adolescents feel out of control, overwhelmed, out of touch. Active intervention strikes straight to the heart of these conditions and is an absolute necessity in promoting a feeling of faith, optimism, and confidence within the client toward therapy and the therapist. With the suicidal adolescent, it will further be necessary to make a special effort to be warm, extending, and befriending, within the bounds of a professional role, while taking the greatest care not to seem condescending or judgmental in a way that the adolescent has come to expect.

Object Loss and the Conflict over Dependency Needs

Replacement of the lost object as a therapeutic goal is a principle of treating the suicidal adolescent. Many suicidal adolescents will struggle with strong needs for attachment fueled by unmet and powerful dependency needs and a tendency toward regression under stress. However, their status as adolescents may present conflict, aversion, and fear of these tendencies that can act against the development of an effective therapeutic relationship. Teenagers have a corresponding and conflicting need to be strong and independent. The clinician needs to walk the middle ground between fostering an unhealthy and possibly frightening degree of dependency in the client, while avoiding seeming too aloof, distant, and inaccessible. This task is made difficult by the need on the part of therapists to extend themselves more to suicidal adolescents than to nonsuicidal clients and the opposing threat of feeling too involved and too responsible. The client and therapist are both best served by the maintenance of a relationship that is accessible and caring, while not becoming controlling, either by the client or the therapist.

Regardless of the best efforts of good therapists, it will not be possible to maintain all adolescents in a close therapeutic relationship. The very closeness of it, while attracting and helping many, will ultimately drive some others away. Failure is inevitable a certain percentage of the time. A case in point from my own experience involves a 16-year-old girl with whom I had begun to work during the spring of her ninth grade year. The age/grade discrepancy is noteworthy in that she had been a chronic truant since the age of 13 and had been retained in both grades 8 and 9. Charlene was referred to me while she was still 15-years-old for evaluation and counseling by order of the Juvenile Court. Failure to comply with the court's order to attend school would have resulted in placement in a residential facility for delinquent girls. Initially, then, Charlene's attendance in both school and counseling sessions was under extreme duress. Rather quickly, however, she began to express a sincere wish to "make something" of herself, to finish school, to get out of the rut of regular drug use and aimlessness that had not only been the pattern of her life for several years, but that of her family for many more years than that. She reported rages, which she did not understand and could not control, feelings of depression that welled up within her without apparent provocation and led her to acts of suicidal recklessness.

Therapy continued through the summer with the relationship eventually becoming very close as Charlene formed a strong attachment both to me and the counseling process. She would go to extraordinary lengths to attend sessions, even coming to my office at her school to see me for scheduled appointments on days when she was cutting school or had been suspended.

Charlene was very frightened at the prospect of becoming like the rest of her family, dissolute individuals, living a chaotic, disorganized life-style unable to effectively maintain themselves independently in society. She viewed them as "bums," "losers." On the other hand she saw much of her family's history and influence in herself. She interpreted her difficulty in attending school, turning down drugs, and her inability to separate from an older, dominating boyfriend as evidence of a weakness in character that was identical to that which she abhorred in her family. Staying in school, she felt, would make her different. Neither her father, mother, or older brother had finished school. Staying in school was impossible in her view, however, without me, therapy, and the support it provided for her.

Staying in school, as it turned out by the fall, would be impossible without a specialized, alternative high school program offering a great deal of structure, supervision, individualized curriculum, and small group instruction, as well as ongoing counseling. At her request (she beat us to it in terms of ascertaining her need for it) she was placed in this program in late October. Her counseling continued and, if anything, seemed to intensify with revelations of a highly abusive (physically, and perhaps sexually) childhood. She wrote me a deeply emotional and moving letter thanking me for helping her to stay in school and for listening to her and caring about her. This was to be my last real communication from her. I never saw her in counseling again. Though she remained in school for the rest of the school year, she kept no further appointments and strenuously resisted efforts on my part to re-engage her. She never explained why she terminated, leaving me, initially, angry and bewildered, but more than anything, incredibly frustrated. I was convinced I could help this person and could help to make a real difference in her life. Further, she had seemed much more than willing to do her part in that work when suddenly the bottom dropped out of it. She herself dropped out of school at the end of that year, allegedly pregnant and quite possibly into an early marriage to the young man whom she had hoped desperately to leave. At any rate, her prospects of living a life much different than her mother's appeared slim.

I can never be sure, of course, without corroboration from Charlene, why she left therapy, but I suspect she feared she had come to need me too much. Her dependence on me had become dangerous and painful and to her, perhaps, more frustrating than my feelings about her leaving. As she came to need me more and more, in part as a way to separate herself from family and past supports, she came to see me as dangerously and painfully limited. I could not be all she hoped. I could not be a new father or new boyfriend. I could not be with her all the time. I, as the ground beneath her feet, may have begun to look terrifyingly amorphous and unreal in comparison to what she wanted. This may have made her feel unbearably alone and helpless. Perhaps then out of frustration and fear she jumped away and back to the solidity of older more familiar ground.

Sensitivity to Rejection or Separation

Suicidal adolescents, due to their histories, are typically hyper-vigilant to signs of rejection, lack of caring, and imminent abandonment on the part of others. For these reasons, therapists need to be aware of the effect episodes of their own personal preoccupation, distraction, or depression may have on their clients. Teenagers may exhibit dramatic fluctuations in mood that are directly related to their estimation of the success they are having in their relationship with the therapist. These will be very difficult to understand or interpret unless therapists are aware of their own possible role in producing them. Therapists will need to pay particular attention to their own punctuality and to be true to their word. Perfection will, of course, be impossible.

Inadvertent insensitivity and misunderstanding on the part of the therapist will occur. When they do, they may precipitate a crisis in therapy. However, rather than creating delay or serious disruption, they can be used as experiences that may help clients to learn something of their own sensitivities, and that, rather than proof of a lack of caring, misunderstandings and errors are a normal part of even the best of relationships.

Ambivalence

The dynamics are, of course, the same as with "conflict over dependency needs." However, the description to follow presents a distinctive manifestation that can severely test the patience and understanding of any therapist. Suicidal adolescents are ambivalent toward the world, toward living, toward people and relationships in general, and toward therapy and the therapist, as well. These clients often behave in an approach/avoidance manner toward life, in general, and people, in particular, displaying their conflicted nature and demonstrating their limited ability to enter fully into relationships that might provide for their needs. These individuals often need to be "chased." Therapists will need to extend themselves a great deal to these clients as proof of their caring. An example from my own practice comes to mind. She was a suicidal 17-year-old girl whom I first met through the process of a psychological evaluation that her school asked me to conduct. I will refer to her as Sheila. Sheila's ambivalence became immediately apparent from her opening comment that "you won't learn anything from me," and her subsequent disclosure of far more personal history and affect than is generally expected during a first session. When testing had been completed it was clear that the girl needed therapy. I discussed this with her and offered to see her myself since it was obvious she had valued her time with me during testing. She vacillated a great deal, denying she needed it, fearful of her family's attitude toward it and appearing most reluctant. Finally, she agreed, asking if she could see me every day!

Early sessions saw her evidencing great difficulty tolerating an entire session. She tended to arrive late and sought to leave early. It could take her some time even to sit down. However, she always came and it seemed very important to her that I encourage her to get the most out of her time by coming on time and staying. Limit setting was necessary, but caused her to turn things on their head and perceive it as rejecting behavior. Though I would assure her that, in fact, the opposite was true, she continued to need to act out her uncertainty. One day, in particular, stands out. Sheila was having trouble making one of her biweekly appointments and I had suggested changing it to another time. She was unwilling to either change it or confirm that she would keep it on this particular day. At that I simply said, "Well, I'll be here waiting." And so I was, with open door, at the appointed hour, when I noted an eye peeking at me through a crack in an outer door. It was Sheila, checking to see if, indeed, I would wait for her. Sheila's ambivalence continues to manifest itself in her interpersonal relationships, though to a greatly diminished degree in therapy, after eight months. As she began to develop a sense of trust in the relationship and a faith in the benign and genuine quality of the caring implicit in it, she allowed herself to approach it with a minimum of avoidance and ambivalence. My persistence with this client was motivated by the firm belief that her apparent avoidance and efforts to "play hard to get" needed to be worn down. Though she often appeared amused at my efforts, she clearly appreciated it.

Low Self-esteem

Feelings of low self-esteem, typically years in the making and continually reinforced and fortified by familial patterns and faulty reality testing, constitute a most difficult challenge to the therapist. Breaking down the client's negative beliefs about him or herself is one of the most problematic aspects of the treatment of the suicidal individual. The therapist must begin by accepting the clients' view of themselves and exploring its origins and sources of sustenance. When these systems are well understood, it is important for the therapist to challenge the clients' negative beliefs and expose to them the role their own internal negative self-statements play in the maintenance of their low self-esteem. Clients will need help in accurately perceiving their own attributes and assessing the positive attitudes others have toward them. Naturally, the therapeutic relationship itself, through the transference which develops, will serve as grist as well. It is of perpetual interest to me how some adolescents, who unceasingly castigate their parents for what they feel is their ignorance, unfairness, and utter incompetence, who consider them to be wrong about virtually everything, will nonetheless, agree with them entirely on the matter of their own worth. This inconsistency of thought is not apparent to most adolescents who are engaged in it. In cases where parental attitudes have played a major role in the etiology and maintenance of the suicidal adolescents' low self-esteem, it is useful to hold up to the adolescents the dichotomy in their beliefs. I will often say to such a teenager, "You seem to feel that your parents are wrong about everything, yet you appear to agree with everything they say about you. How can that be?"

Aggression

Amidst the obvious depression, low self-esteem, ambivalence, and neediness of many suicidal adolescents, there exists powerful aggressive com-

ponents that are sometimes undervalued. These are often very angry individuals whose anger is played out predominately or, at least cyclically, upon
themselves. Further, the client's anger when expressed externally is most
likely to be directed at persons who either, in the present or the past, have
been in a position to provide for his or her needs. Through transference
this may include the therapist. While expression of anger and hostility in
therapy may be initially very frightening to adolescents, given their experience with adult responses in the past, it needs to be accepted as safe
expression of legitimate feelings. Most writers feel that it is a positive sign
in therapy and an important element in the process of reducing the amount
of inner directed aggression (Birtchnell, 1983; Mayer, 1971; Richman, 1979).
It is essential that the adolescent learn to express anger toward others,
perhaps initially to the therapist, and later when it is manageable and can be
appropriately expressed, toward significant others.

Hopelessness

Suicidal adolescents experience a depth of despair and hopelessness that may
appear shocking and even ridiculous to the unprepared adult. It is difficult
not to view the problems of the suicidal adolescent as simply exaggerated
problems of a normal adolescence, that will pass in time. However, these
adolescents seem to have lost faith in time. In a temporal sense they feel
stuck and imprisoned in an age they cannot bear, thus, their despair. They
feel that they will be 15 forever. They have no hopefulness for a future that
they find hard to believe will ever come and certainly not soon enough. It
is important to realize that our temporal sense is very different from theirs.
To us, adult time (alas) passes much more quickly. Further we know
adolescence ends. They do not. It is, therefore, imperative that the therapist
not rush in to try to cheer the adolescent up. To do so is to negate important
feelings. One must guard against impatience. The therapist needs to accept
and stay with the hopelessness, thereby conveying to adolescents that their
feelings are acknowledged and, therefore, they are not alone. It is a helpful
device to help the client to be more aware of passing time and changing
conditions that are positive. This can be done in a variety of ways including
reviewing together, old therapy notes, drawings, letters or diary notations
by the client. Objective evidence of change should be sought. Engendering
a belief in even slight movement and change can be enough to dislodge the
adolescent who is stuck in time and despair.

Constriction

Constriction refers to the narrowing of intellectual focus that occurs in the
individual who has come to believe that only two solutions are possible to a

problem, the idealized, hoped for one, and death. Typically, a high level of perturbation is responsible for this unrealistic narrowing of focus. Once therapists are able to calm the client down with energetic offers of support and alliance, they need to pry open the client's restricted view of possibilities and broaden the scope of potential solutions. Group support is often very helpful in this regard, especially if the group consists of other adolescents who have experience with suicidal behavior. Ultimately, the therapist needs to move the client well away from the choice of death as a reasonable solution by actively exploring the merits of other alternatives. The tendency on the part of many suicidal adolescents to set themselves up for failure in problem solving by seeking unattainable goals and unworkable solutions will need to be explored by the therapist.

Separation and Termination

Any separation between the suicidal adolescent client and the therapist is an enormously important event for the teenager and must be handled with great care and sensitivity.

> The cardinal rule of all therapy with suicidal persons is that separation is to be handled sensitively and with a sense of timing. Separation, in fact, is the major precipitant for seriously suicidal behavior, owing to the suicidal person's intolerance of separation with its subjective finality and association with death. (Richman, 1979, p. 137)

Vacations, then, are to be given a good deal of thought and preparation as regards the therapy. Cancelled appointments by therapists need to be strenuously avoided and, when unavoidable, rescheduled during the same week. Therapists should expect acting out behavior, regression, and a resurfacing of old issues prior to separations and a cool reserve upon return. Clients may retaliate by missing an appointment after the therapist's vacation. Clients should always be called to inquire as to their welfare when such an appointment is missed. Lengthy vacations may require that the therapist send a card to the client as an indication that they still exist and have not forgotten them.

Separations and termination between therapist and client are, of course, not the only meaningful interruptions and endings in the interpersonal worlds of our clients. Separations and terminations elsewhere in their lives need to be paid close attention and heeded. The therapist must note and remember the constellation of important peer, adult, and family relationships and supports that exist for the adolescent and anticipate regression and perhaps increased suicidality if a break in an important relationship occurs. Separations as normal and routine as those that take place when school ends and summertime dispersal of friends to various family vacation homes commences, are experienced by some adolescents as exceedingly painful losses in a way that is often hard for adults to understand or anticipate.

The issue of separation in a different form relates to manifestly pathological and destructive relationships (usually boyfriend/girlfriend, or parent/ adolescent) with which the adolescent may be involved. Separating the suicidal adolescent from such relationships, when the emotional entanglement is strong, is a dangerous and risky undertaking. Except in situations where there exists in the judgment of the therapist a clear and imminent danger to the life of the adolescent or in cases of incest, to act precipitously is to court disaster. The therapist must, in most cases, work gradually in helping adolescents to separate on their own, for their own reasons, enabling them to both take responsibility and credit, if credit be due, for themselves.

Termination must, of course, be treated with at least equal care and will often draw the same client response as separation. Ambivalence on the part of both the client and therapist must be understood and dealt with. Adolescents may attempt to control the therapist with a recurrence of suicidal talk or acts. Therapists need to be sure of themselves at termination and in control. Many clients will need to be weaned away from therapy with bimonthly or monthly sessions. Therapists need to align themselves with the growth forces within the adolescent and convey the idea that termination is evidence of growth and that this is valued for the client's sake. Finally, termination need never be permanent. The adolescent may be encouraged to write or schedule another visit in the future. The impression should never be given that the door is closed forever.

SPECIAL ISSUES

Confidentiality

The assurance of confidentiality is a prerequisite and basic tenet of effective counseling. However, there are few, if any, absolutes in this universe and confidentiality is not one of them. Therapists, by acts of omission or commission must never knowingly ally themselves with death or in any way allow themselves to become a partner in a suicidal act. Though some may say that every individual has a right to take his or her own life, this must never be actively supported by therapists. In dealing with adolescents, who are minors and, therefore, the responsibility of adults, an extra burden exists. If in the judgment of the therapist the adolescent client intends to seriously and perhaps fatally harm him or herself, the therapist must act to prevent it or become ethically and even legally responsible. The therapist needs to make the client fully aware of this at the time and equally aware of the motivations for such an intervention. Therapists must attempt to make clear that their intentions are vested in a strong desire to serve the welfare of the client and, even if proved wrong, their acts stand as a gesture of sincere caring and concern and as an acknowledgment of the fact that responsibility for the life and maintenance of the adolescent client needs to be shared by other responsible adults beyond the therapist. Parents or primary caretakers need to be notified. Hospitalization may need to be discussed and recommended.

It is common for teenagers to react, at least initially, with anger and fear at the suggestion that their parents be notified of their suicidal intent. They will feel betrayed and attempt to pressure and cajole therapists to change their minds about informing the parents or their assessment of suicide risk. It is sometimes a very tough spot for therapists to be in, especially when the adolescent gives them some legitimate reason to believe that the parents are likely to react in such a way as to make matters even worse. However, if therapists continue to believe that a significant suicidal risk is present (they do not have to prove it, just think it), the parents or care-takers must be given the opportunity to share the responsibility. It will be up to the therapist to inform the parents in such a way as to also prepare them to respond to their son or daughter in an appropriate and helpful manner. Hopefully, this communication will take place within the context of a good trusting working relationship between the parents and their child's therapist.

Despite initial reactions, if the therapeutic relationship is a good one, most adolescents will be very appreciative of the therapists' efforts and see them as sincere efforts to help. Responsiveness to the apparent threat of suicidal acts can defuse a potentially lethal situation. To not respond to the threat of suicide is to leave the client with a latent and potentially destructive message.

Anniversaries

Key dates in the lives of our adolescent clients must be recorded and remembered, since they can exert as powerful an impact on their feelings and level of suicidality as can holidays. Holidays have long been recognized as times of increased suicide risk for suicidal individuals. Key dates may include the dates of past traumas, losses, or a previous suicide attempt. Aggression and a resurfacing of feelings and conflicts associated with these events may emerge on or near the anniversary of these important experiences. Anniversaries also provide the therapist and client opportunities to rework and more fully integrate important issues and to review changes in the adolescent's status.

Use of the Telephone

Some therapists feel that it is necessary with a suicidal client to offer one's home number to be used in time of crisis or emergency. In my practice, I give my home phone number to adolescents whom I judge to be suicidal and in need of both the offering and use of that means of reaching me. It has never, in my personal experience, been abused. However, telephone use may become a complex and potentially problematic component in the therapy. Hankoff and Einsider (1979) offer a well thought out commentary and guide on this issue. Obviously, phone availability can lead to intrusiveness and subsequent guilt on the part of the client, manifestations of unhealthy dependency strivings, unrealistic expectations and demands, competition with the therapist's family for the therapist's time and attention, expression of hostility, and aggression. Therapists must first confront their own counter-transference reactions and their impact on their ability to function in therapy. Therapists must also confront clients with their provocative behavior and help them to deal with and explore those feelings that led to the phone calls and the sense of guilt that might, therefore, be aroused. Ultimately, therapists need to define for themselves and their clients the legitimate limits of therapeutic responsibility and of relationships in general.

Family Involvement in the Treatment of the Suicidal Adolescent

Opinions will vary widely as to who should be treated when an adolescent is deemed suicidal and needing of clinical intervention. Modalities will, of course, range from family therapy to individual therapy for the adolescent, with combinations of the two in between. Determining factors will as often be found in the theoretical prejudices, training, and preference of the therapist as much as in the apparent needs of the client. There is clearly no right or wrong modality. Rigid doctrinaire adherence to any one modality is greatly limiting of the therapist. Worse, it can exclude certain potential clients from treatment. Agencies that refuse to see any adolescent without cotherapy for the parents do some adolescents a terrible disservice in the service of their own (agency) needs. A far more critical issue is the competence and appeal of the therapist. However, certain client-centered determinants must be considered. First must be an assessment of the family's ability to enter into, make use of, and support therapy. While it is accepted that the family is often the major component in the development of the problem of suicidality in their adolescent son or daughter, it must be recognized that they may not always be able to become part of the solution. Further, issues of separation or other family dynamics may preclude an adolescent's acceptance of treatment if offered only a family therapy model. Adolescents often insist on individual therapy, at least at first. Initially, client-preference needs to be the major influence on the treatment plan. First and foremost, the adolescent needs to be engaged; and later the family, or those parts of it who are willing and able, may be incorporated into the therapy either on a regular or irregular basis.

Ideally, full and committed family involvement offers the best hope of success whether through family sessions or a combination of family and individual therapy. However, when working with seriously disturbed adolescents and families, circumstances are often less than ideal. For some adolescents, eventual removal from, rather than efforts at reconciliation with, their families may ultimately prove to be in their best interests.

Group Counseling

It has been offered by Slavson (1964) and Yalom (1975) that inclusion of suicidal persons in therapy groups is a risky and discouraged undertaking. Suicidal people were felt to pose a threat to the stability of the individuals in the group and the group as a whole. Pressures of responsibility and guilt, relative to the threat or actuality of suicide attempts among group members were felt to have a debilitating effect on group functioning. Others (Asimos, 1979; Billings, Rosen, Asimos, & Motto, 1974; Farberow, 1972; and Frey, Motto, & Ritholz, 1983), have reported on group process as an effective treatment method for persons at risk for suicide. Further, the social support networks that can be developed through group work have been found to have a positive and health producing effect on suicidal individuals (Antonovsky, 1979; Berkman, 1977; Cobb, 1976; Kaplan, Cassel, & Gore, 1977). However, it is acknowledged that the state of research in this area is as yet poorly developed (Frey et al., 1983). No studies could be found that deal exclusively with groups for adolescent suicide attempters.

Peer Group Counseling

A model that has yet to find its way into the literature and that has received virtually no research attention is one specially adapted for adolescents and which includes critical components of group counseling strategies with adult suicidals.

Research on attitudes toward suicidal behavior is rather emphatic in reporting negative attitudes toward suicidal attempters, particularly when the attempter is young and the attempt appears to be of low lethality and dubious intent. Mental health professionals are not excluded from these findings that suggest feelings of reduced sympathy and readiness to help these individuals (see Chapter 5). Among the various professional and age groups studied for attitudes toward suicidal behavior, only adolescent suicide attempters have been found to hold even mildly positive attitudes toward adolescents who make suicide attempts (Curran, 1984; Limbacher & Domino, 1986). These findings suggest a treatment model which may offer teenage suicide attempters a more supportive and productive postattempt experience than is often extended to them. Peer counseling, in the form of professionally led groups of teenage suicide attempters may be a modality offering a high likelihood of providing the attempter with the support, "help and attention" they often seek, while at the same time dealing with some of the issues underlying the behavior. These groups should also serve to educate the participants as to the attitudes the human environment has toward suicidal behavior and teach coping and communication strategies that are more appropriate and satisfying than the generally very counterproductive suicide attempt. Teenage suicide attempters would be referred to these ongoing, though time-limited groups (say 10 weeks), by parents, police, emergency room personnel, school officials, or whoever may have detected the attempt and is able to facilitate the referral. All attempters should be referred. The group would most likely meet in community mental health centers, schools, or other appropriate settings. Parents and family members would be strongly encouraged to attend concurrent counseling sessions. Finally, the group and the agency with which it affiliates would be in a position to provide crisis management and maintenance both during the 10 week program and after if the person is not by then in some form of individual or family therapy.

The primary intent of such a program would not necessarily be to provide psychotherapy, but rather to make available immediate support and education in the hopes of preventing the attempter from becoming a chronic attempter and ultimately to keep all of them alive.The essential lesson involves the abandonment of suicidal behavior as a means of expression. Peer counseling, by a group that is likely to hold positive attitudes, especially toward first-time attempters, might prove to be an effective short-term treatment modality for the teenage suicide attempter who is otherwise considered among the more difficult and unwanted of clients.

In conclusion, it seems far more important that the suicidal adolescent be referred and treated with respect, empathy, and care than that a particular treatment modality be promulgated or promoted. Therapists working with adolescents must be prepared to extend of themselves, to be active, to accept emotional strain and intrusion into their own lives, and to be a person of central importance to very needy suicidal clients. As such, no therapist should take on more than a couple of highly suicidal clients. Adolescent clients can be exceedingly frustrating, maddening, wearing, and depressing; but there is probably no more exciting, appreciative or gratifying group with which to work.

CASE STUDIES

Following I present two case studies of adolescents with whom I have had extensive involvement as their therapist over many, many months. Both have been suicidal. Both engaged in suicidal behavior that was years in the making. In most other respects, however, they differ markedly. They are presented for the purpose of giving some sense of the problems that exist in the assessment and treatment of suicidality. They each provide a glimpse into the kinds of lives and the kinds of teenagers who become suicidal, while at the same time making clear the futility of thinking in terms of a suicidal adolescent type. They will all be quite different from one another. Finally, these cases will, hopefully, offer some documentation of the kind of openness, honesty, perseverance, and courage that is required of adolescents who seek to struggle against their self-destructive tendencies.

Case 1: Brenda S.

Brenda S. was 16 years old when I first met her in a therapeutic context. However, I had met her once before and I had known of her and her family for about a year. Brenda's younger sister, Terri, had been a client of mine during that time. At any rate, Brenda knew who I was and had been quite impressed with the positive changes that had taken place in her sister's previously very wild behavior since seeing me. She attributed the changes to the therapy. I was not terribly surprised then, when Brenda, who was at that time an 11th grader at a high school in which I sometimes worked, came to my office door one day in January, 1984, asking to speak to me. At first I thought it might have something to do with Terri, but one look at Brenda made it clear that she had her own problems at that point. She could be, when well rested and attentive to her appearance, quite an attractive girl. On this day, however, she appeared haggard and pale. Her hair was disheveled and might have been dirty. It was obvious she had been crying. She wore old, worn jeans, an equally old and worn jean jacket. She came in and sat, but was extremely anxious; she could not make eye contact and was initially unable to even formulate an explanation for her being there. Eventually, it came out that she had been to see a neurologist recently as a result of severe headaches. The physician was unwilling to prescribe any medication for her unless she was also in therapy. Brenda admitted feeling very angry about this. She had not been a fan of therapy, feeling that it had never done her mother (who had a long history of mental health problems that will be described) any good and though Terri had apparently been helped, therapy was not for her. Consequently she had waited for two weeks, suffered the continuing headaches, and now out of desperation she had decided to come to see me. However, by that point, she said, things had gotten much worse. She reported not being able to sleep or eat properly, nor concentrate or attend school. She described a rather violent relationship with a boyfriend who sounded pretty disturbed. She appeared very confused, even disoriented and as mentioned before extremely anxious. She cried off and on throughout our talk. She spoke repeatedly of suicide and a strong desire to escape. To make matters worse, Brenda was a diabetic and she was a heavy drinker, a fact she admitted in explaining how it was she coped with and treated her headaches and other problems. Finally, I knew enough about her family to know they would not be able to provide much help.

It seemed clear that counseling was no longer enough and I, knowing something of how she felt about mental health services gently asked her if she had considered or would consider a psychiatric hospitalization. I was much surprised and greatly relieved when she readily agreed. She was admitted that evening, but to a pediatrics unit since no beds were available in the psychiatric unit. Within 24 hours Brenda had stabilized and, as is so often the case with adolescents, she wanted out. Within a few days she got her wish. I began to see her on an out-patient basis that week. Through my relationship with Brenda, which was to last off and on for two years, I was to experience one of the most chaotic and trauma-filled lives I have yet encountered.

Brenda finds it hard to remember very much of her past. It is even more difficult for her to reconstruct it sequentially from early age. Much has been forgotten.

Brenda is the oldest of her mother's two children. There is a sister (Terri), three years younger. Brenda's parents appeared ill-prepared for marriage and parenthood, both of which they encountered before the age of 20. Mrs. S was admittedly overwhelmed by her maternal responsibilities and relied heavily on her own mother for support and parenting for herself and Brenda. Mr. S appears to have been only minimally involved. He worked long hours and seemed distant and restless in the marriage at that time. Matters did not improve with the passing years. Mrs. S began to experience debilitating bouts of depression. She felt uncared for. Mr. S appeared to want more and more to shake off the burdens of a needy wife and two needy children. They were divorced when Brenda was seven. Brenda remembers that her mother in anger and despair sometimes blamed her and her sister for her husband leaving them saying that their bad behavior drove him out. Two years later, unable to cope with worsening depression, Mrs. S made a series of increasingly serious suicide attempts, the last of which resulted in a four month psychiatric hospitalization. Brenda and her sister were sent to live with their father, his new wife, and their new baby.

Life with father is remembered more as life with stepmother. She is recalled as a harshly rejecting and depriving figure who, from the start, resented their presence in her home, as living symbols of her husband's first marriage. She seemed to demand an allegiance from Mr. S that included his rejection of his two daughters. Growing success in the sales field kept him away much of the time, solving his problem of allegiance quite nicely. Brenda, however, always felt that he had sided with the stepmother at the girls' expense. They were outcasts in this new home, in this new town. Brenda recalls episodes of severe neglect. She states that she and her sister were sometimes locked out of the house all day, their meals put outside on the porch. They felt hated and scorned during those years. Behavioral problems inevitably ensued. After four years with their father and stepmother, years that are recalled with anger and pain, Brenda and her sister returned to live with their mother who had since remarried. She had been in touch intermittently during those four years.

Brenda was now 14. Residences had changed but serious problems remained. Mrs. S had developed a serious drinking problem. Persisting depression, an abusive new husband, and the demands of again parenting two growing children placed her mental health status in continuing jeopardy. To her new husband, the children's return constituted an impediment to his relationship with his wife and their very active social life. Again, Brenda found herself living with a parent whose loyalties were being put to the test by a stepparent. Again, Brenda felt that she had lost, as it seemed her mother was compelled to give her attentions only to the stepfather.

Brenda, however, had found distractions from a chaotic family life in the teenage world of her new town. She plunged headlong into a drug and alcohol pervaded night life. She had complete freedom to come and go as she chose and for the most part she chose to go. She became a very active girl.

One year after Brenda and her sister returned, Mrs. S's second husband left her. Again Mrs. S's initial response was to blame her daughters, but especially, Terri, the younger one. Brenda, in fact, had gotten along rather well with the man. He used to buy beer for her. Mrs. S, at this point began to experience increasing difficulties with depression, anxiety, drinking, and the abuse of prescription Valium and barbituates. Most evenings were spent at area bars. Sometimes she would not return home at night. Brenda continued her own party life with gusto. She began a relationship with a boy that was to last two years.

In the Spring of 1983, Mrs. S had to be hospitalized psychiatrically for what she termed a "nervous breakdown." She remained hospitalized for eight weeks. It was during this time that I actually met Brenda for the first time.

She had asked to speak to me about Terri, but ended up talking about herself. Brenda felt confused and guilty over her reaction to her mother's hospitalization. She felt angry and unsympathetic toward her mother and did not understand why: "I'm a cold person, Terri is so much more caring." It was not her intention to pursue this any further, however, and I did not see her again until January, 1984.

In the months following Mrs. S's return from the hospital and subsequent intensive outpatient psychotherapy, home life and her psychological condition became increasingly stabilized. Mrs. S eventually took in a male friend (whom she later married) who provided her with much support and a steadying influence, without alienating either daughter. However, as family life normalized, greater restrictions and accountability were imposed upon Brenda. This she rebelled against mightily. During the ensuing 12 months she left home three times to live with friends. She had dropped out of school. At the same time, she wondered what was wrong with her that everyone in the family was doing so much better while she was doing so much worse. Her boyfriend, she felt, was her only support, her only constant. They were inseparable. She felt they were kindred spirits and that he was the only person who understood her. This relationship was, however, extremely self-destructive for both. Fights were bitter, breakups frequent, accusations and rejections constant.

It was with this backdrop and within this context that my work with Brenda began. Therapy proved to be very hard for Brenda. Intellectually she was more than capable. Further, she understood essentially, what was wrong with her, what she needed and what she needed to do about it. What she could not do, in the first several months of therapy, was face it. Instead, Brenda vacillated between approach and avoidance of key issues, critical and painful feelings and memories, and me. I often had the feeling with Brenda that she was floating in and out of contact with me. It was hard to feel close to her. I always had the sense that she was holding back a great deal, that she was sitting well back into herself, away from the visible exterior. She expressed her trepidation, her ambivalence during those days in comments such as, "I just can't get the words out that I want to say. I feel like I'm choking on them, but I know what they are." She could admit that she would try to deal with troubling thoughts and feelings by "just blocking it out." Sometimes blocking it out required intensive partying with drugs and alcohol. She also understood that she was denying herself the opportunity to get control of these feelings and in fact, was creating even more problems for herself in trying to avoid so much, but she could not break through the conflict. However, she continued to attend her sessions regularly and expose herself to that which she generally sought to avoid.

Conflict at home continued and worsened with Brenda feeling alternately uncared for and overcontrolled. She felt very left out, alienated from the "exclusive threesome," as she called it, consisting of her mother, her mother's male friend, and her sister, Terri. She was clearly locked in an intense conflict over dependency needs that she felt but angrily refused to acknowledge and instead acted out against. Another move out of the home ensued.

On a weekday morning in March, at 5:45 am, I received a telephone call at my home from Mrs. S. She shakily told me that it had just been reported on the news that Brenda's boyfriend had killed his mother and himself in his home, the afternoon before. Mrs. S drove to where Brenda was living, told her the news and brought her back home. Brenda's initial reaction was a kind of benumbed plunge into activity. She worked, re-entered school in a specialized alternative high school program, remained at home, and in therapy. Though she maintained a placid rather porcelain pleasantness, she continued to have trouble with eating and sleeping. She alternated between powerful feelings of guilt for the boy's death (one of their innumerable breakups had occurred a few days before the murder-suicide) and apparent denial that he had even died. Mrs. S's concerns about Brenda could not be translated into a supportive relationship, however, as conflict between the two of them continued unabated. Brenda reported a dream in which she killed her mother, was rescued by her father, who then abandoned her, leaving Brenda to wake up with cries of "I just want to be loved!" lingering in her mind.

Elsewhere in her life, Brenda's functioning began to erode. Her re-entry into school lasted only a month. Her time was mostly spent working a night shift in a local bakery and sleeping days. Her social life had diminished recently nearly to the point of nonexistence. Her work hours and growing disinterest in her former boy and girl friends precluded her from participating very much in what was once for her an extremely active party life. Further, she was finding herself both fearful of her drinking and increasingly temperamental and argumentative with her peers. She no longer felt anything in common with them and resented them for their differentness. She was beginning to surmise that she was not very good company. It was especially difficult for Brenda to establish or maintain relationships with boys. Since the death of her boyfriend, efforts to mask her depression with a frenetic social life and drug and alcohol use had ceased to attract her or allow her an avenue of denial or escape. Brenda was working in therapy with the intensely conflictual issue of her needs for interpersonal closeness, affiliation and caring and her fears of failed relationships, rejection and loss, and the overwhelming feelings of sadness and anger associated with them. Her relationships were characterized by a critical and demanding attitude toward others and a superficial style which conveyed to others her wish that they stay at arms length. She was, therefore, consistently unable to close the painful gap between herself and others to have her enormous but oft denied needs met. She was feeling increasingly "cold" and empty.

For Brenda, however, matters went from bad to worse. In May, she discovered (acknowledged) that she was four months pregnant with her deceased boyfriend's baby. An abortion was decided upon and arranged. However, preliminary tests at the hospital on the day of the planned procedure revealed that the baby had died at nine weeks. Brenda now felt responsible not only for the death of her boyfriend but his child as well. She was bitterly depressed and felt somehow "cursed with differentness" from all other people and that she was destined to "screw up anything that I get close to." In subsequent sessions her moods varied greatly. She could be humorous and animate or lethargic and unresponsive.

As the summer of 1984 progressed, Brenda's sadness became more a part of our sessions as she began to speak for the first time of her past and her feelings of unrequited love for her father. Her sense of unworthiness and inadequacy was expressed in terms of having come to think of herself as "ugly," "no good," and "a low-level person." She was beginning to make connections between the experiences of her past ("I never felt loved") and her present fears of closeness to others and subsequent loneliness. Brenda's openness was allowing me to feel much closer to her and I was greatly encouraged by what seemed to be her growing trust in me. In actuality, Brenda was moving toward a nearly fatal suicide attempt. My last session with her, prior to her attempt on July 23rd was on July 18th and there were two things about the session that were unusual, both of which I failed to associate with imminent suicidal behavior. First, she brought a friend along (who waited in the waiting room); something she had never done before or since. Second, she was practically buoyant. I thought, at first, that she was high. With her surprisingly elevated mood came a superficiality of manner that brought back the far away and distant quality of relating that she had just recently begun to change. In fact, her plan for suicide was already in progress and her elevation in mood and distancing from me represented a release from the kinds of intolerable feelings of which she had become increasingly aware and burdened.

On July 23, 1984, Brenda was admitted to a hospital suffering from acute acidosis, the result of purposeful mismanagement of her self-administered insulin injections, over a period of almost two weeks. At 4 am she was admitted to the hospital. Feeling fearfully ill and increasingly disoriented, Brenda told her younger sister what she had done and asked for help. Her sister alerted her mother and Brenda was rushed to the hospital where she spent the first 24 hours in critical condition in intensive care. She was very frightened and apologetic to her mother and to me for having attempted suicide. Fortunately, the next two days were marked by rapid improvement without apparent complications. During this time I visited her often as she would not speak to any of the attending psychiatrists or other medical staff. Brenda was able to recount the process in which she initially used her insulin treatments as a suicide attempt, followed by her unsuccessful efforts to stabilize herself and finally, having run out of her monthly supply altogether and becoming increasingly ill, she called upon her sister for help. Brenda was embarrassed and ashamed, both at having tried and having failed. While she had initially intended to die and had in fact planned the attempt, she changed her mind and tried to correct the situation, but by then it was too late. In retrospect, both her mother and sister were able to recall oblique suicidal remarks prior to the attempt. Twelve days before the attempt she had gotten on the phone to call her former boyfriend who had been dead for months.

As for myself, I felt stupid and ashamed having been so optimistic while things were, in reality, apparently moving in the opposite direction. I was confused as to why I had not been offered or perhaps had not perceived any suicidal intimations. Perhaps I had not gotten any closer to Brenda at all as I had so recently thought. I remember feeling embarrassed at meeting her mother and sister. I expected them to be mad at me. On the contrary, the dependence of Brenda and the whole family on me became more intense.

The next few days were spent trying to cool Mrs. S's anger at Brenda for refusing a voluntary two week hospitalization, and helping Brenda to understand what she needed to do to not become suicial again. Mrs. S was helped to express her anger toward Brenda in terms of how frustrating it was to care for someone (Brenda) who did not see it or seem to want it. Brenda, on the other hand, was told that in order to survive she would have to let people care about her and that she was dying of hunger in a bountiful land. I described her as someone in a glass cage who could not get out or let anyone else in. Finally, I told her that I could not be of much help to her if I too was kept out. She must, in the future, share her suicidal feelings so that she would not feel so alone, or be compelled to enact them. Brenda tearfully, responded "it's so hard to." On July 27, only four days after her near fatal suicide attempt, Brenda was released from the hospital at her insistence and since she was deemed to be no longer at immediate risk for another attempt.

Brenda's suicide attempt produced for her some very significant changes. Foremost among them was the reestablishment of her relationship with her father, who responded to the news of her attempt with energy and genuine concern, apparent even to Brenda.

Brenda's relationship with her mother, however, did not improve and became no less conflictual and tense. Mrs. S clearly was anxious having Brenda at home. Memories of her own past suicidality and her strongly held conviction that Brenda belonged in the hospital for psychiatric treatment produced an anger and uneasiness that was easy for Brenda to see. Brenda continued to feel like the odd person out as her sister, mother and mother's male friend grew ever closer and more amicable. Brenda felt very painfully that she was not wanted and did not belong. "My mother wants to just get rid of me. That's why she wants me in the hospital."

Her father, however, was working behind the scenes. He arranged to have Brenda move out of state to live with relatives from his side of the family. He would help her to get a job and to obtain her driver's license. Brenda agreed. She had little choice at this point. Clearly, she had to get away from home. Life with these older relatives proved peaceful but dull, though her health, and the condition of her diabetes improved as she began to lead a more organized existence. She was learning through necessity healthier ways to cope. Soon, however, her depression and loneliness returned as did her guilt at feeling that way considering the efforts on her behalf which she saw her relatives and father making on a daily basis.

Brenda and I maintained phone and mail contact through August and September until she eventually stopped calling and writing. I would hear about her periodically from her mother and the reports were very good. However, while Brenda had learned to cope and learned to live, she had not become a happy person. In October of 1985 she called and asked me if she could begin seeing me again. She had been to a couple of therapists near where she lived but could not talk to them. She was willing to drive the 35 miles each way every week for the appointments and did so without missing a session for the next six months.

She had become a mature young woman and her life no longer featured the mayhem and chaos of her earlier teenage years. She was employed full-time, very successfully, in a secretarial position with many opportunities for advancement. She was taking evening college level business courses. She had a steady boyfriend for the past nine months whom she believed loved her. However, she remained intensely conflicted and fearful of commitment, felt at times very depressed and alone, experienced a return of the severe headaches that precipitated our initial meeting two years before, was drinking again, thinking more and more of her deceased former boyfriend, and of suicide. She had come to see me to talk of all these things and she did. The threat of suicide seemed to abate almost immediately. Brenda forced herself to work very hard in therapy during these months. Though she often "choked" on her words, she would keep trying to get them out and eventually would. She kept her own private diary of her impressions of the sessions and her goals.

Brenda's visits became a highlight of my week and I told her so. She taught me a great deal about how therapy should work, and I told her this as well. We both learned a lot in those six months. Eventually, she felt, with my agreement, that she could go it alone (from therapy) for awhile. However, she often remarked that she thought she would need help off and on for years and I think she may. My hope is that she really has learned to ask for it and how to make use of it.

Case 2: Dean B.

Dean's story is unlike Brenda's almost regardless of the basis of comparison. Aside from Dean's being male, he differed dramatically from Brenda in personality, his use of therapy, his age, and in the circumstances of his eventual suicide attempt. Perhaps the greatest difference is how his story ends, or at least seems to have ended, for now.

I first heard of Dean through an encounter with his school's librarian, who confronted me, red-faced, bug-eyed, shaking and sputtering in an attempt to relate to me "the most difficult experience [she] had ever had with a student in [her] twenty-two years of work in schools." Having, thereby, riveted my attention to her narrative she proceeded to give me my first description of Dean, then a 12-year-old, in October of his seventh grade year. Apparently she had had to reprimand him for some reason in library class for some minor infraction. However, the correction occurred before the rest of the students and Dean at first seemed to be very, even inordinately embarrassed. Then in quick succession, he became anxious, agitated, and finally, explosive. Words suddenly began to fly out of him at her with stunning force from one so small and otherwise angelic-looking. "I'll sue you, you bitch! You're a witch! I'll never stay after school for you. . . well maybe in three years." Even more startling was his then immediate shift to conciliation, "If you let me off, I'll be good forever." and finally, "I hate you!" The librarian concluded her rendition with a veritable shudder as she caricatured for me the manner in that he "sneered" and "bared his teeth" at her. It was fairly obvious that she felt (with good reason!) that the boy might need counseling. I suggested she call and report the incident to the boy's parents, ask them if they had concerns of their own and if they would consider counseling. She was to mention my availability as well.

The next day the librarian told me she had spoken to Mrs. B, the boy's mother and that Dean had been in counseling before, that she and her husband were indeed very concerned about Dean and that Mrs. B was expecting a call from me. I got my first hint that this was not to be an easy case when I called Mrs. B the next day and was told that she had not asked to have me call, that Dean seemed much improved from earlier years and that, no, counseling did not seem necessary at that time. In other words, "don't call us, we'll call you."

By late November of that year there had been a change of heart. Though I had heard no further reports of Dean from teachers, I received a call from Mrs. B asking to meet with me about Dean whom I still had not met or even seen. Mrs. B proved to be an intelligent, attractive, sensitive woman in her mid-thirties. She was well dressed, almost aristocratic in appearance but not strong or confident in manner. She was accompanied, not by her husband as I had suggested and hoped, but by her two-year-old son with whom she struggled ineffectually throughout the session. Mrs. B recounted how Dean had been a management problem for her from the age of two. While her husband seemed to have little trouble with him, she found it practically impossible to cope with him. He seemed, to her, to be constantly demanding of her, testing her, disobeying her, or rejecting her. They had few pleasant moments together. Two years ago, burdened with guilt over her "physical abuse" of Dean, she and Dean went to a private psychologist. Sessions lasted for over a year, eventually being terminated by the parents for reasons that are still disputed and unclear. Throughout most of the session, Mrs. B was teary eyed, seeming very depressed and clearly, admittedly overwhelmed by the demands of motherhood, demonstrating as she spoke, her desperation as she vainly endeavored to occupy her latest two-year-old boy. It was a sad and somewhat frightening sight.

Mr. B's absence from that first session seemed significant as it was in keeping with Mrs. B's description as a good, competent father, but very unsupportive husband. She felt abandoned by him when she felt most needy, as at times such as that. She felt isolated as well, having been uprooted by marriage from her Southern home and deprived of the support and friendship of life-long family and friends that she was unable to replace in any approximated fashion here in New England. She desperately missed her mother. In short, as is probably apparent, the first session developed into one that she directed predominantly to her needs. Thus it appeared to be with her parenting, as her own tremendous neediness conflicted with those of her children, creating for her great confusion, frustration, uncontrollable anger, then guilt, depression, and increased unavailability to her kids. Children tend to become more demanding in situations such as these. Certainly, the child before my eyes did and I suspected Dean had as well, hence the abuse. At any rate, it was agreed that I would see Dean and the parents, though separately.

Dean came to his session willingly with a palpable mixture of suspicion and eagerness. He was as angelic and choir-boy in appearance as he was devilish by description. Dean was a small, exceedingly handsome fellow in a feminine sort of way. He was neat and trim in every way, well dressed, without jeans in a school where jeans were overwhelmingly popular. His size and prepubescent face gave him an appearance two to three years younger than his chronological age. Nonetheless, he was not shy. He knew why he was with me, something of what counseling was for and seemed to have fond memories of his previous therapist (who had since moved out of state). He was willing to continue counseling with me, viewing it as a vehicle by which his relationship with his mother might be improved and to discover something about his problems with peers.

In the following months, Dean expressed much sadness and anger over his feeling unloved, rejected, and disapproved of by his mother. He was extremely bitter over past incidences of abuse that consisted of being hit with fists on his face and all over his body. He was admittedly lonely, had no friends, and reported feeling closest to a hamster, which had died a year ago and which his mother would not allow to be replaced. Talk of his father always brought a change in his depressed or angry mood, always evident when speaking of his mother. He got along much better with his father, who had gotten him into a drama club and who he felt liked him.

Sessions with the parents, usually with his father in attendance, focused on management issues and skills, his mother's distorted, highly personalized perception of Dean's motives for his oppositional behavior, and his father's degree of supportiveness to his wife. Marriage counseling was proposed, but never acted upon. Mrs. B resisted suggestions to seek individual counseling.

Meanwhile, things at home continued to deteriorate. Dean's attention-seeking, demanding behavior made it impossible for his parents to have guests at their home. He would create scenes between himself and his mother, usually in public. He was alternately argumentative and insulting, or be-seeching of conversation and companionship. Mrs. B, for her part, reported simply wanting to get away from him. Both sides of his coin were intolerable to her. Things would consistently devolve into mutual anger and rejection. Mr. B mostly worked.

In April, Mr. and Mrs. B reported money missing from their savings account. As it turned out Dean had been using their bank card to make withdrawals from a money machine. The total came to $240, $60 on each of four episodes. Dean was giving sums away to peers, but it brought him very little social success. He continued to have no friends. A fight between him and another boy at the drama club got him kicked out of it. Conflict with a teacher and a student at his Sunday religion class resulted in his removal from there as well. In his individual sessions, however, he was losing touch with his sadness and feeling only his growing anger. Further, he had come to externalize most of his feelings, putting blame exclusively on others, especially his mother. He became more superficial, more sullen, and more intransigent in his oppositional attitude and behavior. By this point he preferred to use his sessions primarily to castigate his "enemies" with almost paranoid fervor. By June, the situation was critical. Mrs. B was on valium.

Mr. B described his status as "a wreck." Ultimately, it was decided that Dean go to live with his maternal grandparents down South for the summer and, if possible and agreeable, remain there for the next school year. Dean was in favor of this idea as it seemed to be the best thing at the time. He knew and got along very well with his grandparents and they had a positive opinion of him. Dean did remain away for all of his eighth grade year.

I did not see or hear of Dean again for over two years. After returning from his year with his grandparents, a year which had gone well—behaviorally, academically, and socially—he returned home and was enrolled in a private school. In March of his 10th grade year I was called by Mrs. B and asked to meet with herself and her husband about Dean. It had been nearly two and a half years since I had been involved with him and his family. Mr. and Mrs. B began our session with light conversation, moving into a generally positive description of Dean's current functioning. Academically, he had done pretty well for the past two years. Their relationship with him was described as being better than it had been before his year away. He seemed to have friends and had become the object of several girls' attention. His behavioral improprieties sounded like normative adolescent fare and were understood as such by his parents.

Well then, why the visit? Finally, Dean's parents exposed their reason for wanting to see me. They were beginning to fear that Dean may have been contemplating suicide. On a number of occasions, while angry at his parents, he had shouted out "Maybe you'd be happy when I'm dead, see how you'll feel then," and phrases to that effect. Once he said to his mother, "I should kill myself. Then everyone would see you're not so great." Mrs. B relayed most of this quite impassively as if to say "isn't he a weird kid?" Mr. B, on the other hand was agitated, fidgety, constantly crossing and uncrossing his legs, taking deep breaths, and rubbing his eyes. Mrs. B also revealed that she had been into Dean's private possessions, notebooks, etc., and had found numerous poems and diary-like notations which appeared to her to contain themes of violent aggression, death and suicide.

At the end of the session I asked them to discuss their concerns with Dean and to ask him if he would agree to see me again, at least for a few sessions. It was decided that it would be best for the father to do this because of Dean's continued conflictual and oppositional relationship with his mother. He would likely have said "no" to a trip to Hawaii if it was proposed by her. Mr. B was to tell Dean of their visit to see me. The matter of the poems and diary notations was a difficult one. On the one hand it was important, in case of denial on Dean's part, for the father to be able to somehow validate his concerns with objective evidence. On the other hand the "evidence" was gained by a breach of privacy which, if revealed at the point of referral might have produced an anger that would lead to a rejection of anything his parents asked him to do including seeing a therapist. He could not at his age (15) and with his powers of resistance, be forced to go to therapy. It was decided that Mr. B not mention Dean's writings at this point, but that I would have to during our first session, the main goal being to get him to my office for an evaluation.

As it turned out Mr. B had no trouble with Dean. In fact, Dean was very agreeable and was happy to learn that I was still around. I saw Dean the following week. The differences in his manner were striking in comparison to the Dean I had known more than two years ago. Physically, he had not changed much. He was taller but still short and young looking for his age. He was fashionably and expensively dressed. He had remained very handsome. Gone, however, was the sad, lonely boy of seventh grade. In his place was a cool, but obviously angry fellow who exuded a fairly pervasive contempt for people. He seemed hard. It became immediately evident that he had not been a relative angel at all during the past couple of years, but had simply moved his acting out into the community more and away from home, which is where he spent most of his time it seemed, away from home. He was into drugs (pot) on a regular (3, 4 times a week) basis, vandalism, fire-setting, petty theft, and fights. His compatriots seemed less like friends, but rather associates with complementing pathologies. He often took his parents' car without permission (and without a license) and reported that he sneaked out of his house every night after midnight for about two hours. However, he was not getting caught by anybody for anything. He did relate one story of a very close call with chilling possibilities.

He and two friends had taken Dean's mother's new car for a ride to a nearby city to buy pot. On the way, in heavy traffic, they scraped another car. Both cars pulled over to check damages and exchange identification and information. Remaining calm, but realizing he had no information he cared to exchange, Dean tricked the driver of the other car by suggesting they both drive up the street a bit to a nearby parking lot so as not to block traffic. The man got back into his car where his wife and two children waited, only to see Dean go careening by him and onto the entrance ramp to the highway. Dean related the ensuing scene with giddy, triumphant excitement. At one point they thought they were going to be caught. The man was very large and very angry looking in the rear view mirror. As it turned out they made good their escape and survived to laugh about it all the way home in Mom's miraculously undamaged car. I asked Dean what he would have done if he had been caught by the man. He laughed and said, "We'd decided to beat the shit out of him." I said, "He sounded pretty big." Dean replied matter of factly, "We had pipes."

I discussed with Dean his parents concern about him. He admitted having made suicidal comments to his mother but denigrated the notion of an actual attempt. At that point I asked him if he was aware that his parents' concerns and mine were based also on writings of his that had been discovered. I described my impressions of the death and suicide themes. At that, his face got red. His eyes widened and began to well up with tears, which he strained to keep from overflowing, briefly betraying a glimmer of the younger, sadder Dean, "My mother," hissed his only response." "I'd like to kill her, not me." I commented that I was aware that he had been exceedingly angry at his mother for a long time but that in the past he had also felt very sad as well. Were these writings about that sadness? Dean described a fantasy of his depicting his death as a final escape from his family, and a curse to his mother. He felt helpless to hurt her in any other way and hopeless in obtaining her love or approval. "She's a bitch and she can't stand me and I can't stand her," he said, recovering quickly. He stated that he had never attempted suicide and had formed no specific plans for doing so. He insisted that he derived a great deal of support and satisfaction from his male friends, but felt that "all girls are bitches. I'm too nice to them." He seemed to understand the irreversibility of death. Asked to state hypothetically which method he would choose if he were to attempt suicide, he replied pills, but could not say what kind. Dean agreed to see me individually once a week for the purpose of helping him to cope with life at home. We could not agree on an intra-psychic focus. Rather, Dean's preoccupations determined an initial focus on external problems such as life with Mom and Dad. Family therapy was to occur weekly as well.

From here things deteriorated rapidly. In April, I was informed by Mrs. B that Dean had become "like his old self." and that it could not be tolerated. They were intent on foster care for him. Dean provocatively cheered the idea, saying anywhere was better than home. Foster care was a disaster lasting only four days. In that space of time, Dean was accused of stealing from a roommate, broke curfew, had his bike stolen, skipped three days of school, beat up an 8-year-old boy whom he claimed had stolen his bike, and finally ran away from the foster home with another male foster child and spent two nights at the home of a drug dealer.

He returned home, but to anything but harmony. Family therapy sessions became explosive to the verge of physical violence. Mr. B stated that he had had it with Dean and would spend no more money or emotional energy on him. Dean threatened both parents with a severe beating if they ever laid a hand on him again.

Dean's individual sessions remained exercises in externalized blaming, aggressive fantasies, tales of antisocial behavior and demonstrations of a character that seemed increasingly limited in capacity to relate, to trust in, or empathize with others. He valued his time with me, however, and went to some effort to always keeps his appointments, but I felt frustrated as the summer began that my goals with Dean were so circumscribed, while the problems were so enormous. Basically, it amounted to simply helping him to see how he could best get his needs met. Maintaining a peaceful if not loving coexistence with his parents was in his best interest because he had nowhere else to go, not because it was nice to be nice to people. Suicide would not get his needs met because it would punish him for deeds that his mother was supposedly (in his view) responsible for. This left him without an outlet for his anger, however, and I began to be increasingly concerned about homicidal rather than suicidal tendencies. I shared these feelings with Dean and his parents in the form of concerns about the family's ability to continue to live together. I began to talk with Dean more and more about finding another place to live, perhaps with a friend. Things could not continue as they were. The danger of something violent happening appeared to be building much faster than therapy alone could manage.

In mid-July, Mrs. B called to report a terrible fight with Dean. She had slapped him and for the first time he had struck back, throwing her to the floor and leaving the house. A week later Mrs. B cancelled Dean's appointments with me saying that no progress was being made and that they were sending Dean to another doctor. Mrs. B went on to say that she too was leaving to return home to her mother's. Two days later Dean was admitted to the hospital after an overdose of antibiotics, taken that night at home.

I was informed of this by Mrs. B two days after the incident. She had decided not to leave home after all. Dean was still in the hospital and needed to be seen by a psychologist or psychiatrist before he could be released. It being a Sunday, no one else could be found and so I was asked to go in. Mr. and Mrs. B were, however, still intending to switch therapists. I saw Dean that day, and though he appeared sincere, in my judgment, in saying that he felt stupid and frightened the moment he swallowed the pills and was no longer suicidal, I could not feel that he was safe returning to his home. A note written by Dean before the suicide attempt and discovered by his mother, blamed her for his act. He wrote that he could no longer live with her and that now that she had changed her mind and decided to remain, he had to leave. Suicide was the only way out. It would allow him an escape from an intolerable situation and hopefully, he wrote, brand her as the true villain he felt her to be. He concluded with kind words for his father, anger at being taken away from me, and a good-bye to his best friend, Paul.

In my last meeting with Mr. and Mrs. B that same day I told them that therapy, no matter who it was with, was not sufficient at this point. It was dangerous for Dean and his mother to go on living together. A change was needed immediately. Mrs. B renewed her decision to leave with Mr. B's passive acquiescence. In the meantime Dean was to return home with my home phone number in his pocket and my advice to leave home and go to

Paul's house, where he would be welcome, whenever things at home got to be too much. Mrs. B was to leave three days later and I have not heard from Dean or the family since. (At the time of this writing, it has been three months).

Dean, despite his more obvious antisocial and angry characteristics had remained a very depressed boy. He had gotten so far away from feeling depressed, however, that he had lost any chance of understanding it or coping with it. He instead invested in anger and attempted to divest himself from people whom he perceived as ill-willed, uncaring and generally as hostile as he had come to feel. Therefore, he remained alone and ready to burst from all the pent up rage which he could not fully express, could not entirely hold in, and could not effectively neutralize. The longer he felt trapped in a situation (his family) that seemed to swell his anger even greater, the more desperate he became to escape. It was not possible, for me at least, to determine in advance the direction his destructive urges would take. It seemed just as likely that they would continue to be directed against other people or things, possibly with increasing ardor. I was surprised when he turned it against himself. I had not fully appreciated the extent of his depression. He hid it from me about as successfully as he denied it to himself.

Dean's case presented a number of very difficult problems. His lack of insight and lack of willingness to gain insight into the dynamics of his feelings about people, relationships, and himself was a major obstacle to progress in therapy. His increasing adoption of an antisocial attitude and life style served to reinforce his negative view of people and his investment in anger rather than more basic and deeper feelings of sadness. His parents offered lukewarm and inconsistent support to the therapy, at best, eventually under-cutting it altogether as they may have done with the earlier therapist. Dean's distrust of others and fear of his own very powerful inner feelings made it impossible for him to open up in therapy and make optimum use of it. It was a frustrating experience for me and a less than fruitful one for Dean. Situations such as these, however, are not terribly rare.

10

Education and Prevention

There would exist little reason for the creation of this book, if adolescent suicidal behavior was a well understood phenomenon. The general public, as well as those whose lives and professional positions put them in close contact with adolescents, appear rather uninformed and uneducated as to the dynamics behind adolescent suicide. This is expected, of course, on the part of the general public, since national media attention has only recently illuminated this growing problem. Scientific interest had in the past been only slightly more responsive to the subject, though this has begun to change dramatically. It is inevitable and in the nature of things, that a problem, even one as appalling as adolescent suicide, needs to exist and grow for a while before it draws attention. Now, with suicidal behavior threatening to become an aspect of adolescence and adolescent coping with which teenagers are increasingly familiar and attracted to, the problem has reached a point of urgency. The process by which individuals become educated concerning its manifestations, management, and prevention needs to be improved and speeded up. Time has become very precious in this respect. An aggressive effort toward suicide education and prevention needs to be undertaken across the country.

Suicide prevention strategies and programs must be distinguished from crisis intervention. Crisis intervention is a tertiary mode of prevention that refers to efforts to prevent a crisis from leading to a lethal suicide attempt. Organizations such as the Samaritans specialize in this type of prevention, as do suicide prevention centers, various "hot lines" and some mental health organizations. These interventions are usually the result of active solicitations of help on the part of critically suicidal individuals. Their goal is to calm the state of crisis and extreme perturbation, move the person away from suicide, and make referrals. If an attempt has already taken place, assistance will be offered to keep the attempt from becoming fatal by calling in medical assistance and if possible helping the suicide attempter apply his own first aid.

Secondary prevention, on the other hand, refers to programs, whose goal is early intervention. It seeks to prevent suicidal crises from developing or becoming severe. Education programs aimed at teaching people how to identify and respond to potentially suicidal persons prior to a suicidal crisis would be examples of this. For instance, high school teachers and students might be taught how to respond to suicidal feelings expressed as a way of preventing them from reaching crisis proportions.

On a much broader scale, primary prevention refers to community wide programs which would seek to address the root causes of adolescent suicide and depression by involving the family and all other community based sources of potential support for adolescents. The goal here might be to extend the network of social connections available to adolescents, thereby addressing the problems of loneliness and alienation.

This chapter will focus on primary and secondary levels of prevention though any comprehensive community program for suicide prevention must include services on all three levels. The focal point of this effort must be the schools. Strong advocates of this view, aside from myself, include Hill (1984) and Ross (1980). Sudak (1984) summarizes the views of many in writing:

> *Since schools provide captive audiences, they constitute an ideal place in which to attempt preventive, interventive, and postventive efforts with students and faculty. (p. 360)*

It is in our public and private high schools that teenagers are most likely to exhibit suicidal tendencies that will be identified. Teachers are generally excellent observers. Their experience in working, during their careers, with hundreds or thousands of teenagers allows them to develop a very large sample population from which norms are readily, though informally, established. Deviant adolescents and significantly troubled adolescents become apparent to the alert teacher and every school will have many such observant and concerned individuals. Further, it is to teachers or other school personnel (among adults) that adolescents will often entrust a revelation of suicidal ideation or intent. Finally, it is in school, where the suicidal adolescent's deterioration can be most clearly visible in terms of declining grades, attendance, social involvement, or increasing behavioral problems and loss of control. Schools are institutions of normality, consistency, and conformity. Deviations from this channelling effort will be noticeable. Suicidal adolescents will often deviate markedly. They will perhaps be no more distinctive anywhere than in their schools.

While adolescents with problems are often highly visible in schools and teachers adept at spotting them, suicidal adolescents remain very poorly understood by school personnel and peers. Gordon (1979) found that seondary school teachers possessed a low level of knowledge concerning both the problem of teenage suicide and the potential for teacher intervention. My own experience confirms these findings. Gordon further reported that secondary level teachers possessed predominantly negative attitudes toward adolescent suicidal behavior, an orientation that seemed to be supported by relative ignorance of the problem. Both Gordon and Barber et al. (1975) have demonstrated that education about suicide can have a positive effect on the attitudes that one holds toward suicidal individuals.

Studies of adolescents' familiarity with suicide have shown that high school students have extensive contact with suicidality and are often faced with opportunities to respond to suicidal verbalization by peers. Ross (1980) has confirmed in her research the widely held belief that teenagers will tell other teenagers first of suicidal intentions. Though suicidal adolescents are more likely to communicate suicidal intention to a friend rather than an adult, research by Mishara (1982) suggests that adolescents often respond inappropriately and in a nonhelpful manner to suicidal verbalization from peers.

Suicidal behavior (including verbalizations) tended to elicit feelings of anger, shock, and panic in a majority of the respondents in Mishara's study. These feelings, closely associated with ignorance about suicide, appeared to produce more defensive, closed reactions rather than more helpful open communication. The value and even the necessity of basic education for students as well as faculty about suicide and its management is well established. In the belief that a positive, caring response to the suicidal individual serves as a counterforce to suicidality, it would seem that a vigorous educational effort, based in the schools would be most efficacious in coping with the problem on a local and national level.

At this time, two states, California and Florida, have passed laws requiring schools to offer suicide prevention programs at the secondary level. Other states are considering such a move. In California, the mandated program includes requirements for teacher training, parent-awareness programs, and incorporating into the school curriculum a minimum of five hours a year on suicide prevention. Florida's law requires that suicide prevention programs be part of the life-management classes that will be offered to 9th and 10th graders. The legislation also stipulates that to be eligible for certification, teacher candidates must receive suicide prevention training.

Teachers cannot and should not be expected to take on the responsibility of suicide prevention alone. It is essential that every secondary school have available to it supportive mental health services of both a consultative and direct service nature. These services should, ideally, be in-house. This is a prerequisite for any optimally functional preventive mental health program. Programming must fulfill not only the prophylactic purpose of preventing adolescents from becoming suicidal, but provide a service that can cope with them when they do. Adolescents must have available the opportunity to self refer for their own mental health needs, independent of their parents or other adults. Concerned friends need a trusted and easily available professional mental health resource to go to for assistance in responding to a suicidal peer or for help in making a referral.

Adolescents are reputed to be a difficult age group to engage in psychotherapy (Weissman, 1974). In my experience, however, they are a group intensely interested in learning about themselves and very open to accepting adult, if not parental, support in helping them through the difficult adjustments of adolescence. They simply need the option of having access to counseling services, as any adult would, without that process being under some other person's control. Similarly, health services such as the dispensing of birth control pills and even abortion in some states are available to adolescents without parents controlling access. While many parents are certainly willing to assist their teenager in obtaining mental health services if they are asked, few adolescents will make such a request to parents. Once an adolescent has entered therapy, the therapist must, of course, endeavor to involve the parents, but the initial contact between therapist and teenage client is greatly facilitated by the easy access that a school setting affords.

From the therapist's standpoint, work in a nonclinical setting such as a school offers some important advantages. The possibility for independent self-referral insures the therapist a high percentage of highly motivated clients, something often missing in the clinic setting. Since transportation is not a problem, there are far fewer missed appointments to delay and inhibit the process. Since the therapy would be free, provided that the therapist was an employee of the school system, it can last longer, unconstrained by the limitations of cost and insurance coverage. Suicidal teenagers often need more than one or even two sessions a week plus access to the therapist in times of crisis. Placement of the therapist in the adolescent's school allows for a maximum of contact, though limited setting can at times be a problem here.

Finally, placement in the school allows for better monitoring of the adolescent's school and community functioning and peer relationships, as well as for consultation with school personnel on issues of management and educational planning. There is simply tremendous value both to the potentially suicidal adolescent and the therapist to have the therapist out working where the clients live, and in the case of adolescents, most of them live, for 6-7 hours a day, in the school.

At the very least, counseling services should be made convenient and available in an associated agency in the community in which the school is based. Small communities will have to form regional support networks serving several towns together. The staff of the mental health agency needs to have a close working relationship with the teachers and staff of the high school or high schools with which they work. A growing number of school districts around the country are using this model, often with the aid of special education staff, to grapple with what is to schools, a frightening responsibility.

In order for school based counseling services to be most effective as a preventative instrument, an active suicide intervention attitude and policy must prevail. Colleges have long struggled with the problem of suicide on campus. As has been reported, college populations have generally been found to have higher suicide rates than their noncollege peer group (Ishii, 1985; Mishara, 1982; Seiden, 1969). Partly as a consequence, colleges usually have in place, in-house counseling services. In speaking of the suicide problem on the college campus, Dashef (1984) has urged an active policy of identification and outreach to those students who appear to be at risk. Services and ideas discussed and applied on the college level must now be considered for the high school level.

As regards active outreach, neither school personnel, nor the school therapist can afford to sit back and wait for the actively disturbed adolescents to surface and for self-referrals to pour in. We read too often of the suicide victim who is described as having been a quiet person, who pretty much kept to himself, and was not very well known by anyone. A high percentage of young persons who attempt and commit suicide have never been in counseling (Dashef, 1984; Seiden, 1966; Shafii, et al., 1985; Weissman, 1974). Dashef proposes a vigorous education process involving faculty and students focussing on signs of suicide, reasons for suicidal thinking and behavior, and orientation to the counseling services available in the school and community. Further, he suggests that when a student with high suicide risk is identified, active outreach to the student must be initiated by the counseling service and a number of services offered or proposed. All of this is applicable on the high school level. Teachers and students must be sensitized to the signs of depression in order to improve their ability to notice the more quietly unhappy and lonely adolescent. They and/or the counseling service must then be willing to encounter the potentially troubled teenager with offers of services, support, or simply the knowledge that they exist, to establish a connection. However, a broader based program of suicide education and prevention is possible and desirable involving even curriculum additions and a focus on general mental health issues.

Ross (1980), a strong advocate of high school based programs, has outlined and implemented a program that included some essential introductory features. Included are:

1. Distribution of brochures on suicide for all teachers and students
2. Education on basic facts and concepts regarding a suicidal crisis, for students and teachers
3. Guidelines on how to identify presuicidal behavior
4. Guidelines on how to respond to a suicidal communication

Education directed at helpful responses is vital in light of Mishara's (1982) research. Students and teachers need preparation in formulating responses to suicidal communications so as to avoid the closed, avoidant responses that are both unhelpful and potentially dangerous. Students, in particular, as the persons most likely to encounter a suicidal intimation, need help in this regard. Education, including the use of role playing, should also include guidelines on how to make a referral, as well as discuss the issue of confidentiality as presented in Chapter 9 of this book.

Ross utilized a workshop and discussion group format as the educational vehicle of choice. Teachers and students had the opportunity to share ideas and feelings in such a way as to reduce stigma, ignorance, and avoidance in dealing with suicide. Education and consciousness-raising was extended to the community by means of numerous newspaper articles and the presentation of an educational film on adolescent suicide to the public.

These programs, however, can only be effective as a beginning or introduction to an ongoing collective of services and education. Changes in attitudes and behavior of the magnitude being described here require nurturing, development, and reinforcement over time. Information on suicide and its management cannot be effectively internalized and comfortably acted upon by teachers or students unless they begin to feel more comfortable with suicide and death. Services such as counseling must be present and available not only to students in need, but as a source of professional guidance to the students and faculty, who will need continuous bolstering, advice, reassurance and ongoing education as frontline figures in the struggle against suicide. Programs and educators coming from outside the community to drop their well-intentioned wisdom and concern and depart, leave the job unfinished unless designed only as an orientation or enrichment to an ongoing program. A prototypical school-based education/prevention program should, therefore, include permanent mental health staff and permanent curriculum changes (additions) as the best way to keep the process going.

In the area of curriculum, death education, and instruction in coping skills and problem solving strategy development would serve as needed components to an emphasis on good mental health care as a supplement to existing required courses in physical education and health (physical) that already exist in schools. As good physical and mental health have come to be seen as more and more inextricably intertwined, it makes good sense on a variety of levels, not just in reference to suicide, that these two areas find equal billing in high school course offerings.

DEATH EDUCATION

We live in a society in which the experience of human death has become increasingly remote, especially to our children. Deaths nowadays occur far less commonly in the home in view of the family. Death is more hidden now. It does not take place in public very often except in time of war or aberrant violence. It takes place behind closed doors, in hospitals, and nursing homes, more likely to be attended by the facilities' staff than the family. When the family is represented, it is usually in the person of an adult, not a child or adolescent. Most people my age have seen very few dead people, fewer still have seen them die. Death has all but disappeared from our experience. Adolescents are, paradoxically, surrounded by death without often having to witness it, talk about it, or in some way confront it. The adolescent suicide and homicide rates have increased, the harmful use of tobacco, drugs, and alcohol has proliferated, as have abortions. One of every 600 adolescents will die this year, 35 percent from motor vehicle and other accidents. Still death continues to be a taboo subject in the home in that discussion of it, like sex, is largely ignored (Stillion & Wass, 1979). Our society offers little guidance on how families should handle the experience or the subject. While adults have available to them death rituals associated with their religion (wakes, funerals), little is offered by way of a shared, comprehensible experience for children. We are never quite sure what to do about them when a death occurs. Among other things, anxiety and ignorance about the unknown thrive under these conditions.

A rationale then for including death education as a component of suicide education/prevention, within a larger mental health program, would include the issues of death anxiety, development of a mature death concept, and coping with loss as important factors in the psychology of adolescent suicide. Further, it would seem to be an entirely appropriate educational endeavor with adolescents in general considering the salience of issues such as abortion, euthanasia, the nuclear threat, near death phenomena, living wills, and suicide. Cognitively adolescents are more than ready for discussion of these important issues; emotionally they need an opportunity to feel something about death and as regards their life-styles, must acknowledge the health related implications of drug and alcohol use, reckless behavior, and venereal diseases.

Learning about death cannot effectively proceed until anxiety and fear about death are reduced to manageable levels. Coping with death, one's own or another's, cannot develop in a healthy manner until one is able to adopt an open accepting attitude toward it. Suicide, be it completed, attempted, or threatened, cannot be properly responded to without some capacity to deal with death. Mishara (1982) has demonstrated the negative effects of "shock," "panic," "fear and discomfort" on students' responses to suicidal communications from peers. High levels of anxiety about death can prevent people from responding in an open, helpful, and potentially life saving manner to a threat of suicide. Death anxiety can have a dangerous effect in more direct fashion on the suicidal individual himself. Orbach and Glaubman (1979) found that suicidal children who were judged to be anxious about death manifested more distorted personal death concepts than nonsuicidal children. A similar finding has been reported by McIntire, Angle and Stryppler (1972). More mature reasoning on the realities of death can be subverted by the suicidal person's anxieties regarding his own death. So it is possible for a suicidal adolescent, even one of high intelligence, to distort the concept of death's finality, for instance, in order to render less frightening his own suicidal intentions. In fact, death anxiety has been shown to have a greater impact on brighter individuals than cognitively lower subjects in research with a group of preadolescents. Stillion et al. (1984), however, suggested that among adolescents, older subjects with higher IQ might have a more mature concept of death and be less likely to romanticize death or suicide. An ability, then, to think honestly and clearly about death may actually decrease a person's capacity for suicidal behavior.

Whether due to death anxiety, in particular, stress, anxiety, and distorted reality testing in general, low IQ, high IQ, or whatever, suicidal adolescents are sometimes supported in their intentions by faulty reasoning on the issue of death, its finality, and irrevocability. High impulsive suicidal adolescents are particularly dangerous in that they might not have given the concept much thought at all. Further, little if anything in our society has asked them to think about it. Death education would help in cognitizing what for some suicidal adolescents had been a purely emotional response. The benefit of thinking about behavior is greatly valued in suicide prevention. The 17-year-old girl whose thoughts of suicide were altered by the suicide of a friend, described in Chapter 3, serves as an example of the preventive value of a form of death education, tragically presented and very fortuitously absorbed.

Coping with loss is a central issue in both the psychology of suicide and the psychology of adolescence (Tabachnik, 1981). Education about death as a form of loss or separation can serve as a vehicle by which teenagers can learn to deal with the losses so endemic and painful in adolescence. The fragility and mobility of the modern family have brought additional losses and burdens. The potentially suicidal adolescent, in particular, would benefit from an opportunity to learn health coping mechanisms. They, as well as other adolescents, need to learn to accept that loss and death are universal human phenomena, which cannot be avoided, rather than a personal curse, and must ultimately be endured and accepted. Crase and Crase (1984) summarize these hopes in writing

> *While research data are limited, death education for young people may conceivably reduce fears toward death, but more importantly it may provide them with skills that ultimately lead to less suicide and other self-destructive behaviors. (p. 346)*

The teaching of death related issues could take place either as a special unit within a particular (mandatory) course such as health, integrated into several courses, or as an autonomous offering initiated by teachers independently where appropriate and relevant to the curriculum. At any rate, it should do good and not harm as some may fear. Rosenthal (1983) has carried out research in response to the anticipated allegation that death education might cause more death (i.e. suicide) among students as is often stated about sex and drug education. She was able to find no measurable increase in suicide potential among students exposed to death education.

COPING SKILLS

Clinical experience and research regarding suicidal adolescents and their families are replete with observations that coping and problem solving skills are often poorly developed and inadequate to the task of managing the multiple stresses and conflicts that beset them. Education/prevention programs need to include a component that offers alternatives to suicide as a coping mechanism and problem solving strategy. Schools might add a section to the albeit bulging health curriculum dealing with relaxation techniques, organization skills, the physiology of stress, the value of exercise, self-limit setting, assertiveness training, communication skills, and anger management. The guidance and counseling staff might work with teachers in other subject areas in finding ways to incorporate the teaching of healthy problem solving skills into the existing curriculum. Students might be encouraged to discuss what other course of action a suicide victim in history or literature might have taken. It should not be presumed that the modeling of mature and effective coping skills has taken place at home.

Schools have long recognized the need for health education and instruction in the physical realm. Mandatory health and physical education classes for all students bear witness to this fact. The idea that physical and mental health are discrete entities can no longer be justified. To the extent that schools accept as a goal of education the preparation of its young for successful adaptation to its society, they cannot deny the relevance of education in mental health. As adolescents continue to struggle in an increasingly complex and unsupportive environment the need for such an educational focus will grow more urgent. The increased rate for adolescent suicide is only one symptom suggestive of a void in this area of preparation for life.

With preventable deaths such as are due to various forms of stress related heart disease, the leading cause of death among American adults, adults in this nation have been finally compelled to regard good mental health with respect and concern. Corporations have acknowledged the cost effectiveness of stress reduction in the workplace and have made efforts to help employees cope more productively in order to be more productive. It seems rather ludicrous in light of the high levels of stress faced by adolescents, their often self-destructive ways of handling it and the relative ease of instituting programs aimed at stress reduction and teaching coping skills, that more has not been done.

PEER COUNSELING

Involvement of adolescents in the counseling process for suicidal peers has been called for by myself (Curran, 1984) as well as by Ross (1980) and Sudak et al. (1984). A prototype for implementing such a program is described in Chapter 9. However, peer counseling programs require a great deal of professional supervision, training, and preparation. Again, the necessity of an in-house counseling staff qualified to function in a supervisory capacity becomes clear. While it may seem an unnatural and unwieldy burden to entrust adolescents with responsibility for helping maintain the lives of seriously disturbed peers, the demand is already being made by those very peers. Responsibility, therefore, cannot be avoided. In addition to a formalized peer counseling program, adolescents would benefit from training in dealing with the crisis situations that we often thrust upon them. Such an offering would be most welcome by many teenagers. Many schools recognize the life saving capacities, opportunities and responsibilities of adolescents in making CPR training a part of the health curriculum.

Finally, adolescents will need and often will seek guidance on an ongoing basis concerning how to deal with friends who may be approaching a suicidal act. As a therapist in a public high school I have frequently been utilized in this manner. Again, the effectiveness of time-limited orientation/education programs dissipates over time if left untended.

Students also need something in their hands in the form of concrete, step-by-step directions on how to deal with a suicide crisis. Many colleges include material of this nature in student brochures. High schools should begin to do the same. The following guideline, used at the school in which I work, is an example. It is part of the student handbook that is given to each student at the start of each school year. The contents of this guideline are discussed by me with each incoming class, each year as part of a wider school-based suicide education/prevention program.

What to Do if You Feel a Friend Is Thinking of Suicide

Increasing numbers of teenagers struggle with overwhelming levels of stress and depression. Some of these teenagers feel unable to get the support they need and begin to think of suicide as a way out. However, most of them very much want to live. Many will tell another person of their suicidal thoughts and intentions. This is often a way to start to talk about their problems. The person they usually tell first is not their parents or any other adult. It is another teenager, someone in their school.

If a friend of yours makes you feel that they might attempt suicide you should try to do the following things:

1. Do not be afraid to talk about suicide or to use the word. This will *not* put the idea in their heads or influence them to do it.
2. Try to get your friend to talk about what it is in their life that makes them feel the way they do. The more talking *on their part* the better.
3. Try to convince them that they need to speak to a trusted adult: either their parents, a teacher, coach, counselor, etc. Tell them you want them to get more help than just you alone can give. Go with your friend to speak with the adult, if necessary.
4. Unless you are *absolutely certain* that your friend has spoken to an adult *about suicide,* you will need to speak to an adult yourself about your concern for your friend. It is better if you tell your friend you intend to do this.
5. Confidentiality. If your friend asks you not to tell anyone, should you keep the secret? NO. There is no rule of confidentiality when it comes to potential suicide. It does no good to keep the secret and lose the person.
6. Your friend may be angry and try to convince you that you will get them in trouble if you tell. If you still believe that your friend is at risk, you must act. All you can do is try to convey the idea that you are sincerely trying to help.

Suicide threats are a serious sign of trouble and need to be taken seriously so that people will not feel the need to resort to more drastic means of expressing their unhappiness. Responding to a potential suicide in this way can help prevent many suicide attempts or even a committed suicide.

Material presented in this fashion provides a simple formula for student intervention within the school context. It purposely avoids a lengthy discussion of signs of suicide which could not possibly be adequately covered in a short space and should more appropriately be addressed in an instructional unit devoted to the issue. It focuses on the more unequivocal sign of suicide, the suicide threat.

No matter how well conceived, well staffed or energetically implemented, no suicide prevention program can guarantee perfect success. Often it will have been better to be lucky than good. It is probably the lucky communities that have been spared the experience of adolescent suicide whether occurring singly or in clusters. It is not "bad" communities that have been or will be less fortunate. Suicide education and prevention must include preparation and assistance to the potential survivors of an adolescent's suicide. A system must be in place to help peers and adults deal with the feelings of guilt, anger, loss, helplessness, and the attendant reactions of denial, blaming, oversimplification of the reasons for the act, loss of confidence, and confusion; to help them grieve and mourn the loss in a healthy manner. Hill (1984) found students to be receptive to assistance while faculty members tended to be more closed. The spectre of the cluster suicide phenomena lends urgency to the need for an in-place system for helping survivors deal with adolescent suicide. Phillips' (1979) work points out the rapidity with which imitative suicides tend to develop. There simply may not be time to react in a helpful and preventive fashion if reacting has not been previously planned.

Students do not inhabit only their schools. Schools are not their only problem. Schools cannot, all by themselves, provide the solution. Plano, Texas, now known as the site of an especially tragic incidence of adolescent cluster suicides has adopted a community wide program of primary as well as secondary and tertiary suicide prevention that stresses an improved quality of life and a more supportive environment for its adolescents. In a well coordinated effort, Plano mobilized many segments of the community in its reaction to the growing number of youth suicides in their midst. Meetings were held with city officials, police, clergy, the mental health community, Rotarians, Lions Club and the Junior League. Funding for a 24-hour hotline and a community crisis center was acquired. Counselors were added to the elementary schools and a number of student-oriented groups were set up to ease the transition for the vast numbers of newcomers moving into this upwardly mobile and rapidly growing city. Since 6 of the

8 suicide victims had been students at the public high school, SWAT, for Students Working All Together, was organized. It was designed to help students befriend new classmates. Another group, BIONIC, for Believe It Or Not I Care, was formed which sent get-well cards to sick or injured classmates who were not able to attend school. "We never went after just a suicide prevention program; the goal was to create an atmosphere that someone cared," said Larry Guinn, Plano's Director of Student Services (Boston Globe, April 6, 1986). Guinn's comments and Plano's intentions could not be more on the mark in perceiving the critical importance of the issue of caring and support in adolescent suicide.

A school-centered, community-involved suicide education/prevention program should, therefore, be more than just a program to prevent suicide. Rather, it must be a program capable of improving and enriching life as well. Instruction and discussion of death issues and coping profit all and foster healthy growth for maturing adolescents. Efforts aimed at providing services, support and social contact to lonely, new or ailing students promotes well-being in the giver and the receiver. Acknowledgment of the problems that face young people's lives and acceptance of some responsibility in caring for those more severely afflicted promotes a broadened social consciousness as well as an awareness that no man should be an island.

A comprehensive program in Cherry Creek School District in Colorado involving the training of teachers, administrators, counseling staff, students, and parents, has produced measurable results. Formal assessment of the student curriculum showed not only that the students increased their basic knowledge of suicide prevention, but that they felt more comfortable and willing to intervene in suicide, if needed (Barrett, 1985). This is an important finding in light of the findings by Curran (1984) and Limbacher and Domino (1986) on the predominantly negative attitudes which teenagers, uneducated about suicide, held toward peer suicide attempters. Reduced rates of suicide have been reported after the implementation of education/prevention programs. Significantly lowered rates in the Cherry Creek, Colorado and San Mateo, California county school districts have been attributed to their energetic programs (Newslink, March, 1985).

There would appear to be an excellent chance that suicide education/ prevention programs can significantly impact upon the rates of attempted and committed suicide. Unlike adolescent problems with drug, alcohol, and sex, which have become increasingly normative behaviors and are often not viewed as problems or deviant behavior by adolescents, suicidal behavior is considered deviant even by adolescents.

Adolescents who have attempted suicide rarely feel positive toward their behavior. Most teens feel intensely ambivalent about their suicidal acts and experience shame and guilt after an unsuccessful attempt. It should be possible, therefore, to offer group support to the life forces within the individual, while creating and making known a consensus among adolescents which discourages the suicidal alternative as an acceptable form of communication. Education should, at the same time, foster a more caring, understanding, and sympathetic response from teachers and peers when an adolescent does attempt, thus minimizing the likelihood of him making a repeat attempt.

One final note is in regard to the need for better education for those in the medical and nursing professions. Research has established that negative attitudes and a reduced level of sympathy and readiness to help often exist on the part of medical personnel toward suicide attempters, particularly those of the adolescent variety (see Chapter 4). These feelings become possible and problematic when adolescent suicidal behavior is misunderstood and trivialized due to ignorance. Diagnosis, treatment and referral of the adolescent while in the hospital setting for a few hours or a few days is apt to be mishandled under these conditions, leaving the suicidal adolescent potentially more suicidal after contact with hospital staff than before. Education must, therefore, be made available to nurses, physicians, and other emergency room personnel concerning the nature and meaning of adolescent suicide attempts. Recognition of its differences from adult suicidal behavior and the magnitude of the psychological emergency that it signals is of the greatest importance.

References

Abraham, Y. (1978). Patterns of communication and rejection in families of suicidal adolescents. *Dissertation Abstracts International, 38*(8), 4669-A.

Alvarez, A. (1971). *The savage god: A study of suicide.* London: Weidenfeld and Nicolson.

Andreason, N. C., & Noyes, R. (1975) Suicide attempted by self-immolation. *American Journal of Psychiatry, 132*(5), 554–556.

Angle, C. O'Brien, T., & McIntire, M. (1983). Adolescent self-poisoning: A nine year follow-up. *Developmental and Behavioral Pediatrics, 4*(2), 83–87.

Ansel, E., & McGee, R. (1971). Attitudes toward suicide attempters. *Bulletin of Suicidology,* 22–28.

Antonovsky, A. (1979). *Health, stress and coping.* San Francisco: Jossey-Bass.

Ashton, J., & Donnan, S. (1981). Suicide by burning as an epidemic phemonenon: An analysis of 82 deaths and inquests in England and Wales in 1978-9. *Psychological Medicine, 11*(4), 735–739.

Asimos, C. (1979). Dynamic problem-solving in a group for suicidal persons. *International Journal of Group Psychotherapy, 29,* 109–114.

Balser, B., & Masterson, J. (1959). Suicide in adolescents. *American Journal of Psychiatry, 116,* 400–404.

Bancroft, J. H., Hawton, K., Simkin, S., Kingston, B., Cumming, C., & Whitwell, D. (1979). The reasons people give for taking overdoses: A further inquiry. *British Journal of Medical Psychology, 52,* 353–365.

Bancroft, J., & Marsack, P. (1977). The repetitiveness of self-poisoning and self-injury. *British Journal of Psychiatry, 131,* 394–399.

Bancroft, J. H., Skrimshire, A. M., & Simkin, S. (1976). The reasons people give for taking overdoses. *British Journal of Psychiatry, 128,* 538–548.

Barber, J. H., Hodgkin, G. K., Patel, A. A., & Wilson, G. M. (1975). Effect of teaching on students' attitudes to self-poisoning. *British Medical Journal, 2,* 431–434.

Barraclough, B., Shepherd, D., & Jennings, C. (1977). Do newspaper reports of coroner's inquests incite people to commit suicide? *British Journal of Psychiatry, 131,* 528–32.

Barrett, T. C. (1985). Does suicide prevention in the schools have to be a "terrifying" concept? *Newslink* (Newsletter of American Association of Suicidology), *11*(1), 3.8

Barter, J. T., Swaback, D. O., & Todd, D. (1968). Adolescent suicide attempts. *Archives of General Psychiatry, 19,* 523–527.

Beck, A. T., Schuyler, D., & Herman, I. (1974). Development of suicidal intent scales. In A. T. Beck, H. L. P. Resnick, A. J. Lettieri (Eds.). (1974). *The prevention of suicide.* Bowie, MD: Charles Press.

Bell, D. (1978). Sex and chronicity as variables affecting attitudes of undergraduates towards peers with suicidal behaviors. *Dissertation Abstracts International, 38,* 3380-B.

Bellak, L. (1981). Psychotherapy with suicidal patients. *Suicide and Life Threatening Behavior, 11,* 341–348.

Bergstrand, C. G., & Otto, V. (1962). Suicidal attempts in adolescents and childhood. *Acta Paediatrica, 51,* 17–26.

Berkman, L. (1977). *Social networks, host resistance and mortality: A follow-up study of Almeda County residents.* Unpublished doctoral dissertation, University of California at Berkeley.

Berman, A., & Carroll, T. (1984). Adolescent suicide: A critical review. *Death Studies, 8,* 53–63.

Bernard, J. (April, 1974). *Observer Magazine,* 28.

Biller, H. B. (1974c). *Paternal deprivation.* Lexington, MA: Health.

Billings, J., Rosen, D., Asimos, C., & Motto, J. (1974). Observations on long-term group therapy with suicidal and depressed persons. *Life-threatening Behavior, 4,* 160–170.

Birtchnell, J. (1983). Psychotherapeutic considerations in the management of the suicidal patient. *American Journal of Psychotherapy, 37*(1), 24–36.

Birtchnell, J., & Alarcon, J. (1971). The motivation and emotional state of 91 cases of attempted suicide. *British Journal of Medical Psychology, 44,* 45–52.

Black, K. D. (1971). *A descriptive survey of student suicide in higher education within the southwestern Rocky Mountain states.* Unpublished doctoral dissertation, University of Denver, Colorado.

Bloom, V. (1968). An analysis of suicide at a training center. *American Journal Psychiatry, 124,* 1542–1546.

Blos, P. (1963). The concept of acting out in relation to the adolescent process. *Journal of the American Academy of Child Psychiatry, 2,* 118-136.

Boldt, M. (1982). Normative evaluations of suicide and death: A cross-generational study. *Omega, 13*(2), 145-157.

Bollen, K. A., & Phillips, D. P. (1982). Imitative suicides: A national study of the effects of television news stories. *American Sociological Review, 47,* 802-809.

Bosselman, B. C. (1958). *Self-Destruction.* Springfield, IL: C. Thomas.

Brown, J. H. (1973). Suicide—The deserted field. *Canadian Psychiatric Association Journal, 18,* 93-94.

Bruhn, J. G. (1962). Broken homes among attempted suicides and psychiatric out-patients: A comparative study. *Journal of Mental Science, 108,* 772-779.

Burvill, P. W., McCall, M. G., Stenhouse, N. S., & Woodings, T. L. (1982). The relationship between suicide, undetermined deaths and accidental deaths in the Australian born and migrants in Australia. *Australian and New Zealand Journal of Psychiatry, 16*(3), 179-184.

Cobb, S. (1976). Social support as a moderator of life stress. *Psychosomatic Medicine, 36,* 300-314.

Corder, B. F., Shorr, W., & Corder, R. F. (1974). A study of the social and psychological characteristics of adolescent suicide attempts. *Adolescence, 9,* 1-6.

Crosby, K., Rhee, J., & Holland, J. (1977). Suicide by fire: A contemporary method of political protest. *International Journal of Social Psychiatry, 23,* 60-69.

Crumley, F. (1982). The adolescent suicide attempt: A cardinal symptom of a serious psychiatric disorder. *American Journal of Psychotherapy, 36*(2), 158-165.

Curran, D. (1984). *Peer attitudes toward attempted suicide in mid-adolescents.* Unpublished doctoral dissertation, Boston College, Chestnut Hill, Massachusetts.

Dashef, S. (1984). Active suicide intervention by a campus mental health service; operation and rationale. *Journal of American College Health, 33,* 118-122.

Deykin, E., Alpert, J., & McNamara, J. (1985). A pilot study of the effect of exposure to child abuse or neglect on adolescent suicidal behavior. *American Journal of Psychiatry, 142*(11), 1299-1303.

Domino, G. (1985). Clergy's attitudes toward suicide and recognition of suicide lethality. *Death Studies, 9,* 187-199.

Domino, G., & Swain, B. (1986). Recognition of suicide lethality and attitudes toward suicide in mental health professionals. *Omega, 16*(4), 301-307.

Dorpat, T., & Boswell, J. W. (1963). An evaluation of suicidal intent in suicide attempts. *Comprehensive Psychiatry, 4,* 117-125.

Dorpat, T., & Ripley, H. (1967). The relationship between attempted suicide and committed suicide. *Comprehensive Psychiatry, 8*(2), 74-79.

Douglas, J. D. (1967). *Social meaning of suicide.* Princeton, NJ: Princeton University Press.

Dressler, D. M., Prusoff, B., Mark, H., & Shapiro, D. (1975). Clinician attitudes toward the suicide attempter. *Journal of Nervous and Mental Disease, 160*(2), 146–155.

Dublin, L. I., & Bunzel, B. (1933). *To be or not to be: A study of suicide.* New York: Harrison Smith and Robert Haas.

Durkheim, E. (1952). *Suicide: A study in sociology.* (J. A. Spaulding & C. Simpson, Trans.). London: Routledge and Kegan Paul. (Original work published 1897)

Farberow, N. (1970). The suicidal crisis in psychotherapy. In E. Shneidman, N. Farberow, & R. Litman (Eds.), *The Psychology of Suicide.* New York: Science House.

Farberow, N. (1972). Vital process in suicide prevention: Group psychotherapy as a community of concern. *Life-threatening Behavior, 2,* 239–251.

Farberow, N., & Shneidman, E. (1961). *The cry for help.* New York: McGraw-Hill.

Farr, W. (1841). *Third annual report of the Registrar General of births, deaths and marriage in England (for 1839-40).* London: HMSO, 82.

Finch, J. M., & Poznanski, J. (Eds.). (1971). *Adolescent suicide.* Springfield, IL: Charles C. Thomas.

Fisher, S. F. (1973). *The female orgasm: Psychology, physiology, fantasy.* New York: Basic Books.

Fox, R. (1971). Today's students: Suicide among students and its prevention. *Royal Society of Health Journal, 91,* 181–185.

Francis, C. (1976). Adolescent suicide attempts (Doctoral dissertation, California School of Professional Psychology, San Diego, 1976). *Dissertation Abstracts International, 38,* 4453-B.

Frederick, C. (1971). The present suicide taboo in the United States. *Mental Hygiene, 55*(2), 178–183.

Freeman, D. V., Wilson, K., Thigpen, J., & McGee, R. (1974). Assessing intention to die in self-injury behavior. In C. Neuringer (Ed.), *Psychological assessment of suicidal risk* (pp. 18–42). Spingfield, IL: C. Thomas.

Freud, A. (1958). Adolescence. *The psychoanalytic study of the child, 13,* New York: International University Press.

Frey, D. H., Motto, J. A., & Ritholz, M. D. (1983). Group therapy for persons at risk for suicide: An evaluation using the intensive design. *Psychotherapy: Theory, Research and Practice, 20*(3), 281–293.

Getz, W., Allen, D., Myers, R., & Lindner, K. (1983). *Brief counseling with suicidal persons.* Lexington, MA: D. C. Heath.

Ghodse, A. H. (1978). The attitudes of casualty staff and ambulance personnel towards patients who take drug overdoses. *Social Science and Medicine, 12A,* 341–346.

Ginsburg, G. (1971). Public conceptions and attitudes about suicide. *Journal of Health and Social Behavior, 12,* 200–207.

Goodman, P. (1960). *Growing up absurd.* New York: Random House.

Goldacre, M., & Hawton, K. (1985). Repetition of self-poisoning and subsequent death in adolescents who take overdoses. *British Journal of Psychiatry, 146,* 359–398.

Gordon, S. (1979). An analysis of the knowledge and attitudes of secondary school teachers concerning suicide among adolescents and intervention in adolescents Doctoral dissertation, North Texas State University, 1979). *Dissertation Abstracts International, 40,* 1393-4A.

Gould, R. (1965). Suicide problems in children and adolescents. *American Journal of Psychotherapy, 19,* 228–246.

Green, A. H. (1968). Self-destructive behavior in battered children. *American Journal of Psychiatry, 135*(5), 579–582.

Greuling, J., & DeBlassie, R. (1980). Adolescent suicide. *Adolescence, 15* (59), 589–601.

Grollman, E. A. (1971). *Suicide: Prevention, intervention, postvention.* Boston: Beacon Press.

Haim, A. (1974). *Adolescent suicide* (A. A. Sheridon Smith, Trans.). New York: International University Press.

Haldane, J. D., & Harder, R. (1967). Attempted suicide in children and adolescents. *British Journal of Clinical Practice, 21,* 587–591.

Hankoff, L. D., & Einsidler, B. (1979). *Suicide: Theory and clinical aspects.* Littleton, MA: PSG Publishing.

Hawton, K. (1982). Annotation: Attempted suicide in children and adolescents. *Journal of Child Psychology and Psychiatry, 23*(4), 497–503.

Hawton, K., Bancroft, J., & Simkin, S. (1978). Attitudes of psychiatric patients to deliberate self-poisoning. *British Journal of Psychiatry, 132,* 31–35.

Hawton, K., Cole, D., O'Grady, J., & Osborn, M. (1982a). Motivational aspects of deliberate selfpoisoning in adolescents. *British Journal of Psychiatry, 141,* 286–290.

Hawton, K., O'Grady, J., Osborne, M., & Cole, D. (1982b). Adolescents who take overdoses: Their characteristics, problems and contacts with helping agencies. *British Journal of Psychiatry, 140,* 118–123.

Hawton, K., Osborne, M., O'Grady, J., & Cole, D (1982c). Classification of adolescents who take overdoses. *British Journal of Psychiatry, 140,* 124–131.

Hawton, K., Marsack, P., & Fagg, J. (1981). The attitudes of psychiatrists to deliberate self-poisoning: Comparison with physicians and nurses. *British Journal of Medical Psychology, 54,* 341–348.

Herjanic, B., & Welner, Z. (1980). Adolescent suicide. *Advances in Behavioral Pediatrics, 1,* 195–223.

Hetherington, E. M. (1972). Effects of father-absence on personality development in adolescent daughters. *Developmental Psychology, 7,* 313–326.

Hewitt, D., & Milner, J. (1974). Drug related deaths in the United States—First decade of an epidemic. *Health Services Reports, 89,* 211–217.

Hill, W. (1984). Intervention and postvention in schools. In Sudak, H., Ford, A., & Rushforth, N. (Eds.), *Suicide in the Young.* Littleton, MA: Wright PSG.

Hodgman, C. (1985). Recent findings in adolescent depression and suicide. *Journal of Developmental and Behavioral Pediatrics, 6*(3), 162–170.

Holinger, P. (1979). Violent deaths among the young: Recent trends in suicide, homicide and accidents. *American Journal of Psychiatry, 139*(9), 1144–1147.

Holinger, P., & Offer, C. (1982). The prediction of adolescent suicide: A population model. *American Journal of Psychiatry, 139*(3), 302–307.

Hood, R. W. (1973). Dogmatisms and opinions about mental illnesses. *Psychological Reports, 32,* 1283–1290.

Horton, H., & Stack, S. (1984). The effect of television on national suicide rates. *Journal of Social Psychology, 123,* 141–142.

Hudgens, R. (1974). *Psychiatric disorders in adolescents.* Baltimore: Williams and Wilkins.

Ishii, K. (1985). Backgrounds of higher suicide rates among "name university" students: A retrospective study of the past 25 years. *Suicide and Life-Threatening Behavior, 15*(1), 56–68.

Jacobs, J. (1971). *Adolescent suicide.* New York: Wiley Interscience.

Jacobs, J., & Teicher, J. (1966). Broken homes viewed as a process. *International Journal of Social Psychiatry, 13,* 139.

Jacoby, J. (1976). Consumer psychology: An octenium. In M. R. Rosenzweig, & L. W. Porter (Eds.), *Annual Review of Psychology* (pp. 331–358). Palo Alto, CA: Annual Reviews.

Jacobziner, H. (1965). Attempted suicide in adolescence. *Journal of the American Medical Association, 10,* 22–36.

Kalish, R. A., Reynolds, D. K., & Farberow, N. L. (1974). Community attitudes towards suicide. *Community Mental Health Journal, 10*(3), 301–308.

Kerfoot, M. (1979). Self-poisoning by children and adolescents. *Social Work Today, 10,* 9–11.

Kessel, N. (1965). Self-poisoning, *British Medical Journal,* 1265.

Kessel, N. (1966). The respectability of self-poisoning and the fashion of survival. *Journal of Psychosomatic Research, 10,* 22–36.

Kessler, R., & Stipp, H. (1984). The impact of fictional television suicide stories on U. S. fatalities: A replication. *American Journal of Sociology, 90*(1), 151–167.

Kiev, A. (1977). *The suicidal patient: Recognition and management.* Chicago: Nelson-Hall.

Klagsbrun, F. (1976). *Too young to die: Youth and suicide.* Boston: Houghton-Miflin.

Kovacs, M., Beck, A. T., & Weissman, A. (1976). The communication of suicidal intent. *Archives of General Psychiatry, 33,* 198–201.

Krech, D., Crutchfield, R., & Blallachey, E. (1962). *Individual in society.* New York: McGraw-Hill.

Kreitman, N. (1969). Parasuicide. *British Journal of Psychiatry, 115,* 746.

Kreitman, N. (1976). Age and parasuicide. *Psychological Medicine, 6,* 113–121.

Lamb, M. E. (Ed.). (1976). *The role of the father in child development.* New York: Wiley-Interscience.

Lampl de Groot, J. (1960). Adolescence. *The psychoanalytic study of the child.* (Vol. 15). New York: International University Press.

Leese, L. M. (1969). Suicide behavior in twenty adolescents. *British Journal of Psychiatry, 115,* 479–480.

Lester, D. (1967). Fear of death of suicidal persons. *Psychological Reports, 8*(2), 74–79.

Lester, G., & Lester, D. (1971). *Suicide: The gamble with death.* Englewood Cliffs, NJ: Prentice Hall.

Limbacher, M., & Domino, G. (1986). Attitudes toward suicide among attempters, contemplators and non-attempters. *Omega, 16*(4), 325–334.

Linehan, M. (1971). Sex differences of suicide and attempted suicide: A study of differential social acceptability and expectations. *Dissertation Abstracts International* (Doctoral dissertation, Loyola University, Chicago, 1971). *32,* 3076-B.

Litman, R. E. (1968). Psychotherapists' orientations toward suicide. In Resnick, H. L. P. (Ed.), *Suicidal behaviors: Diagnosis and management.* (357–363). Boston, MA: Little, Brown.

Litt, I. F., Cuskey, W. R., & Rudd, S. (1983). Emergency room evaluation of the adolescent who attempts suicide: Compliance with follow-up. *Journal of Adolescent Health Care, 4*(2), 106–108.

Lozoff, M. D. (1974). Fathers and autonomy in women. In R. B. Kundsin (Ed.), *Women and success.* New York: Morrow.

Lyman, J. L. (1961). Student suicide at Oxford University. *Student Medicine, 10,* 218–234.

Malla, A., & Hoenig, J. (1983). Differences in suicide rates: An examination of underreporting. *Canadian Journal of Psychiatry, 28*(4), 291–293.

Maris, R. (1985). The adolescent suicide problem. *Suicide and Life-Threatening Behavior, 15*(a), 91–109.

Marks, J., & Haller, M. (1977). Now I lay me down for keeps. *Journal of Clinical Psychology, 33,* 390.

Mattson, A., Seese, L. R., & Hawkins, J. W. (1969). Suicidal behavior as a child psychiatric emergency. *Archives of General Psychiatry, 20,* 100–109.

Mayer, D. (1971). A psychotherapeutic approach to the suicidal patient. *British Journal of Psychiatry, 119,* 629.

McIntire, M., & Angle, C. A. (1973). Psychological "biopsy" in self-poisoning of children and adolescents. *American Journal of Diseases of Children, 126,* 42–46.

McIntire, M., & Angle, C. (1980). *Suicide attempts in children and youth.* Hagerstown, MD: Harper and Row.

McIntire, M., Angle, C., & Schlicht, M. L. (February, 1980). Suicide and self-poisoning in pediatrics. *Resident and Staff Physician,* 72–85.

McIntire, A., Angle, C., & Struppler, L. (1972). The concept of death in mid-western children and youth. *American Journal of Diseases of Children, 123,* 527–532.

McIntosh, J., Hubbard, R., & Santos, J. (1985). Suicide facts and myths: A study of prevalence. *Death Studies, 9,* 267–281.

McIntosh, J., & Jewell, B. (1986). Sex difference trends in completed suicide. *Suicide and Life Threatening Behavior, 16*(1), 16–27.

McKenry, D., Tishler, C., & Kelley, C. (1982). Adolescent suicide: A comparison of attempters and non-attempters in an emergency room population. *Clinical Pediatrics, 21*(5), 266–270.

McKenry, D., Tishler, C., & Kelley, C. (1983). The role of drugs in adolescent suicide attempts. *Suicide and Life Threatening Behavior, 13*(3), 166–175.

Miles, C. P. (1977). Conditions pre-disposing to suicide: A review. *The Journal of Nervous and Mental Disease, 164,* 231–246.

Millen, L., & Roll, S. (1985). A case study in failure: on doing everything right in suicide prevention. *Death Studies, 9,* 483–492.

Mintz, R. S. (1968). Psychotherapy of the suicidal patient. In Resnick, H. L. P. (Ed.), *Suicidal behaviors: Diagnosis and management* (271–296). Boston, MA: Little, Brown.

Mishara, B. (1975). The extent of suicidality in adolescence. *Psychiatric Opinion, 12*(6), 32–37.

Mishara, B. (1982). College students' experiences with suicide and reactions to suicidal verbalizations: A model for prevention. *Journal of Community Psychology, 10,* 142–150.

Motto, J. A. (1965). Suicide attempts: A longitudinal view. *Archives of General Psychiatry, 13,* 516–520.

Motto, J. A. (1967). Suicide and suggestability—The role of the press. *American Journal of Psychiatry, 124,* 156–160.

Motto, J. A. (1970). Newspaper influence on suicide. *Archives of General Psychiatry, 23,* 143–148.

Murray, M. (1972). Unpublished 4th year dissertation, University of Glasgow, Scotland.

National Center for Health Statistics. (1968–1981). Death rates by age, race, sex—5 and 10 year age groupings. *Vital Statistics of the United States.* Hyattsville, MD.

Nicol, D. (1973). Factors affecting the negativity of attitudes toward suicide. (Doctoral dissertation, York University. Canada, 1973). *Dissertation Abstracts International, 36,* 5235–5236B.

Niemi, T. (1975). The time-space distances of suicides committed in the lock-up in Finland in 1963–67. *Psychiatria Fennica,* 267–270.

Novick, J. (1984). Attempted suicide in adolescents: The suicide sequence.

In H. Sudak, A. Ford, & N. Rushforth, (Eds.), *Suicide in the young.* Littleton, MA: Wright PSG.

Offer, D. (1979). Normal adolescent development. In P. Novello (Ed.), *The short course in adolescent psychiatry* (Chap. 4). New York: Bruner/ Mazel.

Oldham, D. G. (1978). Adolescent turmoil: A myth revisited. In S. C. Feomsteom (Ed.), *Adolescent psychiatry, 6* (Ch. 14). Chicago, IL: University of Chicago Press.

Orbach, I., & Glaubman, H. (1979). Children's perception of death as a defensive process. *Journal of Abnormal Psychology, 88,* 671–674.

Orbach, I., Gross, Y., Glaubman, H., & Berman, D. (1985). Children's perception of death in humans and animals as a function of age, anxiety and cognitive ability. *Journal of Child Psychology and Psychiatry, 26*(3), 453–463.

Osgood, C. (1957). *The measurement of meaning.* Urbana: University of Illinois Press.

Otto, V. (1972). Suicidal attempts in childhood and adolescents today and after ten years: A follow-up study. In A. L. Annell (Ed.), *Depressive states in childhood and adolescence.* New York: Halstead Press, 357–366.

Patel, A. R. (1975). Attitudes toward self-poisoning. *British Medical Journal, 24,* 426–429.

Paulson, J. J., & Stone, D. (1974). Suicidal behavior of latency-age children. *Journal of Clinical Child Psychology, 3,* 50–53.

Peck, M. (1968). Suicide motivation in adolescents. *Adolescence, 3*(9), 109–118.

Peck, M., & Schrut, A. (1971). Suicidal behavior among college students. *HSMHA Health Reports, 86,* 149–156.

Peck, M., & Litman, R. (1972). Current trends in youthful suicide. *Tribuna Medica. 5,* 120–126.

Phillips, D. (1974). The influence of suggestion on suicide: Substantive and theoretical implications of the Werther effect. *American Sociological Review, 39,* 340–354.

Phillips, D. (1979). Suicide, motor vehicle fatalities, and the mass media: Evidence toward a theory of suggestion. *American Journal of Sociology, 84*(5), 1150–1174.

Pinkerton, W. S., Jr., (1969). The lethal impulse. *Wall Street Journal,* (March 6).

Porot, M., Coudert, A., & Collett, M. (1968). Suicidal behavior of adolescents. *Psychiatrie de l'enfant, 11,* 317–369.

Powers, D. (October, 1954). Youthful suicide attempts. *Northwest Medicine,* 1001–1002.

Ramon, S. Bancroft, J. H., & Skrimshire, A. M. (1975). Attitudes towards self-poisoning among physicians and nurses in a general hospital. *British Journal of Psychiatry, 127,* 257–264.

Reubin, R. H. (1973). A study of the factors involved in the decision to treat suicidal clients. (Doctoral dissertation, University of Michigan, 1973). *Dissertation Abstracts International, 24,* 296–297B.

Richman, J. (1979). The family therapy of attempted suicide. *Family Process, 18,* 131–142.

Robbins, D., & Alessi, N. (1985). Depressive symptoms and suicidal behavior in adolescents. *American Journal of Psychiatry, 142*(5), 588–592.

Robertson, I. (1980). *Social problems.* New York: Random House.

Rohn, R. D., Sarles, R. M., Kenny, T. J., Reynolds, B. J., & Heald, F. P. (1977). Adolescents who attempt suicide. *Journal of Pediatrics, 90,* 636–638.

Rosen, B., Bahn, A., Shellow, R., & Bower, E. (1965). Adolescent patients served in out-patient psychiatric clinics. *American Journal of Public Health, 55,* 1563–1577.

Rosenbaum, M., & Richman, J. (1970). Suicide: The role of hostility and death wishes from the family and significant others. *American Journal of Psychiatry, 126*(11), 128–131.

Rosenkrantz, A. L. (1978). A note on adolescent suicide: Incidence, dynamics and some suggestions for treatment. *Adolescence, 13*(50), 209–213.

Rosenthal, N. (1983). Death education and suicide potentiality. *Death Education, 7,* 39–51.

Ross, C. (1980). Mobilizing schools for suicide prevention. *Suicide and Life Threatening Behavior, 10,* 239–243.

Ross, M. (1969). Suicide among college students. *American Journal of Psychiatry, 126,* 220–225.

Sabbath, J. C. (1969). The suicidal adolescent—The expendable child. *Journal of American Academy of Child Psychiatry, 8,* 272.

Sale, I., Williams, C., Clark, J., & Mills, J. (1975). Suicidal behavior: Community attitudes and beliefs. *Suicide, 5*(3), 158–159.

Schneer, H. I., & Kay, P. (1961). The suicidal adolescent. In S. Lorand and H. I. Schneer (Eds.), *Adolescents: Psychoanalytic approach to problems and therapy* (pp. 180–201). New York: Hoeber.

Schneer, H. I., Kay, P., & Brozobsky, M. (1961). Events and conscious ideation leading to suicidal behavior in adolescents. *Psychiatric Quarterly, 35,* 507–515.

Schneer, H. I., Perlstein, A., & Brozobsky, M. (1975). Hospitalized suicidal adolescents: Two generations. *Journal of American Academy of Child Psychiatry, 14,* 268.

Schrut, A. (1964). Suicidal adolescents and children. *Journal of American Medical Association, 188*(3), 1103–1107.

Seiden, R. (1966). Campus tragedy: A study of student suicide. *Journal of Abnormal Psychology, 71,* 389–399.

Seiden, R. H. (1969) Suicide among youth. *National Clearinghouse for Mental Health Information.* Washington, D.C.

Selby, J., & Calhoun, L. (1975). Social perception of suicide: Effects of three factors on causal attribution. *Journal of Consulting and Clinical Psychology, 43*(3), 431.

Senseman, L. A. (1969). Attempted suicide in adolescents. A suicide prevention center in Rhode Island is in urgent need. *Rhode Island Medical Journal, 52,* 449–451.

Shaffer, A. (1974). Suicide in childhood and early adolescence. *Journal of Child Psychology and Psychiatry, 15,* 275–291.

Shafii, M., Carrigan, S., Whittinghill, J., & Derrick, A. (1985). Psychological autopsy of completed suicide in children and adolescents. *American Journal of Psychiatry, 142*(9), 1061–1064.

Shneidman, E. (1968). Orientations toward cessation: A re-examination of current modes of death. *Journal of Forensic Science, 13,* 33–45.

Shneidman, E. (1974). *Orientation toward death: A vital aspect of the study of lives.* Baltimore: Williams and Williams.

Shneidman, E. (1981). Psychotherapy with suicidal patients. *Suicide and Life-Threatening Behavior, 11*(4), 341–348.

Sifneos, P. (1966). Manipulative suicide. *Psychiatric Quarterly, 40,* 525–537.

Silving, H. (1957). Suicide and the law. In E. S. Shneidman and N. L. Farberow (Eds.), *Clues to suicide.* New York: McGraw-Hill.

Slavson, S. (1964). *A textbook of analytic group psychotherapy.* New York: International University Press.

Smith, K., Conroy, R. W., & Ehler, B. D. (1984). Lethality of suicide attempt rating scale. *Suicide and Life-Threatening Behavior, 14*(4), 215–242.

Smith, K., & Crawford, S. (1986). Suicidal behavior among "normal" high school students. *Suicide and Life Threatening Behavior, 16*(3), 313–325.

Sorrel, W. E. (1972). Violence toward self. *Diseases of the Nervous System, 33*(8), 503.

Stack, S. (1980a). The effects of interstate migration on suicide. *The International Journal of Social Psychiatry, 26,* 17–26.

Stanley, E. J., & Barter, J. T. (1970). Adolescent suicidal behavior. *American Journal of Orthopsychiatry, 40,* 87.

Stanton, M. (1977). The addict as savior: Heroin, death and the family. *Family Process, 16,* 191–197.

Stengel, E. (1964). *Suicide and attempted suicide.* Baltimore: Penguin Books.

Stillion, J., McDowell, E., & May, J. (1984). Developmental trends and sex differences in adolescent attitudes toward suicide. *Death Studies, 8,* 81–90.

Stillion, J., McDowell, E., & Shamblin, J. (1984). The suicide attitude vignette experience: A method for measuring adolescent attitudes toward suicide. *Death Studies, 8,* 65–79.

Stillion, J., & Wass, H. (1979). Children and death. In H. Wass (Ed.), *Dying: Facing the facts.* (208–235). Washington, DC: Hemisphere.

Sudak, H., Ford, A., & Rushforth, N. (1984). Adolescent suicide: An overview. *American Journal of Psychotherapy, 38*(3), 350–369.

Surtees, S. J., Taylor, D. C., & Cooper, R. W. (1976). Suicide and accidental deaths at Beachy Head. *Eastbourne Medical Gazette, 2,* 22–24.

Swain, B., & Domino, G. (1985). Attitudes toward suicide among mental health professionals. *Death Studies, 9,* 455–468.

Tabachnick, N. (1975). Subintentioned self-destruction in teenagers. *Psychiatric Opinion, 12*(6), 21–26.

Tabachnick, N. (1981). The interlocking psychologies of suicide and adolescence. *Adolescent Psychiatry, 9,* 399–410.

Teicher, J. (1973). A solution to the chronic problem of living: Adolescent attempted suicide. In J. C. Schoolar (Ed.), *Current issues in adolescent psychiatry.* New York: Bruner/Mazel.

Teicher, J., & Jacobs, J. (1966). Adolescents who attempt suicide. *American Journal of Psychiatry, 122,* 1248.

Teicher, J., & Jacobs, J. (1966a). The phsyician and the adolescent suicide attempter. *Journal of School Health, 36,* 406.

Tishler, C. L., & McKenry, P. C. (1983). Intrapsychic symptoms dimensions of adolescent suicide attempters. *Journal of Family Practice, 16*(4), 731–734.

Tishler, C., McKenry, P., & Morgan, K. (1981). Adolescent suicide attempts: Some significant factors. *Suicide and Life Threatening Behavior, 11*(2), 86–92.

Toolan, J. (1971). Depression in adolescents. In J. Howell (Ed.), *Modern perspectives in adolescent psychiatry.* New York: Bruner/Mazel.

Toolan, J. (1975). Suicide in children and adolescents. *American Journal of Psychotherapy, 29,* 339–344.

Topol, P., & Reznikoff, M. (1982). Perceived peer and family relationships, hopelessness, locus of control as factors in adolescent suicide attempts. *Suicide and Life-Threatening Behavior, 12*(3), 141–150.

Triolo, S., McKenry, P., Tishler, C., & Blythe, D. (1984). Social and psychological discriminants of adolescent suicide: age and sex differences. *Journal of Early Adolescence, 4*(3), 239–251.

Tuckman, J., & Connor, H. E. (1962). Attempted suicide in adolescents. *American Journal of Psychiatry, 119,* 228–232.

Walch, S. (1977). Adolescent attempted suicide: Analysis of the differences in male and female behavior. (Doctoral dissertation, California School of Professional Psychology, 1977). *Dissertation Abstracts International, 38*(6-B), 2892B.

Walker, W. L. (1980). Intentional self-injury in school age children. *Journal of Adolescence, 3,* 217–228.

Wass, H., & Corr, C. (1984). *Childhood and Death.* Washington, DC: Hemisphere.

Wasserman, I. (1984). Imitation and suicide: A re-examination of the Werther effect. *American Sociological Review, 49,* 427–436.

Weiner, I. (1970). *Psychological disturbance in adolescence.* New York: Wiley-Interscience.

Weisman, A. D., & Worden, J. W. (1974). Risk-rescue rating in suicidal assessment. In A. T. Beck, H. L. P. Resnick, & A. J. Lettieri (Eds.), *The prevention of suicide* (pp. 193–213). Bowie, MD: Charles Press.

Weissman, M. (1974). The epidemiology of suicide attempts 1960–1971. *Archives of General Psychiatry, 30,* 737–746.

Wenz, F. (1978). Multiple suicide attempts and informal labelling: An exploratory study. *Suicide and Life-Threatening Behavior, 8*(1), 3–13.

Wenz, F. (1979). Sociological correlates of alienation among adolescent suicide attempts. *Adolescence, 14,* (5–3), 19–30.

White, H. C. (1974). Self-poisoning in adolescents. *British Journal of Psychiatry, 124,* 24–35.

Wilkinson, K., & Isreal, G. (1984). Suicide and rurality in urban society. *Suicide and Life-Threatening Behavior, 14*(3), 187–200.

Yalom, I. (1975). *The theory and practice of group psychotherapy.* (2nd ed.). New York: Basic Books.

Index